Dear Jamie,

The pathways of life continue to amaze me as we connect & reconnect in unexpected ways and times. Thank you for being an early reader. May the stories resonate for you as you are continuing to embrace all that shows up.

Lots of love,

Kathy xox

EMBRACING THE STRANGER IN ME:

A JOURNEY TO OPEN HEARTEDNESS

KATHY JOURDAIN

BALBOA
PRESS
A DIVISION OF HAY HOUSE

Cover Design by Tania Marie, visionary artist,
sacred tattoo designer, and Reiki Master Teacher.
www.taniamarie.com
www.spiritualskin.com

Balboa Press books may be ordered through booksellers or by contacting:

Balboa Press
A Division of Hay House
1663 Liberty Drive
Bloomington, IN 47403
www.balboapress.com
1-(877) 407-4847

Because of the dynamic nature of the Internet, any web addresses or links contained in this book may have changed since publication and may no longer be valid. The views expressed in this work are solely those of the author and do not necessarily reflect the views of the publisher, and the publisher hereby disclaims any responsibility for them.

The author of this book does not dispense medical advice or prescribe the use of any technique as a form of treatment for physical, emotional, or medical problems without the advice of a physician, either directly or indirectly. The intent of the author is only to offer information of a general nature to help you in your quest for emotional and spiritual well-being. In the event you use any of the information in this book for yourself, which is your constitutional right, the author and the publisher assume no responsibility for your actions.

Any people depicted in stock imagery provided by Thinkstock are models, and such images are being used for illustrative purposes only.
Certain stock imagery © Thinkstock.

ISBN: 978-1-4525-7572-8 (sc)
ISBN: 978-1-4525-7574-2 (hc)
ISBN: 978-1-4525-7573-5 (e)

Library of Congress Control Number: 2013910355

Printed in the United States of America.

Balboa Press rev. date: 06/28/2013

TABLE OF CONTENTS

DEDICATION

This book is dedicated with love to:

My parents
Mary Patricia Ann Ritcey Jourdain
(living in spirit) and Raoul Hector Jourdain

My brother
Robert Jourdain

My birth parents
Joanne Saulnier (living in spirit) and Fred Hanson

My sisters
Debbie Van Soest
Robyn Hanson

ACKNOWLEDGEMENTS

A memoir is a strange beast. It is an attempt to distill an individual's life's lessons in story form with a hope that in the storytelling someone else sees a thread that resonates with their own life journey. Life journey does not happen in isolation. I have a keen awareness that these are my reflections and stories of specific moments in my life, moments that have intersected with others on the journey. The way others have experienced the same elements of journey may be somewhat or vastly different than the way I have experienced them. Their experiences are their stories to tell but I would not be the person I am today without having crossed paths with these fellow journeyers, without having had the experiences that I did in relation to them and for each and all of them I am grateful.

You are too many to begin to acknowledge you all individually so here are only a few.

For life journey, I acknowledge the two people who brought me into the world and then let me go: Joanne Saulnier and Fred Hanson, without whom I would not exist in this world. My birth parents released me to my parents Mary and Hector Jourdain who took me in as an infant, embraced me as their own and journeyed with me over the course of a lifetime.

Although sometimes we are like ships passing in the night as we are not always in frequent contact, my brother Robert Jourdain is a soul journey partner too. We are aligned in philosophy and approach to life and a strong family unit.

There was a silent human guardian of my soul journey for decades, holding the memory of me close while following the path of her own journey: my sister Debbie van Soest, who thought of me often, wanted to honor my path, even when it meant not being in my life for decades. Without the lifelong curiosity of my half-sister Robyn Hanson about someone she had never met but who was an absent part of her life, some of this story may never have unfolded, as she was a first point of contact.

When it came time to get serious about writing this book, I sent my first tenuous writing out to a small group of new friends. Heather Plett responded with a long offering of suggestions and an apology, hoping to have not offended me in her comments. It was a gift, starting a conversation I embraced. Heather's guidance radically expanded the vision for this book. She introduced to me to books on how to write a memoir and stuck with me through three rewrites of the chapter on finding out I was adopted, which I had imagined was going to be the first chapter of this book. She questioned me three different times before I realized, with the third rewrite of the chapter that she was right and it was not the starting point.

Much of this book was drafted and edited on airplanes and in airports, particularly when my flights were disrupted and I ended up staying overnight unexpectedly in a city I never planned to be in. It started, not with fully formulated chapters set out in order, but with stories, some written a decade ago and newly discovered during the writing of the book. During one trip interruption in July 2011, I entered into a full round of editing stories that had been written in anticipation of them turning into chapters. When I got home, I laid out each block of writing on my kitchen table and for the first time saw the book in its entirety with the gaps that needed to be filled in. I wrote two more chapters, did a full edit and then sent my manuscript out to a few friends for feedback in the spring of 2012.

I have much gratitude to my brother Robert for his sitting down and reading it from start to finish in one late night, offering his impressions and how he relived the stories. And also for his filling in gaps for me. Every time I had a question about our family history I turned to him for answers.

My friend Jamey Walsh, a university friend newly reentered into my life after my mother died, who learned my life story through reading a first iteration of the book and offering his impressions.

My son Jacob Dwyer read an early version and shared with me how he felt it was a fair depiction of my story and fair to people I write about who touched my life.

Deep gratitude to my good friend Tenneson Woolf who read the manuscript and then sat with me over skype tea one evening giving me chapter by chapter feedback. Tenneson's feedback was instrumental in the next full edit of the manuscript.

Summer of 2012, the newly re-edited manuscript was ready for more feedback. Deep gratitude to Jeanie Cockell and Joan MacArthur-Blair, who had just gone through their own editing process in publishing a book they co-wrote, who offered to read my manuscript and then sat down on the dock on their lake to offer me valuable feedback that significantly influenced the next full edit of the book.

At the end December 2012, the manuscript was ready for the next stage. It was either me doing a next round of edits or releasing it to someone else, someone who did not know me, someone to prepare it for publication. And that is when I began my conversations with Balboa Press.

Zackary DePew, my Balboa editor, who reviewed the manuscript offered exactly what I was looking for—gentle guidance on where clarity was needed and helping me track the proper tense in the story lines. Grateful for his eyes on this and for validating the quality of writing and strength of story.

The final acknowledgement is to my children: Jacob Dwyer, Spencer Dwyer and Shasta Tangri. They are soul journey partners, in it with me for the long haul. They recognize, each in their own way, the quirkiness of their mother and they love me anyway. We have, individually and collectively, been in some crazy intensity of journey and also in some lovely patterns of relationship full of discovery, trust, compassion, love and joy. Some of the reasons I have deconstructed my life twice and put it back together, now finally in what feels a more true path, is to live a journey and a life as authentically as I know how to live it in the moment, to look in the reflection of my children's eyes and know I have done the best I know how in any given moment. My legacy to them is in embracing the stranger, embracing all of me and living as openheartedly as I know how. May your paths rise up to meet you in the journey of love, wherever it takes you.

PRELUDE

DRUMMING CIRCLE

It is summer in the year 2000.

I'm lying on my back on top of blankets that are directly on the ground. There are twenty-six of us lying on our backs in a tent. The tent is so crowded that we are almost touching each other, but not quite. We're not supposed to touch each other; we're not supposed to be in each other's journey.

The shaman is drumming. It's a rhythmical sound intended to free our consciousness to journey to the sound of the drum, a drum beating like a heartbeat, like my heart beating.

I'm aware of the drum. I focus my attention on it just as the shaman has instructed. He told us we might journey below or journey above. Most commonly, in a first journey, people go below. Most of us are first-time journeyers.

We are told to look for a tree that might be familiar to us and travel down through a hole near the tree or along its roots until we come out the other side—wherever that might be. A power animal will greet us there.

I already know my power animal is a lion. Over the previous days, images of lions have appeared to me in at least three different ways: in a particular cloud formation, in the limbs of a tree, and behind my closed eyes, where an image of a lion seemed to hover just inside my eyelids. So I know the animal that greets me will be a lion.

Once we have been greeted, the power animal will take us on a journey. Maybe. The shaman said that for many people, sometimes a first-time journey is just an inkling of something. Many people have to journey often to have a powerful experience, although it does happen for first-time journeyers too. He doesn't want our hopes and expectations to be too high. He wants us to know there is a broad array of possible experiences—no right or wrong, no one way that it has to be.

As the drumming begins, the shaman calls in spirits from seven directions: east, south, west, north, sky, earth, and center. I feel them coming in. When I close my eyes, I see the silhouette of the head and shoulders of a man. I gasp! I can feel the look of astonishment on my own face.

I lie on the ground, breathing deeply, my focus on the drumming, everything else melting away. I quickly find the tree and the hole. The hole resembles the ribbed drainage pipe that goes around our property. As I go down the pipe, the lion is roaring beside me.

And then . . . nothing.

I see nothing.

I wait. I look. No journey. Nothing. I am aware of the lion being there, but there doesn't seem to be anything else. The drum continues to beat in my awareness. No grandiose experience. I can't see anything. I think, *Maybe this is all I will get.* The drumming continues. I try harder. Still nothing happens.

Disappointment registers with a sinking feeling. *Great. Just like the shaman said, I'm going to be one of those people who experiences just a little inkling of something.*

Just as I think this, the person beside me involuntarily convulses. She is close enough to me that I feel it, and I also convulse. My consciousness comes flooding fully back into my body, and my mind is once again alert. I tell myself, *Refocus on the drumbeat.* I take a deep breath, relax back into the blanket, and feel my body melt into the ground.

As I refocus on the drumbeat, I suddenly know that although I can't see it, I can feel it—if I let my senses go. Now I sense a field, a meadow full of flowers. It is the oddest thing. I wonder if I'm forcing it, willing myself to see something, anything. But in surrendering to sensing it, I am able to "see" it. I look across the meadow, with the sun shining overhead and colorful flowers in bloom. It is a warm day in the meadow. I feel the gentle breeze blowing, lightly touching my skin. I become aware of the aromatic flowers and the meadow scent that lingers in the air. I am standing in the meadow with the lion beside me. Delight, surprise, and joy fill me as I surrender more deeply into this experience.

My lion is also delighted. It means he can do his job, fulfill his purpose in being available to me as a guide.

Now I'm curious. If this meadow can all of a sudden appear, what more is here? Is there something in the meadow? What about beyond it?

Silently, I put my arm around the lion, and he begins to fly. A thought intervenes. *This is wrong. Lions don't fly.* Ah. Hmm. Maybe in this space they can. Well, why not? Maybe it doesn't matter. Maybe I just need to surrender the constraints of the physical world, be on his back, and go with it.

What an amazing sense of freedom! We take flight. He flies high up in the air and literally dances as he carries me on his back. We fly over the meadow and come to a forest. We fly over the forest, and I become curious about what is below. I look. People. Is that really so? Yes, it is people. As we fly, day turns into night, and the stars and the moon shine brightly in the night sky. I am filled with wonder.

I see a huge bonfire in the middle of a clearing. We circle round and join the people who are singing, dancing, and chanting around the fire. Lost in the experience of the dance, they don't seem to notice our arrival. Joy and celebration energize this group and float upward in our direction, washing over us, wave after wave. We land. Without a thought, I shape-shift into the lion; we shape-shift into each other. I no longer question my experience or what is or is not possible.

We become one of the dancers moving around the fire with fluidity and grace, weaving in and out of other dancers, carried away by the sound of the drum, the chanting, and the intense joy in this group. We feel at home, as though we belong in this place with these people. It seems as if shape-shifting is an everyday occurrence for me. The experience is incredible, powerful, and overflowing with joy. I feel the joy flowing through my veins, sinking into my cells, and washing through my energy field.

Then the drumbeat changes. We are being called back. The shaman made us promise we would come back when the drumbeat called for us. I'm good to go. My nothing journey has turned into something quite spectacular. I am more than satisfied with this little glimpse of something beyond the scope of my understanding.

The lion and I swiftly take flight and travel back over the forest and meadow, to the entrance of the hole. He will stay in the meadow. I'm not even sure when I separated from him. I am aware of going back up the drainpipe and arriving in the tent, where my body is waiting for me, lying on the ground on top of my blankets with the friends who have gathered together for this experience. I do not want to end my journey, but I am delighted that a very powerful experience has emerged for me.

The shaman tells us he drummed for about ten minutes—a shorter time than usual, but it felt right for this group. It is one of my first remembered experiences of time out of time, with time standing still, and nothing else important occurring in that moment. Ten minutes seemed to be a lifetime beyond lifetimes. A lingering experience. A beautiful journey.

The shaman invites us to tell stories about our journeys. He says this is important, as it will ground the experience for us and allow us to discover what more is there, what symbols are alive for us, and what lasting impressions we will carry away. We are invited to speak about what the drumbeat has shared with us and to say at the end of it, "This is my medicine."

The shaman offers a talking piece for us to pass around the circle. It is a beautifully carved wooden stick adorned with feathers. It's purpose is to invite the person holding it to speak and the rest of us into silence to bear witness to the story teller, create a space to catch the stories that arrive in our circle. It is my first experience with a talking piece.

One by one we share our stories. There are bits of medicine or meaning for me in each person's story, and bits of medicine for others in mine. I have a vague awareness or impression of somehow having broken through a barrier in my own mind about what is real and is not real, what is possible and not possible.

I carry the sense of celebration and joy deep within me. I am told how radiant I look, my joy shining from the inside out.

CHAPTER 1

SHAPING LIFE AND MEANING THROUGH STORYTELLING

I walk into a restaurant ten minutes early for my meeting. There are two moms sitting at a table with their young daughters. The little girls are not yet a year old.

One of them spies me as I walk in. She squeals in delight. Her face lights up. The other one turns to see what has her little friend so bubbly. She also lets out a beautiful little squeal of delight.

For the next ten minutes, these two little girls amuse themselves, each other, and me with delicious baby laughter sparked by engaging me, fully openhearted, in this nonverbal encounter.

Their mothers, curious about what has their daughters' attention, turn to look at me. I smile reassuringly back at them and continue in this dance with the girls until

1

their mothers pack them up, leaving me richer for the exchange.

Another time, I am in a line at the Halifax airport, getting ready for a flight to Newark on my way to Switzerland. In front of me is a couple with a young boy, also under a year old. He is acting out a little. It is very early in the morning. We are on one of those flights that seem like a good idea when you book them, but when you set the alarm to wake up, you wonder what on earth you were thinking.

As I stand behind this family in the line, the boy catches sight of me. All of a sudden, he is paying rapt, delighted attention. As I engage with him, his parents turn to look at me. We begin one of those little conversations about babies and early mornings. They are grateful for the distraction that quiets their child.

We end up on the same small plane. They are a row ahead of me on the opposite side of the plane. The boy keeps leaning into the aisle to catch glimpses of me. A couple of times, he practically crawls out of his father's arms trying to get to me, to his parents' puzzlement and amazement.

The central theme or thread of *Embracing the Stranger in Me: A Journey to Openheartedness* is sense making or finding meaning. How do we make sense of our lives, of the things that happen to us—our experiences, relationships, journeys, or paths? We do this by telling stories—stories that then also shape our experiences and allow us to discover further meaning.

Stories can shift and change over time in the retelling of them through the remembering of long-forgotten details and the nuances that appear as we see different aspects of the same story. We tell ourselves and each other stories about work, children, parents, friends, joys, grief, struggles, frustrations, anger, and more.

Many of us have fallen into unconscious storytelling, lacking awareness of the kinds of stories we tell and the impact they have on us. We tell stories that stress us, make us prematurely age, make us ill, and make us the victims of our own circumstances. We also tell stories of appreciation, gratitude, love, and curiosity. These are the stories that enrich and enliven us, spark joy, give us energy and strength, make it effortless for us to go about our day, allow us to surrender into the flow of what wants to happen, and help us stay present. Often, we don't realize we have a choice about which stories to tell—the ones that give us grief or the ones that give us joy. But we do have choice. Every time we tell a story. We have a choice of what story we want to focus on and how we want to tell it.

The things we focus our attention on are the things we will get more of. This is why we sometimes seem to be spiraling in time. There are days, weeks, months, and even years when everything seems to go right or everything seems to go wrong. We are not always aware of the turning point. We just become aware of the pattern. When it is a pattern we do not like, we want to externalize it, to point to people, conditions or situations outside of ourselves. Point blame and point it somewhere else.

When it is a pattern we do like, we might be more willing to take credit for it, but often we still externalize it—as if it happens *to* us—rather than being attracted by us, rather than being aware of our choices and taking responsibility for those choices, claiming our ability to shift the shape of our own lives.

Taking responsibility is so simple and so difficult at the same time; it is as simple as noticing, yet it is as difficult as practicing it day after day until it becomes simple.

When did you last take notice of the focus of your stories—whether they make you feel bad or good, drag you down or uplift you, disempower you or empower you—the ones you tell yourself and those you tell others?

When we are unconscious of the stories we tell, we are not aware of their effect on us or on others. When we become more conscious, we notice and become more aware of choice. With choice comes the opportunity for intentionality and the ability to shift the shape of our lives and our experiences. We can do this simply through the focus of the stories we tell, the lens through which we see the unfolding of our lives.

In my life, I have told many stories that externalize or give away my power. Learning to own my own experience and my own power has been, and continues to be, a significant part of my journey. I have told many disempowering stories, even when I thought I wasn't doing so. With great intentionality, I have been shifting my focus to tell more and more of the stories of appreciation, gratitude, and love. I am telling more of the stories of the way I want my life to be rather than of how I don't want it to be—so I can focus on and attract what I want, rather than what I don't want. Using story to create new truths in my life.

I have come to understand that all things in my life are here by my invitation or attraction of them in one way or another. If I were not attracting these experience, the insights that arise from them could not be in my experience. This includes people, events, situations, timing, and flow.

This supposition, that everything that has shown up in my life is here by my invitation, is a lot to contemplate, and it becomes truer the more I lean into it. This knowledge is a good thing. I realize that there is no out, no one else to blame, and no finger to point. I accept full responsibility. Full stop.

You might think this would be weighty. Surprisingly, it is not. It is freeing and allows me to step fully into my path with strength, courage and power.

Knowing that everything is here by my invitation has contributed to my journey to openheartedness. We build walls around ourselves when

4

we fear being vulnerable, fear for our emotional well-being. We intend to protect ourselves by shutting out attack, shutting out hurt before it happens, shutting out people before they can hurt us more. It does not work. It does not work because instead of shutting others out, we shut ourselves in. Our heart becomes fragile and brittle. Sadness, frustration, grief envelops us and has no escape through the barricades we build until something seeps out or explodes out in ways we never intended and can't easily recover from. Then we are convinced we need to close down further. Nothing can be further from the path of power and strength than this supposition.

The journey to open heartedness is not about being exposed in a way that is threatening or harmful. It is about waking up and opening to the full range of emotional melody that resides within us—the full range, the rich textures of symphony that wants to make itself heard, not just a narrow range of notes played in isolation. Through the journey to openheartedness, I am learning to live in and with vulnerability—not as weakness but as strength—and I am relying on emotions as a guidance system that is unfailing the more I learn how to use it.

In this book, I share stories of my life. They are stories that spoke to me. They are threads that shaped my journey to embracing the stranger in me. They comprise the journey to openheartedness, to making peace with soul—both my own and the souls of others whose journeys have touched me. Some are sorrowful. Some are joyful. Some are stories that more rightly belong to others, such as to family members. But I am the storyteller here, and it is the way these stories have shaped and influenced the larger narrative of my life that feels important to convey.

They are stories of things that eventually became possible with increasing levels of awareness. They describe my way of being in the world and of being more fully in the world as a result of my journey. I share my stories as a way to dive into deeper patterns that shape life, relationships, healing, and journeys. Even as I reread and edit them, they move me— sometimes to laughter, sometimes to tears. Even though I have spent a lot of time unearthing and living with these stories, some of them still have the capacity to delight and surprise me. My hope is that they do the same for you.

Confluence of Events

This book took shape and form at the confluence of three significant threads in my life over a five-year period. One was coming to know a spiritual lineage that awakened in startling ways after having been deeply buried in my consciousness; this has been called a shamanic journey by friends, an awareness I might not have had or named as such on my own. Another was discovering a physical lineage I had no idea existed. The third was discovering how to walk in the world in my strength, joy, and compassion and to be powerful in my vulnerability in ways that have increased my depth of presence, connection in relationships, and capacity to do deep, meaningful work in the world.

The first two threads speak to the stranger in me—parts of myself I was not familiar with and did not even know existed. The last speaks to the journey to openheartedness, although getting to an openhearted state has been a long and, at times, difficult journey that I am now experiencing with increasing ease most of the time.

Like the fabric of life itself, this book is not just one story; it is a weave of many stories. It is not linear, although there is a path it follows. It is not a chronological account, for the most part, because the stories wanted to be shared in the way we tell them—as associated stories of life where one story sparks another story in the same thread, following the threads through time rather than the weave of all story threads at the same time, in the same telling. In this book there are threads that follow my parents and their stories, and threads following different aspects of my own story unfolding over time.

The writing experience, like the journey itself, took me in unexpected directions. Sometimes, I would sit down to write expecting the process to go forward into the future. To my surprise, it would go back into the past instead—into my family's lineage and into things that shaped me without my knowing or without me even being in the world. This helped me understand that we are not just shaped by our own experiences but that we are also shaped by the stories that are alive in our families, in our lineages, and even the stories that are alive in our collective consciousness. The stories themselves are not what shape us, for we all tell them differently; instead it is our interpretations of and responses to those stories that make us who we are. Changing the shape of the stories and changing the shape of our responses shifts the shape of our lives. It is surprisingly, beautifully true, and easy enough for anyone to test.

Human Tragedy and Soul Journey Lenses

I have thought of my life's experiences as part of a greater journey that transcends birth and death, and the physical experience as we know it. It is a soul journey bridging life and death.

Soul journey is rooted in spirit, in energy, in the essence of who we are before we are born, before any naming of who we are in the physical journey occurs. We are named first as human, baby, toddler, child, teenager, young adult, middle aged, old or any other words we use to place people in our understanding and knowing. We are defined by birth, family, lineage, gender, color, race, place of birth, and so much more even before the name by which we will be called is given to us upon our arrival. These things will linger in physical time and space long after our physical body breathes its last breath.

Soul journey encompasses non-physical experiences, before we come into physical being, while we are in physical form and after we leave the body behind. It is consciousness, not contained in or identified by physical form. It is choices we make and agreements we enter before coming into physical form that guide, but don't necessarily predetermine—what we want our experiences to be. It includes all those we meet on our path—physical and non-physical—and the experiences we invite—intentionally or not.

Purpose and meaning mark our path and call us home—home to the soul, home to longing of the soul—over and over again. This compels us to respond—if and when we pay attention. Embarking on soul journey is like opening a door that will not close, no matter how many ways we try, once we venture through it.

Soul journey is easy to lose track of when we are confronted by the immediacy of the physical experience, which often appears as human tragedy. We see what happens in the physical experience (illness, death, conflict, destruction, failure) as overwhelming, discouraging, tragic—things that should never happen. In my soul journey, I learned to know them as things to be embraced rather than feared, transcending human tragedy to marvel at the potency of soul journey.

Through the experience of soul journey, I have come to a place of knowing that we are both physical form and energetic or spiritual form. The physical form has most of our attention, but the spiritual form is so much larger and expansive than we often know. We find that it is richer than our physical focus when we choose to divert our attention to it. Deep in our cognitive and intellectual sense-making, we disbelieve the energetic component of ourselves. Yet it is in the energetic component that a vast expanse of territory lies to be discovered and explored. When we tune in to it, we shift the shape of our perception and illuminate horizons not available through ordinary sight.

Some of the sense-making of my life involves exploring and illuminating the expansion that becomes possible when we tune in to the energetic aspect of ourselves. It influences how we show up in the world, even when we are not aware of it. Tuning in to the physical is one way to tell the story of our lives. Tuning in to the emotional is another, and tuning in to the spiritual is yet another. These methods are all "right," and there are many combinations of what that could also look like. The question is, how does it influence how you live your life, how tuned-in you are, or how present you are from day to day? Does it serve you or hinder you?

Progress in my soul journey is reflected back to me through many relationships, circumstances, and events and through learning how to enjoy my own company and solitude. And, I have learned to enjoy the company of people dear to me through the work I am called to do, through walking the path with my parents in their health challenges, and through finding my way in marriage and divorce and as a parent. I am also someone who has struggled financially, emotionally, and spiritually for far longer than I care to remember or admit.

Deeper spiritual awakening unfolded in me in the most startling and beautiful of ways: in becoming aware of spirit, spirit guides, and power animals; in finding my voice and learning the power of expressing it; and in experiencing and being witness to my mother's journey with dementia and death. My mother's journey, more than many other things has helped me see how the human tragedy perspective often obscures the soul-journey perspective for many of us.

We are multidimensional human beings. We are not just one version of one story we want to imagine true; we are complex humans known by and through the many stories we tell and live into.

Secrets Shape the Stranger Within

One thing I have discovered in verbally telling many of my stories is that everyone has stories. People have stories. Families have stories. Countries, cities, towns, communities, and organizations have stories. Some stories are told often. Some are funny. Some are sad. Some are tragic. Some are deeply buried.

Some of those stories are also secrets that have been hidden, to greater and lesser degrees, for periods ranging from short amounts of time to generations. There is power in those stories, in those secrets. They have energy that gives them holding power. The power in those secrets is directly proportional to the fear we hold about the secrets being revealed. But these skeletons in the closet, scary though they may be in the dark, are not so scary when illuminated by the light of day, by courage, by boldness, and by love. We all have secrets. We all have failures, frailties, and imperfections, for we are all human.

Secrets take on a life force and energy of their own. They influence the shape of people's lives. Secrets are intended to be a protective mechanism for ourselves, others, the innocent, and our children although they don't often end up serving that way, partly because little people are sponges, and walls have ears. Secrets are not as secret as we think. Even when not spoken, they have an energetic field that shows up in physical space through a person's posture and through interpersonal dynamics. We often sense them even if we do not know what we are sensing.

Secrets reinforce the idea of a stranger lurking in shadows somewhere within ourselves, others, and our families. When we look at ourselves, we want to embrace only the good parts and ignore the rest, imagining in the ignoring of it that it will just go away and leave us with the good. That is not how it works. The more we try to ignore it, box it up, and banish it, the deeper the stranger is submerged in shadow.

When we look at others, especially those we love, we want to embrace the things we see that resonate with what we want to know of them and deny the rest. This is why we have "honeymoon periods" with people we marry and our friends. We embrace the parts of them we like and pretend the other parts do not exist. This leads us to more shadow and then disappointment when we are forced, by things that show up in our path, to face the things we try to deny about ourselves, our situation, our relationships, and people dear to us.

Layers of secrets, little and big, separate us from the essence of who we are. Of course, we didn't mean for this to happen. We didn't intend it. For most of us, by the time we come to awareness we are already full-on in the business of secret making. This is why we fear being exposed as an impostor. In some ways we have this fear because we are impostors to ourselves, having lost our way. Somewhere along the way, we become strangers to ourselves.

We fragment within ourselves, letting ourselves see what we want to see, trying to ignore or disavow the parts we do not want to see or do not want to acknowledge. We become afraid to reveal ourselves—not just to others but also, especially, to ourselves. We don't tell anyone about shoplifting as a child, bullying we may have been involved with, supplies we took from work, extra drinks we consume (especially when alone), pills we pop, times we've been mean, little white lies we tell, the full extent of our culpability, or our responsibility in broken relationships. We want to hide some of it and blame others for most of the rest of it.

No wonder we feel fragmented, incoherent, and incongruent, like a stranger we don't know and sometimes don't even like. It's not the size of the secret that causes problems; it's the power of it, the energetic hold of it. The more we fear other people knowing a secret, the more power it has. The more we are afraid to reveal the stranger within, the larger it looms. The stranger becomes the "other." We make up stories about it and then try to bury it, as if we can separate out and dissociate from a part of ourselves. But when we come to know the "other," we discover the other is not the story we have made up about the other, just as the stranger within is not the story we have made up about it that causes us to want to avoid our innermost being and keep it secret even from ourselves.

I always felt there were secrets in my family. I didn't realize some of those secrets had to do with me. Things that were hidden from me, that I had no way of knowing about, contributed to making me a stranger in my own life. There were parts of me or of my life I did not even know existed.

Discovering I was a stranger in my own life invited me into a contemplation of what that meant and a curiosity about where else and how else I was a stranger in my own life. I began to wonder about what parts of myself I knew and what parts I did not know and did not want to believe or acknowledge existed. Parts of me shut down and parts I shut out in order to not acknowledge or see them in me. I was a stranger of my own making—a stranger I was afraid to know.

I was a long way from how I had come into the world—how we all come into the world: powerfully gifted, tapped into spirit, tuned in to the ability to manifest easily and effortlessly with the clarity of knowing in our being that has and needs no words to express it. We are closest to spirit form when we have just arrived in the physical world. Our inner beauty and light shines through brilliant eyes, smiles, and giggles, just like those of the babies I described at the beginning of this chapter. We all come into the world without the ability to speak verbally. But we do know how to communicate. We are hardwired for it. We learn rapidly.

Babies see things many adults no longer see—guardians, angels, and other benevolent spirit entities. They gravitate to soul essence in others. They see through the veils that separate the physical world from the nonphysical world. For many of us, as adults, the veils seem to be walls that deny ease of communication between worlds, between states of consciousness. The nonphysical world feels separate, with access solidly blocked. It is hard to believe these walls are illusions, learned constraints constructed on the basis of fragmentation through the focus on and distraction caused by the physical world.

The walls are belief systems. Beliefs are simply the things we tell ourselves over and over again. They become part of our filters and perceptions. We come to know them as truth. We forget that many truths can exist side by side. We forget we can shift our learned belief systems from what no longer serves to what will now serve better.

In reflecting on what engaged those young children so much, I believe that it was likely less my physical being and more what they could see surrounding me in the nonphysical field, the things many of us have learned not to see anymore. But what if we could learn to "see" again? Not just a privileged few, but all of us.

Embracing the Stranger

My dances with these children and others are road marks along my journey to openheartedness. Becoming aware of and living into my core essence only became possible by wading into the shadows, discovering and then facing and learning to embrace the stranger in me bit-by-bit, step-by-step, reluctantly, disbelievingly, actively resisting before ever being ready to surrender into what was awaiting me.

Some of what was awaiting me was an awareness of nonphysical beings or entities: protectors, guardians, angels. Whether I was aware of them or not, they were always with me, guiding my journey. With my first awareness of this spiritual expression, I was in denial. I was sure it couldn't be me, a part of me or a reflection of me. I was not that "kind" of person. I was not powerful or gifted in that way. As more and more instances of awareness arrived, I begrudgingly accepted them, but I did not know what to do with this foray into extra-ordinary reality or that which exists beyond the physical, beyond the veil. This was another element of the stranger in me. Who or what was this person who could sense the energetic realm and "see" guides, who could help others see or know their guides? This was another aspect of fragmentation. When people told me I was powerful, I was sure they were mistaken.

Embracing the stranger in me required the acceptance of gifts I found hard to believe I had, gifts of essential soul qualities and inner essence. We all come into this world with these gifts. We are intimately connected to them before we become estranged from the very essence of who we are. We know our soul qualities when we are very young, before we learn concepts of right and wrong, good and evil. We know our soul qualities before we build constructs around ourselves that we fool ourselves into believing are truth and essential to survival. We shape life to fit in and shape ourselves in trying to make other people happy, particularly parents, others we look up to, and authoritative figures we depend upon for survival when we are young. Later it is good friends and family, significant others, and those we work with and for. Peer pressure and those we believe have power over us. Conditional love and conditional acceptance with criteria to meet, often unspoken but communicated nonetheless.

As we move from infancy to toddlerhood, we learn it is not always safe to expose our inner being. When it shows up in innocent ways, it somehow seems to be a threat to others through the openness, authenticity and honesty of it. It is a looking glass for what we are afraid to face in our lives—how separated we feel from essence, how much like a stranger we've become to ourselves. It contains such sweet anguish; even as little beings, we feel the projection on us.

Our soul essence begins to feel fragile instead of strong. Without and beyond words, protective instincts kick in. We are not even aware that we are beginning to create these protective patterns. We begin to hide our inner being in little bits at first, but this grows to "at all costs." We know how precious it is, but we lose sight of it, connection with it and forget it is there. This continues to the point that our inner essence becomes a stranger—the stranger within. Not the dark, foreboding stranger we imagine it to be, but rather a light-filled, joyful, loving stranger trying to make itself known and heard. But when this stranger, our essence, calls out or whispers, it is like an echo with a source that one cannot discern. We imagine it outside ourselves and look around to catch a glimpse.

And so begins the journey of the stranger. We don't even notice. We don't have awareness of the process we are in. We build defenses, construct walls, and create personas to protect our inner essence. Bit by bit, we begin to imagine the constructs we have created are our inner essence. Disengaged from our inner essence, we imagine that the shadowy construct we have created is who we really are. We summon shadow to protect our inner core and imagine a stranger resides there— someone we don't know, aren't connected with, and should fear. We know we should fear it, because every time we make a decision that is not in alignment with our core essence, with our values, we attribute it to this stranger we have crafted. "This isn't like me," we say, looking to excuse the poor choices, bad behavior, or emotional responses we have become uncomfortable with—usually anger, sadness, grief, and frustration. In our confusion, we seek this stranger out less often. Then we forget what it is we have hidden from ourselves or how to unbury it, often for a long, long time. For some of us, maybe even forever.

The inner being of beauty and light—the very essence of who we are that we see in the purity and innocence of children—goes undercover, shifts into a stranger.

We spend much of our life trying to thwart this stranger, running from the fear instead of facing it. In so doing we generate more shadow, obscuring our soul essence more completely and expanding the construct of the stranger within, even more certain that what lurks within is to be feared, not embraced. We make choices about our life, our path, our relationships, and our work. When we perceive those choices to be bad, we begin to imagine we must be bad—otherwise, why would we make bad choices that hurt us or hurt other people? And if this badness—this evil, even—resides at the core, why would we ever want to know it? And why would anybody ever want to know us or, more than that, love us? We must be unlovable.

If we believe this story—that we are unlovable—we will look around and find all kinds of proof to support our belief in the story we make up. We make ourselves unlovable to ourselves. We look outside ourselves to find that love and are disappointed time and time again. No one can love us enough. We cannot get from others what we have not given ourselves. We cannot receive all the goodness, love, beauty, and joy that is awaiting us. We shut it out. We believe ourselves unworthy. And we shut down more. It hurts to love. We build excuses to barricade our hearts. We externalize the source of our pain.

The answer doesn't lie out there or with someone else. It lies inside, beyond the shadows we fear. It is only by embracing the stranger in the shadow that we release its hold, the power we imagine it has over us. It is by heading into the shadow with curiosity and compassion rather than fear and judgment that we can begin to see the stranger for what it actually is—a part of us we mistakenly fear, a part of us that needs to be embraced with love and openheartedness. By shifting the shape of the story of the stranger, we gain the power and the strength to shift the shape of our lives.

The openings to embracing the stranger appear all the time if we are paying attention. Every now and then, the stranger—our inner essence—finds an opening and bubbles to the surface. We glimpse it, but it is so unlike what we are expecting that we don't recognize it. We are expecting a monster, but we glimpse something else. Maybe we have been inspired or encouraged by it and now want to find it, but it seems elusive. We find it hard to believe that what we have glimpsed lives in us, because we are convinced the shadow shields an unsavory stranger we do not want to know. If that constructed stranger is within, then purity, light, love, joy, and redemption must be somewhere else— anywhere else, not inside. We look elsewhere for it, everywhere other than where it actually lives.

We look outside of ourselves to see what we are afraid to look within to find. We look to others to validate us and our experiences and tell us what a good job we've done, what a good person we are. We compare ourselves to others. On occasion, we take false joy in our journey because we can measure our progress and success externally. But deep inside, the stranger, our core essence, is rumbling, calling to us—sometimes gently, sometimes with a strength and persistence that rattles our cage. It is trying to guide us, but we cannot hear it and cannot feel it except for the deep tremble we interpret as fear, the image of this constructed stranger that is larger than life itself.

Journey to Openheartedness

Things happen in life—conspire, even—to force us on a journey to discover who or what the stranger really is. It becomes time to step fully into the journey, to intentionally shift the shape of who we are and how we show up in our own lives. It is only by going to the edges of our fear and a bit beyond that we become ready to face it without even understanding what that means or what we have begun.

Taking those first tentative steps to meet the stranger, we peer into the shadow. What is there, really? Is the stranger within what it seems, or is it something different? What is truth? What is construct? What is alive because we have imagined it to be so and because we have told ourselves, over and over again, the stories that reinforce the constructed stranger? What if we dared to let ourselves dream a different story that could also be true if we gave it life and breath? What if we began to let our defenses down, even a little bit, to open our hearts to what awaits?

This stranger we have feared is at the core of all our failings, all our struggles, all our misguided actions maybe this stranger is an illusion conjured up by the shadow we have both created and feared in order to keep us from the exploration of what is really at the core. This constructed stranger was intended to keep us safe, but instead our resistance to and fear of it causes countless struggles and detours along the way.

Stepping into the shadows and embracing the stranger within is a necessary step to passing through the shadows to our core essence. Our core essence resides not in the dark but in a light that is ready to shine brilliantly as we brush away the shadow we no longer need to fear or construct. As we respond to the longing of our soul by embracing the stranger within. As we step into the journey to openheartedness.

Some of the fear and the trembling that we experience is attributable to the knowing we have that to allow the true essence of who we are to emerge, and to walk with power and strength in life, may require changes in life and lifestyle, changes in relationships, and changes in us—things we need to let go of to allow our full essence to come into being. These are often not easy shifts to make, because they involve other people and us, our notions of who we are, who we think we are, and who we are capable and deserving of becoming.

The real stranger is no stranger at all. It is a shadow disarmed by embracing it, by opening our heart to it. Underneath or within it, it is the incredibly gifted, talented, beautiful, authentic soul essence residing inside each of us, waiting for the opportunity, the growth, the courage, the love, and the joy to burst out in full bloom.

This is what the step into the darkness exposes—that it is actually a step into the light. It is a journey to the core, to the stranger, who is embraced and remembered not as a stranger, but as a gift, a friend, and an essential aspect of self. What is the courage needed to meet and embrace the stranger within? What is the courage needed to step into the journey to openheartedness? It's different for each one of us.

Embracing the stranger is a key premise in this book. In the course of my life's journey, I made decisions and choices that I believed surely must have emanated from some unsavory, unlikable inner self: the stranger within to be feared and shunned, certainly not disturbed to greater awakeness. It was easier to believe that than to accept full responsibility for the decisions and choices in my life. Yet the call to a deep inner dive of self-discovery was so strong I could not ignore it. The more I resisted, the more trauma and struggle showed up in my life. Beginning to embrace the journey and the stranger attracted things and knowing to me beyond my wildest imagination—things that happen to other people you read or hear about, not to someone you actually know, and certainly not to yourself.

I grew up in a small town, moved to a small city, and have lived in a small province all my life. My life began as ordinary—or so I thought. The extraordinary things that have unfolded in my life at times have seemed unreal to me, as though I were going through the motions of someone else's story—things that happen to other people.

You would think that any one of these events would have been enough to handle in a life journey, enough to spark authenticity and strength. Yet in my life, as in many of our lives, one event alone was not all that was needed. A multiplicity of events and experiences shapes who we are. There are many things that call us to journey deep into our essence. I tried to shut it out and shut it down. I feared the places in me that I was being called to travel to. I feared what I thought was the stranger in me. I ran headlong from her into trial, tribulation, conflict, and confusion, fueled by feelings of unworthiness and insecurity.

My greatest teachers showed up in the most unexpected of ways and the most unexpected of places, with the most unexpected of gifts. Some of them were benevolent, and more of them were harsh—until I learned to embrace all that showed up along the way.

I discovered healing in my path. There are many ways to encounter healing through embracing the secrets and the shadow, as well as those things we believe to be beautiful about ourselves. Many people have had spiritual experiences they do not know how to name or talk about or are not willing to share for fear of being exposed as somehow less credible, less reliable, less rational. And many have walked paths while cloaking themselves to make themselves as invisible as possible in journeys screaming at them to be visible and have voice. Sometimes the life path is easier than we imagine it can be through the stories we tell ourselves about ourselves and our life. We tell stories about trauma, difficulty, and suffering as necessary pathways to enlightenment, enrichment. That suffering is a part of life. That there can only be so much joy. Imagine how the shape of your life can shift when you shift the narrative you tell yourself in order to allow, invite and welcome more of what you want and less of what you do not want into your life.

Storytelling gets to the heart of things that resonate for us all. I imagine that for those of you who are drawn to this book and my writing, this is the case because it calls out something in you that connects you to me and my journey and connects me to you too. Maybe reading my stories will illuminate something in you because you witness your own experience in someone else. Maybe your own experience will be more real for you because a similar experience is real for someone else.

I write what is in my heart and from my heart. I try to write with compassion—for me and my journey, as well as for those whose journeys have intersected mine and who show up in the telling of my stories. We don't live in a vacuum; we live in an interconnected weave of relationships. Relationships hold up a mirror to us if we can be both bold and aware enough to gaze at what is reflected back. They give us a road marker to let us know where we are in our journey, where we are free, and where we still need to heal. And all of that shows up in the stories we tell.

You might not believe everything I write. I almost have not believed some of my own experiences at times, and I have been living these stories. They are my stories of what has happened to me, and they are true—true to me, and true to what I remember. They may, however, not be "the facts". I am acutely aware that the people whose lives have been entwined with mine may have very different stories to tell of the exact same moments, shaped by their experiences, their perspectives, their lenses, their journeys. Of course their stories are different from mine. Those are their stories for the telling, not mine. I cannot write their stories, although initially I tried to write some of them. I discovered I can only write mine. I was challenged to only write of my stories to fully own and embrace them.

I welcome you into these stories of my life, of embracing the stranger within and the journey to openheartedness in the same way you would open any book of adventure—with curiosity and a willingness to suspend both belief and disbelief, to be carried along on the many rivers of life that show up, and find yourself reflected in these words at times when that is true for you. Imagine your own story unfolding as you read and discover how much of your life you interpret from a human tragedy lens and how much from a soul-journey perspective. Notice where your preference might lie. What courage rises up in you to meet yourself in your own meaning making?

I have started these stories with what I know—or, rather, what I thought I knew. These are the stories of my life. Then I move on to stories I did not know and never imagined possible, but they are also true nonetheless. Some of them are the stories of people related to me who I did not know at the time of the story I tell. Then I move back to the stories I now know, because I walk the path with more intentionality, consciousness, and purposefulness, although I still walk that path imperfectly. I celebrate imperfection, spirit, growth, joy, release, friendship, and, above all, the journey to openheartedness.

> I hear the stranger within me. I hear the calling of my soul. At times her voice is a whisper. At other times it is a strident calling of my name that is clearly not to be ignored.
>
> "Kathy, wake up!" she whispers to me.
>
> When I don't quite hear her, she grows louder. Then louder still. "Kathy, pay attention!" she eventually screams at me. "See, Kathy, I am pointing the way, and I know you know it. What will you do with what I place in your path? You can't ignore me, although you try. You already know you cannot hide.
>
> "Step in. Uncover. Lean in. Claim. Own. Embrace. Embrace the stranger within. Befriend me so you can remember who you are. This stranger can teach you. As you learn from the stranger within, you move beyond the shadow to the core. I am in you, and you are in me. You are much more than the shadow would have you believe.
>
> "Embrace me," she calls. "Come and find me. I am waiting for you to remember who you are. Invite the darkness as

21

a teacher. Move through it and beyond it with grace and compassion."

I discover she is waiting for me. She helps me find my way to birthing the second half of my life. She guides me in the journey to openheartedness. I don't always like the path. In fact, I often don't like the path. Sometimes I resent it; sometimes I loathe it. But the path has been so because of my deep resistance to embracing the stranger in me and the depth of barriers I created to protect myself, fearing that openheartedness will expose my weaknesses, making me vulnerable and a target rather than making me strong.

I discover I am wrong—about so many things—and not necessarily the things I thought I was wrong about. What a journey to joy a journey to openheartedness and embracing the stranger turns out to be.

CHAPTER 2

THE LINEAGE I KNOW

I am alone, standing in a lush field of tall grass and flowers on a hill overlooking the water. It is ocean water, although it is enclosed in a bay. It is near Martin's Brook, near Lunenburg, near where my grandmother lives. Not too far away is the yacht club.

It is a summer day, and the sun is shining. I already know what's going to happen next, because it has happened many, many times before when I have been standing in this exact spot.

Warships come into the harbor. It's startling, really. Unexpected. A juxtaposition in this day, the early 1970s. The ships are big and gray. In the clear day, cannon fire sounds. I feel moisture land on my skin. Droplets. Droplets of blood. They rain down on me. Where did they come from? I haven't seen other people, but I know these droplets of blood have come from people. Where else could they have come from? Where are the people? Why is blood raining down on me?

I was eight or nine years old, or maybe eleven or twelve, when I had this dream. It recurred many times, so maybe I was all these ages. It was the late '60s or early '70s; it was not the age of social media or video games, and nothing this graphic was represented anywhere I would have seen it. Where did this dream come from? It is like another dream I had when I was four years old. I only had this dream once, but I have never forgotten it.

> We are living in Shelburne, where we lived for just a short period of time. My brother is two. He is just a toddler. We two are just small children. He and I are out walking on our street. We cross the street to visit our neighbor, who is a friend of our family.
>
> A strange man appears. I don't remember exactly what happens next. Somehow I get separated from my brother. When I find him again, he has been chopped into little pieces and left on the front lawn of our neighbor's house.
>
> Terror grips me. My heart races.

After having this dream, I startled awake in my fear and ran into my brother's room, scared to death of what I might find. He was there, whole, lying peacefully sound asleep in his crib.

My imagination has been forever gripped by this nightmare. I don't remember much from when I was this age. I remember this dream. I remember the dream of blood raining down on me too.

We are not just who we are. We are also our forefathers and mothers. Maybe we are also our children even before they are born. The stories we grow up with shape our sense of who we are and how we walk in the world. The stories we hear over and over again give us a sense of footing in the world. The stories we tell are the ones we live into—bringing the past into the present and making them the future. Unless we change the stories we tell to shape a different future.

Stories of our families are not told in chronological order. They are told as memory stirs, when the occasion invites them, or when listeners appear. They are hard to track in the right order of occurrence in time, and usually this doesn't matter to us.

We derive identity, lineage, and heritage from our stories, the stories of our families, and the stories of our places and our travels. We tell them as the moment presents. They come one after another not because that's how they played out, but because one story reminds us of another and that one reminds us of another.

The stories in this chapter inform the lineage I knew—the one I grew up with, and the one that stays with me even as the notion of my lineage expands as I come to know how I am a stranger in my own life and as I come to know the stranger in me.

Ten-Year High School Reunion

I am in Lunenburg, where I grew up. This is the same town my mother grew up in and the same town her parents, my grandparents, made home. It's my ten-year high school reunion. While I come back to Lunenburg, Nova Scotia, often to visit with my parents and my grandmother, I don't spend much time in the town. I haven't kept in contact with the people I graduated with from high school. My life has become centered in Halifax, where I now live and work, just an hour from where I grew up. I have a circle of friends and network of colleagues there. It doesn't feel like there is much for me in this small town. I was so happy to leave, to step into a larger circle of friends and a larger area. There I can hide if I want or find community where it calls.

Lunenburg is a small town with a population of about three thousand. It is a quaint little town. Even now it retains its character with heritage buildings and colorful homes. It was declared a Unesco Heritage Site in 1996. Pictures of the town, the waterfront, and key historical buildings, such as the school and the many churches from two or three hundred years ago, are readily identifiable.

My parents moved back to Lunenburg when I was five after a few years of living in Digby, where they were living when both my brother and I were born, via a short detour through Shelburne, Nova Scotia. My mother grew up in Lunenburg. It was a fishing town when she grew up there. It was a fishing town when my brother and I were growing up too. The town revolved around fishing; the industry there serviced the ships and equipment that made the fishing industry possible.

My mother's father, my grandfather, Loran Ritcey, known fondly to all our family as Pops, was the captain of a fishing vessel until he retired at the age of sixty-five in the early 1970s. He loved being out on the water so much that he filled in for other captains during the summer of his retirement. He was filling in for the captain of a scalloper, the *Kathryn M*, out of Scotia Trawlers Ltd. when the boat ran into some engine trouble and headed back into port. In the brief time he was in port, he came around to our house to say good-bye to my mother, more emotional than he normally was. He told her to make sure she took care of her mother, my grandmother, Kathleen, who was affectionately known as Casey by everyone, a nickname arising from the poem "Casey at the Bat" because of her love of baseball.

In the normal course of ordinary events, the ship headed back out to sea. Pops died at the helm while at sea on August 9, 1973.

Later, the family found out that he knew he had a heart condition and his time was limited. He wanted to do what he loved and preferred to die at sea than at home where my grandmother would find him. Was it a choice? Who's to say? Was it part of his soul journey? And my grandmother's too? Might have been.

My mother's brother came to our house to give my mother the news. Mom met him at the front door. He said, "Mary, Dad passed away." She broke into tears in an outpouring of disbelief and grief.

I was thirteen years old. I witnessed the scene but was puzzled. I was not sure what had just happened. There was so much confusion in my house that I left. I went to the only place I knew to go to—my friends' house a couple of doors down the street. I wasn't really sure of the language I had heard. I didn't know whether my uncle had said "passed out" or "passed away." I knew there was a significant difference, but I was unsure if "passed away" meant my grandfather had died. My friends and I tried to figure it out.

Well, of course, I later learned the answer.

While Pops was out at sea, one of Casey's nieces was visiting with her three-year-old daughter. The basement of my grandparents' house was a rec room where the TV and my grandfather's favorite chair were, a chair he often fell asleep in. During this particular visit, as the little girl started to go down the stairs to the rec room, she stopped midway and called out, "Mommy, there's a ghost down here!" She had the full attention of her mother and my grandmother. Undeterred, she went over to Pops's chair, kneeled in front of it, and put her head down on the seat. Later, they knew this was exactly the moment Pops died.

My grandmother, Kathleen Hackett Ritcey, grew up in Corner Brook, Newfoundland, a ruggedly beautiful province affectionately known as the Rock. The family was large, and to this day you will find a lot of Hacketts there. Kathleen went to a convent in the United States to be educated with a view to becoming a nun. When she decided that wasn't for her, she left the convent and went to Gloucester, Massachusetts, to visit friends for a while.

Loran Ritcey, my grandfather, was born in Kingsburg, Nova Scotia, just down the road from Lunenburg. He was drawn to the sea from a young age. He met and married my grandmother in Gloucester in 1930. They came back to Lunenburg afterward, where they lived most of their married life.

27

A life at sea can show up in many forms. This was the case for my grandfather. He was a fisherman who became a sea captain. But during Prohibition, rum-running was far more lucrative than fishing and my grandfather became a rumrunner. Casey didn't know this, though. She wasn't supposed to find out. It became impossible to guard this secret when Pops' ship was caught off of New York and he stood trial. He was convicted, and his adventures became front-page news in the local paper. The headline "Captain Loran Ritcey of the *Audrey B* Seized in New York Harbor," with aliases listed below, caught my grandmother's attention. In fact, it caught the whole town's attention. There is no doubt there was hell to pay when he got home from that trip.

There were a few harrowing near misses during Pops' time as a rumrunner. Once, a bullet that was intended to cross the bow as a warning shot hit the hull instead and went right through the captain's cabin. Fortunately it went through his sea chest and not him. Casey had the sea chest repaired, and it was used as a piece of furniture in their home for many years after that. It was a good reminder of adventures, the stuff of which stories are made.

After Prohibition, Pops returned to fishing and captained several boats over the years. The second boat he skippered was the *Jean and Shirley*, which was run down by a freighter during the war. Fortunately no lives were lost in the accident. One of his scallop draggers, built in Metaghan in the late '50s, was named the *Mary Patricia* after my mother.

My mother, Mary Patricia Ann Ritcey, was the middle child in her family. She had an older and a younger brother. They teased her mercilessly while she was growing up. There are stories of them chasing her, one of which involved her diving under the bed to escape them and breaking her nose in the process. It never healed quite right. She forever had a little bend in her nose that became quite pronounced in the latter years of her life.

In Lunenburg there is an amazing building on top of a hill surrounded by the town's cemetery. From one of the entrances to the town, you can see this building from a long way off. When I worked at the tourist bureau the summer I finished high school, people always asked about the castle on the hill. They were inevitably surprised to hear it was a school—a still-functioning school at that. This beautiful, majestic building had all the grades in it when my mother went there. When my brother and I were there, it was a primary to fifth-grade school.

My mother only attended the Lunenburg Academy until grade nine, which she failed—maybe because she was too easily distracted by the social dimension of school. A good friend of hers also failed grade nine that same year. Her parents decided to send her away to Halifax to attend the Mount Saint Vincent Academy, which was at that time a school for girls run by the Sisters of Charity. It later became a women's university and then a co-ed university which I attended many years later.

Mom had stories to tell about that place. Judging by her stories, I think that maybe this academy was not quite ready for her or the friends she made there. She often talked about sliding down the banisters in the gracious old building. And she talked about the fire.

In January 1951, Mom's last year there, a fire completely destroyed the original building called the Motherhouse. It happened at night. My mother told stories about the young girls, their faces plastered with night cream, running into the firemen. She always laughed as she wondered if that must not have been quite a frightful scene for those firemen. After the fire, the students and the Sisters were temporarily housed elsewhere in the city, billeted in people's homes, while classes were held in borrowed space. Fortunately a new building was already under construction, so they were soon back on campus.

When she graduated from Grade 12, my mother went back to Lunenburg. She earned her highest grades in math and bookkeeping. This took her to a job in a bank.

My mother met my father one of the times he pulled into port aboard his father's boat. The sea was also in my father's blood.

My dad, Raoul Hector Jourdain, grew up in Quebec. He is the youngest of six children, two girls and four boys. He was forever teased as being the "baby" of the family. He grew up in Cap Chat, a small village on the Gaspe Peninsula on the St. Lawrence Seaway. His parents, Edgar and Alvine (née Pelletier) Jourdain, had grown up across the river on the North Shore and relocated. They had grown up with nothing. Over the years, they amassed a small fortune through hard work. My grandfather became one of the most prominent citizens in his small community.

From a young age, all of the six children contributed to the work and welfare of the family. It was a difficult family to grow up in. Expectations were high, and consequences were harsh. My grandparents were strict disciplinarians; they didn't step away from that role no matter how old—or far away—their children were.

My father struggled with schoolwork until he began to study diesel engines. Then he excelled. Because his performance in that area was so markedly different from his performance in many of his other areas of study, at first his teachers thought he must be cheating or copying off of someone else's work. The problem with that theory was that there was no one else in the class with marks even close to his. This was work and knowledge that came easily to him; it was his purpose and passion in work. He graduated at the age of seventeen and began a career as a marine diesel engineer.

He went to sea on one of his father's boats to earn his papers. Shipping was one of the many business ventures my grandfather was involved in. Because my grandfather was so strict, the money my father earned mostly went to pay his way on the boat.

Lunenburg was well known for its shipbuilding and repair industry. Eventually Dad found his way there when the boat he was on went into dry dock. He was responsible for overseeing the dry dock work and was stationed in Lunenburg for weeks and months at a time.

Handsome Frenchmen who didn't speak much English were quite the exotic attraction in a small town like Lunenburg in the 1950s. All the girls were aflutter. My father met my mother in church, and they began a courtship that became long-distance when Dad went back to sea. Mom didn't speak any French, and Dad was just learning English.

It wasn't long before my father asked my mother to marry him. He proposed in a letter. Because he did it by mail, it took a while for him to get the response. But she did say yes.

They married January 11, 1958, in St. Norbett's Roman Catholic Church in Lunenburg, where they'd met. Their parents stood for them, and they had a small reception at the Boscawen Inn before heading out on a little honeymoon.

In the early days of their marriage, they moved around a bit, mostly in Nova Scotia, before landing back in Lunenburg with their two children—me and my brother Robert, who is two years, less a day, younger than I am.

When we first moved back to Lunenburg, we lived in the bottom flat of a large house on Fox Street. I used to tease friends by saying that it was named Fox Street because a real fox lived there. I was pretty convincing at times, but I don't believe I ever fully convinced my friends it was true.

Across the street was the Lutheran church and the home of the minister and his family. When we moved into the neighborhood, there were already quite a few kids in that family. As I was sitting on the curb playing one day soon after we moved in, one of girls ventured across the street.

I was five years old and happy to meet a possible new playmate. "What's your name?" I asked her.

"Kathy," she said.

Now that was a bit of a conundrum for me. "Your name can't be Kathy," I said. "That's my name."

The two of us put our heads together, drawing from the limited experiences of our short lifetimes, trying to figure out how it was that we both had the same name. We eventually concluded that this was possible because we were different ages (she was four years old). We made up a story between the two of us that we could use to make sense of our colliding worlds, and we made up rules where none existed as often happens in the course of our lives.

Just up the street from where we lived was the graveyard, and just around the corner was the school, the majestic Lunenburg Academy. Not far from the school and the graveyard was Gallows Hill. The graveyard and Gallows Hill served as playgrounds with lots of possibility for those who weren't spooked by the notion of ghosts or restless spirits. I heard quite a few invented stories about ghosts and goblins, but none that I knew or experienced to be true. We played a lot of hide-and-seek in these spots.

My family moved off of Fox Street and onto Dufferin Street, one of the main roadways into town, while I was still in elementary school. At first we rented. Then we moved into the house next door when the opportunity came up to buy it. This is the house my dad still lives in.

When my brother and I were young, we had a metal swing set in our backyard. As young children we swung on the swings and played on the teeter-totter. As we grew older, this became far less entertaining. We would wind the swings around the top bar as far as we could and still sit on them. We would get on the swing with the upper part of our bodies over the top of the swing set.

Later we did away with the swings altogether and just swung around the bar. We hoisted ourselves up, sat on top of the bar, and then dropped backward, wrapping our legs around the bar, swinging off of it to land on our feet—usually. Doing this was, of course, not without incident.

I remember several times lying on the ground with the wind totally knocked out of me, gasping for breath. That is a frightening experience the first time it happens. And the second, and so on. Fortunately it is not so frightening as to ward off a sense of adventure.

For curious children, there was always an adventure to be had: jumping off the roof of a garage; walking the railroad tracks; stealing berries from the neighbor's raspberry and blackberry bushes; or pickup games of hide-and-seek, baseball, kick-the-can, or tag.

Growing up in a small town, you pretty much know everybody and everybody knows you. If you are the least bit physically active, you get to do a lot of sports and play on a lot of teams—not necessarily because you are really good, although some were, but because there is a shortage of choice.

I loved sports and physical activity. In junior high and high school, I played on the volleyball, basketball, and soccer teams. I also played extracurricular softball and figure skated.

I was a little under the radar at times. There was a physical fitness program in the schools that required us to take part in six different physical fitness activities. We were timed or counted or measured for each. There were awards for bronze, silver, and gold, and there was an award of excellence—which I received every year I took part in the test. One year, as the awards were being handed out in our gym class, someone spied the award of excellence badge. She wondered aloud who it was for. When I told her it was me, she laughed. The last laugh was on her. She had a look of utter surprise on her face when I turned out to be telling the truth.

I was the neighborhood organizer; I rounded up the kids to play baseball at an empty lot or down at the train station behind our house. We would begin a game as soon after supper as we could get enough kids assembled, and we played until it got dark and too dangerous to keep playing.

On summer days I would grab a friend or two, and we would go for long walks along back roads all around the town and surrounding areas, or we would walk the train tracks. We often walked to my grandmother's house a few miles away just for something to do. She enjoyed our visits and would entertain us with her endless supply of cookies before we headed back into town. Whole afternoons would pass by with these kinds of activities. There were only two channels on the black-and-white television. There was no sense of urgency. There was hardly any worry on behalf of the parents about where their kids might be; they always showed up eventually. But in my house, we didn't want to be late for supper or bedtime, as there were consequences.

During summers, my family spent a lot of time on the water. It was one of the ways the sea in my father's blood manifested itself. He couldn't stay away from it. When my brother and I were young, Dad had a boat called the *Robert K.* We would go out on that boat almost every summer weekend. One year, we were out late in the summer with two other small cabin cruisers. There were nine children altogether in these three boats, all of them pretty young at the time. It was Labour Day weekend, and there were storm warnings. Despite the fact that fishing boats were coming back into port to wait out the storm, my father and his friends decided to stay out at a popular anchoring spot that was pretty sheltered. The outside boats put down bow anchors and the middle boat, ours, put down a stern anchor.

> In the middle of the night, with the wind high, the anchors begin to drift. My father and his friends decide to haul them up and head for port. My father hauls up the stern anchor. It catches in the propeller of our boat. Dad cuts the anchor, but some of the rope remains. When he turns on the engine, the rope tightens around the propeller, stalling it. In the middle of the night, in the middle of the storm, with winds whipping around, we are adrift. We two small children, my brother and I, are in life jackets. My mother, who cannot swim, is without one.

The roar of the storm is so loud it is almost impossible for the other boats to hear my parents' cries for help. They scream and scream at the top of their lungs and ring the bell, trying to get the attention of their friends. My mother is in a panic. Her life is flashing in front of her, and she fears for the lives of her children as the boat drifts closer to the rocks.

Finally, someone looks back and sees the plight of the *Robert K* as the fury of the storm drives us toward the shoals of the nearby island. One of the boats comes back, and a passenger throws us a line. It takes a while for my father to catch it. It is dangerous for us to get too close to the other boat, especially since we have no maneuvering capability. When my father finally catches the line, he secures it to the bit at the back of the boat. We are towed into port, saving us from disaster and possibly even saving our lives. My father feels an eternal debt of gratitude to his friends.

Later Dad sold the *Robert K*. For a couple of years he had a beautiful mahogany speedboat. But a speedboat is not his style, so when the opportunity came up to buy one of the most beautiful old wooden boats around, he couldn't resist. The previous owner of the *Bluefin* sold it to my dad because he could no longer take care of it. Selling it to my dad was more like entrusting a treasured possession to a friend he knew would take care of it. Soon after he sold the boat, he died.

The *Bluefin* came fully equipped with engraved silverware, linens, matching curtains, pillows, and deck chairs. My father rebuilt it from stem to stern in the thirty years he owned it. It may well have been his greatest love. My mother was certain of that at times. Dad changed aspects of the boat; he built a flying bridge, installed marine technology, and remodeled the galley, but the lines, look, and colors of the boat stayed true to their original form. During the years of the Mahone Bay Wooden Boat Festival, the *Bluefin* always won awards, and Dad was a proud skipper, happy to share the stories of the *Bluefin* and its heritage with anyone who asked.

The joy of going out on the boat, however, was drowned out for my mother by the fear that had been invoked in her during the storm. She became a white-knuckled passenger after that, always reluctant to go. When my father came home from work on Friday afternoons, we would go out on the boat for the weekend. Inevitably my mother wasn't ready. This usually invoked an argument. I could never understand why she wasn't ready, because we always went, for sure. But I also didn't understand the depth of her fear. Years later I realized she harbored a silent hope that if she wasn't ready, maybe we wouldn't go. I don't know if she imagined what that kind of weekend would be like though.

Fortunately, my mother's strong extroverted nature won out while on the boat. It made her an excellent social director even after that harrowing encounter with the sea. She loved the social aspect of boating but hated water that was the least bit rough. Dad respected her fear, even if it made him cranky at times, and stayed close to shore, which was easy enough to do in a bay with over three hundred islands. Occasionally he risked going a little farther afield, but he always kept a close eye on the weather and sea conditions and would rarely knowingly take risks that he knew would frighten my mother.

Another dimension of life while I was growing up was visiting my father's hometown of Cap Chat, on the Gaspé Peninsula in Quebec, for family vacations. When my brother and I were very young, we would stay for two weeks. My grandparents and an uncle owned chalets back in the woods where they had built a swimming pool and a pond. They kept ducks in the pond over the summer, fattening them up for the fall; the ducks then became dinner over the fall and winter. My brother and I preferred to stay in the chalet when we visited rather than in the house, which was located right on the St. Lawrence Seaway. It was more relaxed at the chalet, devoid of the energetic patterns of family dynamics, and we found more to do there.

The Red Cross was allowed to use the pool to teach swimming lessons to local kids. It was one of the many ways my grandparents contributed to their community. My brother and I looked forward to those vacations, to swimming in the pool and meeting up with cousins we rarely saw. There was something exotic about the whole exchange. In addition to a couple who lived in Cap Chat, Dad's siblings lived in Montreal, in the mountains, and in Rimouski. My brother and I didn't know how to speak French, and our cousins knew only little bits of English, but having fun was never a problem for us. My mother didn't know how to speak French either, although a short time into our visits—especially after a drink or two—she would begin speaking English with a French accent. And she did know how to swear in French!

As the years went by, our annual summer trek to Quebec grew shorter. It began at two weeks, became ten days, and then was reduced to just a week. As I got older, not surprisingly, I became less interested in going. I wanted to stay with my friends or my boyfriend, or work.

I didn't realize how much stress my parents, my father in particular, were under during those trips. Deeply entrenched family dynamics continued to play themselves out. Both of my father's parents were strong and demanding personalities, each in their own way.

I was pretty oblivious to all that transpired. I have very few clear memories of the early part of my childhood. My brother remembers with startling clarity events, people, and dates, so I usually defer to him on anything that demands that kind of recall.

Along with those jaunts to Quebec, trips to Digby, was one of the biggest shaping forces on my early life long after we lived there when I was a baby, because my parents had developed close relationships to friends in Digby—friends we visited for years after living there, our visits dwindling as my brother and I got older.

My dad, the best diesel mechanic around, bar none, traveled a lot with his work at National Sea Products Ltd. My mother was often home alone with us. Her greatest joy was working as a hostess at either the Bluenose Lodge or at Captain Angus during the summers. Later she worked at my brother's lunch bar, his entrepreneurial initiative in his early twenties. She talked about those summers and her interactions with her customers—mostly tourists who were often on bus tours— long after she didn't work there anymore, as though it had happened just a year before instead of fifteen or twenty years previous.

When my mother was working and Dad was away, I had the days of greatest freedom I ever remember experiencing as a child. My brother and I were expected to do some things, but we could do them our own time. I read for long hours, watched the afternoon movie on TV, or hung out with my friends. It was completely relaxed, and we had so much fun.

There was a lot of tension in our household while I was growing up. My parents fought a lot. My dad worked hard as the breadwinner. Stress at work showed up at home. My mother escaped into Harlequin romance novels and didn't always take care of the home as Dad would have liked.

There were many times during my teenage years that I wished I were adopted and that my real family would come along and rescue me from the drudgery and dreariness of growing up in a small town. Of course, it never happened.

I only came to understand how much my father loved my mother years later when I was married with my own children. Mom and Dad were driving up to Halifax from Lunenburg. My mother was eating an apple and almost choked on a bite. It was bad enough that Dad had to stop the car and do the Heimlich maneuver.

When they arrived at my place, he was livid. I saw, maybe for the first time, that his anger was born out of fear—fear he would lose her. In this moment, I also saw the depth of love and connection between them, which had not always been easy for me to see.

My dad was away so much that he missed my high school graduation. He had to be in Japan at that time. I was the valedictorian for my graduating class. Anyone who wished could write a speech and submit it for consideration. I wrote one. I was in the middle of writing an exam when the English teacher made his way across the gymnasium floor right toward me. I knew he had my speech in his hand. It was quite an honor and it was terrifying at the same time. That was my first public speaking engagement.

Following high school, I went to Mount Saint Vincent University in Halifax. I didn't go because my mother had gone there; I went because it had the only public relations degree program in the country. Because of my love of writing, it seemed an apt choice; however, like many young people, I changed my mind about my career choice. After a summer of working at the Confederation Centre of the Arts in Charlottetown, Prince Edward Island, I came back to Halifax stirred up, until the awareness dawned on me that public relations was not for me and I needed to shift my major. I was only home for a couple of weeks. I was at my grandmother's house when the clarity came to me and I left there to drop this little bombshell on my parents and tell them I needed to go back to university to drop my courses and pick up new ones. I am not sure how shocked they were, but they were beautifully, lovingly supportive.

I moved to the Bachelor of Arts program and majored in sociology with a minor in psychology. After graduating with my BA, I decided to go for an honors diploma in sociology; I was the first ever sociology honors student at MSVU. I did it over two years so I could get a job and no longer rely on my father funding my education; this pattern of fierce independence shows up in my life in many ways. I had a part-time job working as a receptionist in an optometrist's office. It was a great work environment. The job turned full-time when I graduated. They were willing to train me as an optician, but I was deeply unhappy. This was not what I had imagined as a career—although I'm not quite sure what I did imagine or what I thought I would be able to do with a BA in sociology.

I searched for jobs, but because I had been born at the tail end of the baby boom generation, jobs were scarce. One day in a job interview I was asked, "What do you want to do in five years' time?"—a pretty standard interview question.

Much to my surprise, out of my mouth popped "I don't know. I think I might do anMBA."

I swear I looked around to see where that had come from. It was not in my plan. One of the reasons I'd left the public relations program was because of the business courses.

My answer, though, set an intention that soon became action. I wrote the GMATs and applied to two local universities. While waiting to hear back, I had a job interview for an exciting new project and landed a new job that was more interesting and engaging to me and significantly better paying than what I had been doing. Soon after I started my new job, I got acceptance letters from both universities.

By this time I was in a serious relationship, and I and my boyfriend were living together. I thought I might want to keep my job and study part-time. I wanted to have this conversation with my boyfriend, but he was reluctant to engage in it with me. He had seen how challenged I was while working and studying when I was finishing up my honors diploma, and he wanted me to decide on my own. The only way I could make the decision was to imagine what I would decide if I were on my own and it wouldn't impact anyone else.

I knew in my heart what I wanted to do. I decided to work full-time and study part-time. In the making of this decision, my boyfriend unconsciously and unawares set up a pattern of independent decision making that would haunt us later, in our marriage.

In the most unplanned of ways, my life path and my first career began to find their way to me. Instead of a business focus, I found myself in the not-for-profit sector, quite without meaning to go there. As I was finishing up my MBA, I began applying for jobs again. One job I applied for was an executive director position for an Atlantic-based health charity. I looked at the ad and thought, "I don't really want that job, but I'll apply for it anyway."

I got an interview, then a second interview, and I landed the job—a job that at twenty-seven years of age I had no idea how to do. I had never managed staff. Or a budget that large. Or volunteers on that scale. I dove into it without experience, without training, and without much support, not knowing the real power of the human equation. But I found my way as I went along. I was excited; I was ready to offer up all I had and more.

Ten years after graduation, I found myself back in Lunenburg for my high school reunion. At twenty-eight, I was married to a handsome engineer, had been an executive director for over a year, had newly graduated with my MBA, and was expecting my first baby.

My husband and I never fought. There was rarely tension between us. It was so calm compared to what I witnessed in my parents' relationship that it felt as though I had found the holy grail of marriage. I was seduced by the calm. It felt expansive. This was also part illusion; we didn't fight, but we also hadn't learned how to engage in conversation about things that matter. As issues came along that should have received our attention, we ignored them. They passed. Or, rather, they were swept under the rug so we could ignore them. I had no understanding of the importance of testing our relationship as we went, of learning how to argue, or of learning how to have conversations of fundamental importance to staying in a relationship with each other. No fighting was simply false harmony.

As bigger issues came along, we had not learned ways to find our way through them. We were isolated as individuals inside of our marriage. I felt I had no voice. I retreated into myself, into my work, and into relationships—mostly work or volunteer work—where I did have a voice, where I felt seen and heard, and where I felt people understood me.

Finally, the issues grew so big that there was no way through. We moved to a new, bigger house in a new neighborhood. One day, soon after we moved in, I was standing in the bedroom, looking out over the front yard to the street beyond. An awareness unexpectedly and surprisingly popped into my mind. *The next time I move will be when we get divorced.* The thought startled me. I had no idea where it came from, but it was prescient.

A year and a half later, life was crashing down around me; I was divorcing and moving. This was a far different scenario than that at the time of my high school reunion, when I was living life large. I never anticipated that ten short years following graduation I would be so successful. Sweet. In that moment, it felt as though I had it made. What more could one want? What more could I want?

It is good we don't always know what the future will hold. It was to be the best and the worst of times and just the beginning. By the time I was thirty-eight, my life had completely crumbled—I had divorced, had been fired from my job under difficult circumstances, and was laying some of the foundations for my life for the next decade. By the time I was forty-eight, I was twice divorced and, while continuing rewarding work as a consultant, had launched my third company. This decade of my life heralded some of the most amazing discovery and growth ever, precipitated by my hearing the calling of my soul, the voice of the stranger within, and feeling myself compelled to respond, even when all I wanted to do was run and hide.

For a person who came from such unassuming and humble beginnings, I had little foundation for making meaning of what was laying in wait for me. I had no idea how much of a stranger I was in my own life.

CHAPTER 3

SEEDS OF SOUL-
JOURNEY AWARENESS

December 4, 1997

Dear sons,

I am so sorry. I lost my job today. Coming on the heels
of the separation from your dad and the move into our
new house that you will share when you are with me, I
know you must be wondering why your world is changing
so much. You are both too young to really understand
everything yet. Maybe someday you will.

I know it looks like everything has come crashing down
around me and, consequently, at least part of your life. But
out of every ending is a new beginning. This is part of a
new beginning for me and for you too. It doesn't mean
that it will be easy. The path ahead will be difficult for me,
but I will make it as easy for you as I can. I won't lie to
you. Your world has changed, and things will be different
from here on in. But you will also be in safe environments,

because one thing is for sure: your dad and I both still love you very much. Your well-being is our top priority. The one thing about the future I know with certainty is that I love you both and you are a big priority for me.

Love Mom.

December 19, 1997

Dear sons,

These days leading up to Christmas are so difficult for me. I feel very much as though I'm going through the motions, without feeling a whole lot. Christmas for me is not the same this year. I know it won't be the same for you either, but I want it to still be wondrous and special. Santa will find you in your new home, and you will have more than one Christmas—with your dad on Christmas Eve, and then here with me, and then one with your grandparents.

Christmas 1997

Dear sons,

Thank you for once again showing me the wonders of the world through the eyes of a child. This Christmas morning dawned with a stunningly beautiful sky, the horizon lit up in a deep red colour as the sun rose. You looked out the window, instantly wide awake, and exclaimed, "Look, Mom! It's Rudolph's nose!"

What a great start to this day. Miracles on the horizon,

Love, Mom.

I move into a new house, my own house, near the end of November 1997. I am thirty-seven years old. The new house is around the corner from the one I moved into with the boys and their dad a year and a half before. Their dad and I have agreed that the boys' welfare is top priority. This is why I move close by—so the boys will go to the same school and have the same after-school care, bus arrangements, and friends.

I move because I feel responsible for the divorce. I ignored—or didn't recognize—the impending signs of marriage breakdown. We didn't talk to each other; we grew increasingly apart; and I became engrossed in work, study, and volunteer activities, all the while raising young children. He and I gradually increased our alcohol consumption until most nights we were not sober when we went to bed. Our sex life all but disappeared. I visited my parents more and more on my own with the children.

We did not agree on the number of children we wanted to have. He never wanted any. Now we have two. I didn't know if I wanted to be done having children, but I felt I had no voice in stopping. We didn't know how to talk about it.

I lost a piece of myself, and I buried it in the shadows where the stranger lives. I looked for that missing piece elsewhere: in success at work, in how often I was asked to chair committees or events, in taking on more. I was running from an existence I did not know how to enrich; running from a life that looked pretty perfect on the outside looking in. We were a successful couple with good jobs, good incomes, two beautiful boys and a fabulous caregiver for them, great friends and family, and a beautiful house.

Some friends saw it coming. Some friends were shocked. Most do not understand. I don't understand. What is wrong with me that I would throw it all away?

I tell my parents, "We are living under the same roof, but it is like we are living totally separate lives." My father says, "Yes, I can see that."

My father can see it! I thought this news would shock him. Instead it is me who almost falls off my chair.

Coming out of our situation, our divorce, as financially intact as possible is our second priority, after the boys' well-being. We calculate the value of our house and separate our assets. He remortgages. I buy a new house. We agree we will have joint custody of our boys, who are five and seven. It is quite the decision. Very few people have 50/50 custody arrangements at this time. Everyone tells us it will not work—counselors, lawyers, friends. "The boys will need a more 'stable' arrangement," they tell us. In the end, we know we have to try.

Since we have similar incomes, we do not want a child support or alimony arrangement. Before the divorce is finalized, I lose my job. My lawyer suggests I reconsider and think about child support. I decide not to take her advice. The most important thing to me is to keep our finances as simple as possible. And I feel guilty for wanting the divorce, for wreaking havoc on our lives. I feel fully responsible. Only later would I understanding that I took it all on—my own responsibility and more. This is a pattern that has dominated much of my life.

Ten days after I move into my new house, I lose my job. It is not unexpected, but it is painful. More than painful, really; it is devastating. My self-confidence, self-esteem, and self-worth are shattered. I wonder if they are—if I am—shattered beyond repair.

Many of the relationships that I had in my organization had been rapidly deteriorating over a brief span of time. I am beyond any means of repairing them. It has been incredibly stressful, and there is some relief in finally knowing what the plan is.

Before I lost my job, I talked to my brother, sharing with him my distress, my despair, how lost I am, how afraid. I knew I would get fired. It was just a matter of time, and now it is too late to find a new job, although I had been looking. I cannot afford to just quit. Especially now. My biggest fear is that I will be fired without severance. Then what would I do? My brother is almost speechless. He has never heard me like this before, as I have never been like this before. "You don't sound like yourself!" he says. Where is the calm, self-assured sister he knows?

I was lost in the fear of not knowing, consumed by shadow, disconnected from self, and doubting everything—except that my days in this job were numbered.

Sure enough, the day finally arrived. My office window overlooked the parking lot. I saw the president of my board arrive with another volunteer. I knew this was the moment. I steeled myself for the encounter. I was told I could stay and use the office into the New Year. Even though I was numb, I locked into an efficiency mode. Really it was a dissociated mode, so I wouldn't feel the experience. It would be too hard. Too heartbreaking. Too soul wrenching. It was clear it was in my best interest—and the organization's too—to leave right away. So I packed up my office and carted my personal things home at the end of a very long day.

There was an unsuspecting alarm system installation guy at my house to install an alarm system. In the polite way we all do, he asked me, "How was your day?"

"I've had better," I replied. "I lost my job today." The poor guy was speechless, not knowing what to do but no longer inviting casual chit chat.

My children, who overheard me, say to me, "But Mommy, how can you lose your job? You're the boss!" Not anymore. Not in that capacity anyway. With the slamming shut of that door came an opening to the unknown.

Now, what is next? One thing is for sure; I need to begin a concerted job search. The trouble is that I don't know where to begin. I know I do not want to work in the same sector I was in, but I don't know what else I want to do. It seems that the only jobs I'm really qualified for are in the old sector. I do apply for them; that seems to be an obvious move to make. I do not seem to get considered for anything that I apply for in other sectors even though I know my skills are transferable.

I know there is more I could be doing. My job loss has devastated me, creating a foggy paralysis. I am trying to walk on the seas of change, but I have no foundation. I have no self-esteem or self-confidence. I feel unsuccessful, as if I am a failure. I have lost eight years of my professional life. Even the successes I have had are elusive, as if they no longer count, or have been erased. I do not know who I am. I am a stranger in my own life. At the moment, this has more impact on me than the separation. It is of more immediate concern because I need to pay my mortgage, pay other bills, and support my children.

In the meantime, there are threads of normalcy that need to be distributed throughout my days, weeks, and months. Most of those are times when my children are with me. Two very different streams of life emerge in the weeks I have the boys and the weeks they are not with me. Every other week, I seem to experience empty-nest syndrome.

In one of the threads of normalcy, we go to an animal shelter to add to our family by adopting two new four-month-old kittens. The divorce books I read suggested thinking of divorce as an opportunity to do something you weren't able to do when you were married. For me that something was getting cats. I grew up with cats and have always loved animals. I thought not having pets wouldn't matter. But, in the end, it did—not in a significant way, but in a subtler way. And maybe it wasn't about pets at all; perhaps it was just about everything that was missing in my life—in me—during this time in my life.

The excitement mounts as we prepare to meet them in advance of bringing them home. We don't pick them; they pick us. A brown tabby comes right over and snuggles affectionately. A gray British shorthair saunters over in her own good time and is affectionate in her own subtler way. It is a match.

It is good for the boys to have their own animals in their lives. It teaches them empathy and caring at levels deep within. I am reminded of just how delightful and wonderful it is to have cats around. They make me smile and laugh out loud. They remind me of the simple pleasures in life. They are undemanding, need little, and give much. They are my company on long days at home. When I nap, as I do frequently in these days, they are right there, snuggled close. I thank God for my cats as days grow into weeks and weeks grow into months with very little seeming to change.

These are difficult months for me, but they open the way for healing. My days are marked by tremendous mood swings. I have good days and bad days, and often they are the same day. The days drag by and speed by at the same time.

Most days are long. I feel like I am not doing enough to find a job. I also feel as though I am doing all I can. I am drifting and rootless because I do not know where to focus. I do not know how to find my bearings.

Spending a few hours doing what needs to be done drains me. I need to nap just about every day. The kittens are in their glory.

I send and respond to e-mails. It is an integral part of my support network at a time when I've lost half my network personally and professionally. It is unobtrusive. I can send out a mass e-mail to people who still care about me, despite everything, and get numerous responses back. Every day there are always one or two e-mails, phone calls, or visits that provide support and encouragement for me when I most need it, which seems to be all the time.

The e-mails make me cry. The support of friends makes me cry. I cry often. I cry for whatever sparks the tears, and then I cry for many things. There seems to be an unending well of tears within me, just waiting to be released.

Some days I am hopeless and full of despair. I keep plugging through them. Other days I feel energetic, full of optimism, and certain that everything will be fine.

I spend endless evenings escaping from reality. I don't really have the capacity to read, so I watch movies. The local video store loves to see me coming. I am the easiest upsell customer they have. I walk into the store expecting to rent one or two movies, but I walk out with six—the deal of the week. It is not unusual for me to watch two movies a night, night after night. I settle in with a glass or two of wine and tune in to someone else's world, someone else's story, because I cannot deal with mine. And more of my tears are evoked by those stores, even when they are not that sad.

Some days my escape is made through drinking wine and gabbing with a good friend who is a neighbor. She is a godsend to me. There are days she walks into my house, after tension has been rising within me without my full awareness, and I blow off steam by talking uninterrupted for a half hour or more. Then I relax. She is here often. She watches out for me and takes care of me in many ways.

The weeks go by. I am looking for a job, but what does one do at thirty-seven years of age when one has run an organization, managed a staff, been responsible to a board, and had the freedom to volunteer in a variety of capacities for organizations related to one's work and profession? I know my skills are transferable. I know that if I can decide what I want to do, I will be able to focus and land a job. But I don't know what I want to do. I don't have the energy to figure it out. I am devastated by my job loss; my self-esteem is destroyed, and my confidence is nonexistent.

Finally I land an interview. It is for a job I first heard about the day after I lost my job. I called the recruiter. He paused as I asked about the job. Finally he laughed. He said to me, "You must be really well connected. We only just got this file yesterday. How do you know about it?" He becomes one of my steadfast fans in that process.

He does extensive reference checks. He and I chat a couple of times. The references are solid—as I knew they would be. I am grateful for the support of my friends and colleagues. Unfortunately, my contact at the recruitment firm is not part of the interview. He and his wife are having their first baby. A colleague of his I have not met sits in. There are four or five people on the interview panel for this new startup organization.

The interview is grueling. I am exhausted at the end of it. I am close to tears. One of the interviewers in particular grills me on why I left my previous job. We leave the topic. She comes back to it. I give an answer but do not have a solid explanation to give. I have not answered the question in my own mind. Why? Why? Why? How can I possibly answer the question for someone else? I am nervous and stressed, feeling as though I am not good enough—not then, not now, not later.

At the end of the hour and a half, the headhunter leaves with me. "What do you think?" he asks. I say to him, "I don't know what to think."

After some time goes by, though, I do know—I bombed! Later I hear that one of the interviewers admonished the woman who grilled me, saying that she should have left it alone.

A couple of weeks go by, and I have another interview. I get the interview because of my Masters in Business Administration. This one is in a totally different field. I'm not at all nervous, the interviewer and I connect well, and the interview goes well. This pharmaceutical company is looking for candidates who can quickly be promoted . . . and move to Toronto within a year or two. Relocation is out of the question for me because of my children, and I clearly say that. I suspect it is the reason I do not get a second interview.

In the meantime, I hear from my recruiter friend that the other job is likely to be offered to another candidate with a sales and marketing background. In a way, I am relieved. I am beginning to understand even more clearly that I do not want to continue to work in the not-for-profit sector.

As I think about the interview, I know it would be helpful to get feedback on how I did. I take a deep breath and call the recruiter, expecting a five-minute phone debriefing. We set up an hour face-to-face meeting.

In the meeting he says to me, "Your leadership ability did not come through. They felt you were detail-oriented and stilted." He pauses. "Do you sing?" he asks.

This is an unexpected question. "No," I say, "I don't."

"Oh," he says. "There was a singsong tone in your voice that made me wonder." It must have been an indication of how nervous I was.

He tells me about some of the interaction among the interviewers, and we talk about my job loss and my responses to the questions regarding it. I still have no answers.

He says to me, "You say you are looking for an entrepreneurial, innovative work environment. I think what you really want is to be left alone to work independently."

That hits home. Hard. Might it be true?

As I leave this meeting, I am on the verge of tears yet again. A wreck, once more. Suddenly, staring me in the face are the unresolved issues around my job loss. I know intuitively I need to find a way to deal with them before I can really move forward. But how? The shadows within are swirling so densely I am lost, swallowed up in my own fear of the stranger who stirs the shadows, certain if I disturb these shadows any more I will come face-to-face with the vile human being I surely must be to have made such a wreck of what had been such a good life.

Desperate to find my way, I send an e-mail out to my support network telling them the results of the interview debriefing. Friends write back. "The recruiter must be wrong," one insists. "He must have some kind of grudge against you," another says. "His feedback can't be right." But it is. And I know it. I sink deeper into the shadows.

There seems to be a large divide between the public persona I have created and my inner self. Most of my friends know this public persona. It truly does encompass my inner being. It has shown up as my leadership capacity, my ability to create safe space and enduring friendships, as well as the inner turmoil and despair that has been brewing for years. The stranger within, I'm sure, has attracted these events and circumstances into my life to create openings for me to journey within to find her, but I am so paralyzed and afraid now that my deep inner soul essence is completely obscured. My fear overshadows my own sense of my leadership. Most of my friends do not understand just how devastated I am. It is hard for them to comprehend how this is possible when they have seen me only in my strength.

One of my colleagues says to me, "Let your natural energy and enthusiasm show through."

Thoughts fly through my mind, tumbling over each other. *My natural energy and enthusiasm? Where is it? Where did it go? Will I ever be able to find it again? Will I ever be able to convincingly sell myself to a prospective employer? I am not sold on me. I can't sell anyone else on me. No wonder my job search is stilted and halting. No wonder the job interviews are few and far between. No wonder it is impossible to do a thorough corporate search. What do I have to offer anyone? Despair, frustration, anger, self-doubt?*

My spirit is broken. I am grateful and appreciative for the support of my friends and colleagues. Their belief in me is powerful. Later I know they believed in me when I no longer believed in myself and didn't know I didn't believe in myself.

There are times I cannot understand, for the life of me, what these wonderful people see in me, why they continue to support me. More than that, many of them have expressed admiration and respect for me for how I am handling the tumultuous events in my life. These genuine offerings seem incongruous to me, when I'm certain that there is a stranger within, obscured by the shadows, who must be a monster. When my friends discover this truth I am sure they will abandon me too.

I think about counseling. The husband of a friend offers to counsel me for free. He knows the impact of job loss and divorce each by themselves, let alone at the same time. Do I need counseling? I feel fine in my remote, detached view of the world. I also recognize, ironically enough, that I probably am not the best judge of whether or not I need counseling.

Later I know my reluctance to go to counseling is wrapped up in my reluctance to tell anyone my full story. It is too deeply personal and it hurts far too much for me to let it out. If truth be known, I am not willing or ready to face myself yet. I am deeply ashamed and cannot name it. A part of me knows this and so believes it would be pointless to go to counseling, so I keep my own counsel. I keep the stranger under wraps in the shadow.

Then the middle of my severance period arrives. Time is running out. I am no further ahead. Emotionally, I'm further behind. I am overwhelmed, deeply overwhelmed. Despondent even. Jobwise, there is so little happening. When I look down the road, I panic. My breathing gets shallow. Tears play at the corner of my eyes often. I am paralyzed with uncertainty and fear. The story I make up about life now is about the vile stranger who makes me not nice, not wise, a sinister character in the plot of my own life. Though I try not to play into that story, it is hovering in the mists swirling around the stranger. This is why I drink wine and watch movies.

It takes every ounce of energy I have to get out of bed, get dressed, and go about my day. My head aches. My body is all hunched in on itself. How on earth will I pull it all together before the severance runs out? How will I survive? How will I pay my mortgage? Feed my kids? Rescue my credibility?

I have an abundance of nervous energy. I go for walks. Fast ones. I walk on the nearby golf course. It is quiet and peaceful. I walk for hours, talking to God. Not sure what I say, but I feel better.

I discover a new coping mechanism. I live in today, the now, the present. I wake up in the morning and get through the day to the night. I might plan for tomorrow. I cannot look down the road any further than that. It is like looking into the abyss. It is too frightening. But if I stay in this moment, I can cope—barely. Later I learn that living in this moment actually is not new and is a path; it becomes the path to openheartedness. However, it is more than a decade before I truly discover this, because there are so many ways to veer off the path, to forget what I know.

One day my mother calls. "Kathy," she says. "Celine Dion is coming to Halifax for a concert!" My mother loves Celine Dion. She wants to go to the concert.

"When is the concert, Mom?" I ask.

"December," she says.

December? This is March. I can barely get by day-to-day, and my mother wants to go to a concert nine months away! The irony is not lost on me as I buy us tickets. My mother is thrilled.

Then comes a pivotal day. A breakthrough day. Sometime before this day, I was in a bookstore and picked up three books on self-discovery, self-healing, and self-love. The store clerk chuckled and said, "Someone has an intense weekend ahead." Little did she know. Little did I know.

The first book I start to read is _The Dragon Doesn't Live Here Anymore_ by Alan Cohen. This day I am sitting in my favorite part of my kitchen, overlooking the trees in the backyard. I have two books handy—the practical *What Color is Your Parachute?* and *The Dragon Doesn't Live Here Anymore.*

I hover. I should really be reading *What Color is Your Parachute?* but I pick up the book I am drawn to: *The Dragon Doesn't Live Here Anymore.* I am lost for the rest of the day in a rapid, emotional roller-coaster journey.

I begin to read. I laugh. I cry. I write in my journal. Everything Cohen writes makes so much sense to me. He describes and explains just about everything that has happened to me over the last few years. Suddenly, I have something I have not had in months, maybe even years. I have hope! My future is not defined by my past—unless, of course, I let it be. I am relieved. Huge waves of relief wash over me, again and again, with each new insight.

Cohen talks about the power of the mind and how we attract things to us. We attract that which we focus on. I find that I have been attracting my fears: my fear that friends and family would find out that my life was not perfect harmony; my fear that my colleagues, staff, and board would find out I didn't really have all the answers and that I wasn't as wonderful, effective, or efficient as others made me out to be.

I had been living a life of illusion—illusion of my own creation—and I had been afraid I would be found out. I built so much stress and pressure on myself that I couldn't deal with it anymore. My illusory house of cards had tumbled down. The dissonance in my life was so great I could not stand it anymore. The stranger within, misunderstood, was knocking on the door of my life to wake me up. I didn't want to hear. The more I tried to shut it down, the more insistent the stranger became, attracting increasingly more of the unbearable dissonance that led to my divorce and job loss.

The Dragon Doesn't Live Here Anymore is my first introduction to the concepts and principles that begin to guide my life in powerful ways, that eventually I will teach to others, as I begin to follow them with consciousness and intentionality—as best as anyone can in the imperfectness that makes us human.

In this moment in my life, *The Dragon Doesn't Live Here Anymore* provides me with a framework for understanding. Now everything that has happened doesn't seem quite so senseless anymore. More than that, I come to understand that everything that has happened serves to shape and define who I am at this exact moment—but it does not have to serve, shape, and define who I will continue to be. I do not have to be a "failure" forever. How I respond to what I now know will play a great role in shaping my future. How I want my future to be plays the greatest role.

Up to this point, I was using one set of stories to makes sense of what happened to me. I am being invited by the new awareness generated by my reading to retell my experiences in ways that support and serve me better. This is when I wish I could wave my magic wand and have insights instantly manifest into new patterns. It seems my soul journey is calling for a longer process, although the stranger within is delighted to be glimpsed for who she really is rather than the vile stranger I have been giving life to through story. I am beginning to glimpse what more there is beyond the shadows, the possibility of my inner essence, with hope and delight.

Early in this period of time I become aware of this little thought: "Start your own company." It is just a whisper. It is the stranger within, the one I don't recognize because I imagine her to be the source of my pain and suffering, not the source of my joy and inspiration. She is whispering to me. It is hard for me to hear her, and I easily ignore her quiet voice. Of course, I've become quite practiced at ignoring her quiet—and sometimes not so quiet—voice. It is why I'm in this mess to begin with.

She is persistent, though. I am dismissive as I respond to the call, at first. "What do you mean, 'Start your own business'? What can I do? How could I generate enough revenue to support myself?" I ask the voice of the stranger I do not want to hear.

"What did you love to do in your job?" she whispers back to me.

"I loved the leadership learning. I loved facilitating and the team development work when it went well. I loved the strategy work and long-term thinking." The list flows in my mind easily, intriguing me even in my denial.

"Do that," she whispers to me.

"Do that?" I reply disparagingly. "Do that? That requires me to sell my knowledge as my product. Who's going to want to buy the knowledge of a woman who couldn't make her marriage work, who's been fired from her job and has caused her whole life to come crashing down around her? Really? Who would buy that?"

Years later, I know this is the stuff of experience. It is what makes me wiser, stronger, kinder, gentler and more compassionate in what I have to offer; I have so much hubris to draw on.

In this moment, though, in this conversation between my mind and the stranger or the stirrings of my soul, I resist the idea of starting my own business. The seed, however, is deeply planted in my being. I have an awareness, which I've had before and will have again, that I have already made a decision but am not yet ready to own it or claim it or live into it. I need to catch up to the momentum of it. It is a seed of knowledge that needs time to root in my being, to gain strength so I can get my arms around it to hold onto it. I have forgotten that years before this, I entertained the idea of starting a business that I could run out of home. The man I am divorcing reminds me of this. He is not surprised when I tell him I might start my own business, even as I am surprising myself.

The stranger within, my soul essence, she's the one who holds this crazy idea, nurtures it, grows it, and pushes it back into my awareness through the shadow that surrounds her, over and over again. She is becoming more insistent. "Kathy, wake up to your path. It's here, right in front of you, just waiting for you to step into it. Feel it. Imagine it. Taste it. Dream what is possible."

The stuff of dreams. Am I really allowed to go there after the disaster my life has turned into? Isn't the stuff of dreams for those few pristine, fortunate, born-to-it individuals?

The stranger within wonders aloud in my head and heart, "Kathy, how long, how often, and in how many different ways will you punish yourself? Do you not know you have already paid for your mistakes? For what you consider your transgressions? Suffering is optional. It's a choice. Of course you are allowed the stuff of dreams! Your dreams call to you. Pay attention. Respond." Such a hard lesson to learn in the human tragedy experience. Human tragedy begets more human tragedy. Who am I to dream? I carry the notion that I have to pay for my sins over and over again. The angst I lived with in my marriage was not payment enough. The devastation of my confidence and self esteem was not payment enough. How much is enough? At what point do I come to terms with the idea that I am now making overpayments that will not get paid back? Guilt and shame linger, exacerbated by worry and fear. I believe I am not worthy because I am a bad person; I believe the stranger within must be bad. Not worthy of success. Not worthy of love. The loss of my job was not enough payment.

Ah, but such a gift in the soul journey, to be leaned into lightly—those moments of being fully present, illuminating something I have not yet experienced consciously and cannot yet name.

The soul journey is not to be thwarted. The dream does not lie still. The stranger within will not be silenced.

Little things show up on my path. I begin to explore a variety of options. The possibility of opening a homebrewing and winemaking store shows up. Making wine has become a bit of a hobby, and a friend of mine is in the business. As I think about it though, I am aware that a retail business owns you; you don't own it. It dictates the hours. I need more flexibility in my life than being tied to a physical space and retail hours.

When I go to an entrepreneurial expo where franchises are featured, I become aware that I do not want to own a franchise either, but a little idea germinates in my mind. If I own my own business, my revenue does not all need to come from the same place. This is such an obvious thought, yet it is so different from earning a salary with a regular paycheck. This straightforward little notion creates an expansion and freedom in my thinking that opens a doorway to further exploration. Now I begin to seriously entertain the possibility of starting a business, even one where what I have to offer is me, my experience, and my knowledge, such as it is.

Months before I was fired from my job, I had received a leadership award from the Canadian Society of Association Executives (CSAE), a scholarship, to attend a Guiding People and Organizational Change program at the Banff Management Centre in Alberta. I was supposed to go to one of the programs just prior to losing my job and postponed the trip because of the chaos in my life at that moment. Even having lost my job, the Banff Management Centre assured me that scholarship was mine to use as soon as I was able.

I meet all kinds of interesting people from all across Canada who are attending the course. It is a two-part program, two one-week sessions separated by a few months. I feel connected to many of the people I meet and they see me—the depth of me even though I have lost my job, even though there is nothing on my employment horizon.

When I go back for the second week of the program, I share with the other participants and program leaders that I am thinking of launching my own consulting practice, a shift for me since taking the first part of the program a few months before.

One of the instructors is building an international strategic planning organization based out of California. He invites me into considering aligning my path with his organization. I consider this a high honor. He knows some of my story, and he's still willing to invite this conversation with me. He sees the stranger in me, my soul essence and strength, in ways I cannot.

He says to me, as I am concerned about my lack of experience as a consultant, "Fake it till you make it. You have it in you. Don't let anyone tell you any different."

The whole of my experience in Banff is affirming. I meet people who did not know me before, learn that I've lost my job, and still like me. They like me for what they see of me and in me. I know I never want to repeat this experience of job loss and divorce at the same time, but I want to remember it. If I can remember it, maybe I can remember how to walk a better path, one truer to who I think I am, who I might be, the me I lost along the way in pursuit of ego driven success and validation from others. I want it to keep me humble. I imagine a humble person would not make the same mistakes I have made, would not act out of a need for success, and would know better how to serve others and maybe even a higher purpose.

One of the things my husband said to me as were divorcing was, "You've lost sight of the little people. You've forgotten your roots." He was disturbingly right. I was propelled by ego and a lot of recognition and success at a young age—recognition and success I was not prepared for, had no training for.

I am humbled by the friends I meet in Banff. One night as we head out to dinner, I am late because of a phone call. When I finally show up in the lobby, my friends are still waiting for me. I am grateful and say so. One of them says to me, "Kathy, you attract people to you." Not because I'm an executive director, a chapter president, or a national board member. Because I am me. The stranger within is smiling as I learn these things about the essence of who I am. Although I hardly dare to believe this could be true.

Back home, I step more fully into the idea of starting my own consulting practice. My good friend comes by. We brainstorm company names and come up with verve strategies inc. "Verve" means "inspired enthusiasm." If I can't bring inspired enthusiasm to the work I do for clients, I have no business doing the work.

I incorporate my company and find a graphic facilitation company to develop a logo and materials for me. I buy a proper desk and set up an office in my home. The desk is going to be delivered. I am wondering what is the best way for them to bring it in. I am dumbfounded when it is delivered in boxes. Of course it does not come assembled!

I launch verve strategies inc. at the end of my severance period. The first work shows up within a few weeks. A friend of mine, who runs a national association, asks me to complete an environmental scan for his organization in Nova Scotia. He gives me my first dollar. Another friend invites me to submit a bid for strategic planning work his national association will do in Prince Edward Island. I win the bid, despite being higher in price than the other contenders, because of my background in the not-for-profit sector. It appears that the years I have invested in relationship building just might pay off, and I learn a thing or two about value propositions.

I am asked by another organization to deliver a speech on change management at a conference they are having. I will get paid well for a one-hour talk. My father is bemused. "Who would pay you that much money to hear you speak?" he wonders out loud. Who indeed?

So I'm off. Not exactly on a roll, but with enough bites to know this is possible. I begin a monthly newsletter called *Approaching Change*. It is mostly sent by fax, but a few are sent by e-mail, although that technology is still pretty new. The newsletter is a marketing tool for me, a way to keep my name, my company, my work, and my thinking unobtrusively in front of people.

One client asks me to write for a new publication his organization is launching. Clients come in interesting and strange ways. One calls me for a reference on someone who used to work for me. I'm surprised. I ask, "Has that person listed me as reference?" The answer is no. I say, "I'm sorry, but I'm not able to answer your questions then."

The call turns into a conversation about what I am doing now, what the immediate needs of her organization are, and a contract that is the beginning of a long-term client relationship. I learn many things with this client, including that sometimes when the client is not calling me, it has nothing to do with me and everything to do with other things that have her attention and priority. If I believe my clients' lack of contact is about me, it feeds my insecurity about whether they like me or whether the work I have done with them has been worthwhile. If I understand that they have multiple priorities and that things other than the work I have done with them have their attention, I can let go and relax. Either way, it is a story I create about my experience. Which story serves me better—the one that allows me to be more resourced, the one that allows me to pay better attention to what is really going on?

There is a client I choose not to bill for a session. I have been working with this client on values for his team. I am ill as I go to do this work one evening. At some point, the client is speaking to me. There is ringing in my ears. I cannot hear him. I feel as though I will faint. This has never happened to me, ever. It is all I can do to stay conscious and stay on my feet. I do a dismal job. The client does most of the facilitation. Afterward we have a beautiful conversation. He is so supportive. He says to me, "Kathy, you have a choice. You can choose to bill me."

"Thank you," I say to him. "I will think about what you have offered and let you know."

The next day I write him a note. "Yes, I realize I have a choice. I have to say, what happened last night is not up to the quality of my usual client service, and I choose not to invoice you. I hope that I have another chance to do some work with you." And I did. It felt right and good to honor my service delivery expectations, even though I could have used that money.

I have enough work to know this is work I want to do, but not enough to support myself. I am still on the roller-coaster ride of my own experience. Some days are new and exciting, living into the dream and the soul-story experience. Other days are stressful and draining as I worry about finances, living into the human tragedy lens of the same story, imagining how hard it is, how I will never make it as a consultant.

There are days the strain is so prevalent for me that I walk around the block. I ask myself the question, "If I wasn't doing this, what would I prefer to be doing?" The key word is "prefer." I cast around in my mind for the answer. What would I prefer to be doing? Nothing comes to me. There is nothing I would prefer to be doing. So I say to myself, "Well, then, Katherine Anne, you better make it work."

The only way I can make it work financially is to dip into my retirement savings fund. It is a step I am reluctant to take, but my other option is to accumulate debt. I come to the conclusion that these funds are for my future, and while technically they were for retirement, I need a financial cushion now.

As my new business takes its baby steps into being, I meet my future second husband. A friend of mine calls one day to say, "Kathy, there's a guy giving a talk at the Chamber Luncheon in a few weeks. It seems in line with what you're doing now and you might find it interesting."

I check it out, decide it does look interesting, and sign up to go.

On the day of the lunch, there are a lot of people in attendance. The talk is both interesting and compelling; it is about innovation and creativity. I take lots of notes but do not approach the speaker because so many others are lined up to talk to him. I don't give it much thought at all.

A month or so later, I get an invitation from his company to come to a half-day demonstration event where he will showcase three different service offerings. I accept. This time I meet him and learn more about his work, and he learns about my new venture. He says to me, "It sounds like we are doing some similar things. Maybe we should have a conversation."

I'm thrilled. I am just starting out, and he has been in business—successfully, it seems—for a few years. It is an amazing opportunity.

As soon as my print material is ready, I send it off to him indicating I'm ready for the conversation any time. I don't hear anything from him. At first I find this curious; my hopes are dashed. But then, after placing him, like everyone else I've met, on my newsletter distribution list, I pretty much forget about him as I focus on other things that come to fruition, giving him no more thought.

A year goes by. My business plods along with high and low points. I'm struggling. I'm still struggling with issues of self-esteem and self-confidence, reliant on a few key friendships to keep me going. I engage in some short-term romantic relationships, mostly with men who live in other parts of the country, but nothing lasts.

Interesting chunks of work come my way. I am aware at times of my insecurity in what I have to offer. I am also aware of how draining some of the work is as I struggle with believing I am being hired because I am supposed to know the answers and solve all their problems. I am experiencing steep learning curves regarding process design and content, building my experience with unsuspecting clients. I am still also experiencing a steep learning curve regarding my life as I work out the new living arrangements with my kids.

I join a group focused on mentoring and masterminds. I am looking for ways to grow my capacity to build my business. I really like my little group and feel grateful for the support and the conversations. There is a depth of conversation about real-life issues that is appealing to me.

One day, the topic of divorce comes up. One of the men in the group is going through a rough patch in his marriage. He asks me about my experience. I say to him, "Think really carefully about what you want. I don't regret my choice, but nothing is ever the same again. You still have your kids and your relationships with your kids, but you never again will be a family unit in the same way. Never again will you celebrate key events in life the same way. Never again will you go on a family vacation with everyone or interact with each other in exactly the same way. There is sadness. It is more than the relationship itself that you lose, more than just memories of what's been. You also lose all the hopes and dreams you've had alone and together of what your life was going to be, how you would look back over a lifetime of experiences, good and bad, how you would be there for each other no matter what.

"I'm not saying don't do it, but be really sure that this is what you want, because there is no going back."

While in the mastermind group, during the summer, as things slow down, I decide to take matters into my own hands and run a change workshop. The change management information I've been working with really has my attention. I love both the understanding of human response elicited by the change curve and the practical, tactical ideas for successful change. I am building up a bit of a list for my newsletter. I figure I can go through the Chamber of Commerce list and just add fax numbers for distribution.

I set a target of twenty to thirty people for this workshop. As the days and weeks pass, it becomes increasingly clear that I am not going to reach this target. I grow increasingly more disappointed as the days pass, wondering how else to grow the numbers, who else to reach out to.

Getting people in seats is a numbers game; I had no idea just how much so. I simply don't have enough numbers in my database.

The whole workshop is becoming weighty for me, bearing down on me. It is increasingly difficult to think optimistically about what it is I want to accomplish.

As I bend under the weight, I am failing. I am failing at this one thing I am trying to do to infuse my business with flow. My thoughts run rampant, building a story of gigantic proportions, without the conscious awareness that this is what I'm doing: "What was I thinking? How could I be so off base? How could I be such a failure?"

The light bulbs go off in my brain as realization dawns. Somewhere over the last weeks of dealing with my disappointment, I have generalized a failure to meet my people-in-seats target to a larger episode of a failed workshop, and further, to me being a failure in life! I have created a whole story of failure, a human tragedy story that tells me how unworthy and undeserving I am. No wonder this workshop is weighing me down. I am unconsciously allowing it to take on gigantic proportions and feeding this growth with my thoughts such that I now see myself as a failure. Period.

It is just a little workshop. It has a dozen people registered. It is a playing ground, not a condemnation of who I am. Failure is an action, not an identity; but I have made it my identity through the story I have been telling and retelling myself over the course of weeks. The experience of this workshop personifies every wrong thing that has happened in my life, especially over the last few years! It illuminates every single doubt and fear that has ever surfaced for me and created a few new ones too. The shadow swirling around the stranger within is stirred. Part of me is once again convinced this is a stranger of ill will, the human tragedy story I live into these days.

Enormous waves of relief wash over me as I pluck this assumed identity of failure off of me and hold it a distance away so I can see the illusion of it. Tears flow, releasing the energy and emotion that have been pent up inside of me.

Now what to do? How to move forward? I can now see the path in front of me. With so much weight having been lifted off of me, I dance lightly on the path instead of crawling along on my knees, weighted down by shadows I cannot see, by a story that does not serve me, by a projection into the future that assumes I will be unsuccessful, not just for the workshop but for any undertaking I might assume, for my very life path, now unto eternity.

What if this is just a workshop on change and not a harbinger of success or failure of my entire life? What would be my next step? Returning to the present. Bringing my awareness back to now. Planning the workshop and welcoming those who signed on, of course. Simple when you bring it back to its essence, bring it back to what it is before the story grew.

Three unexpected things happen as a result of the workshop. One of the people who I allow to participate at a much-reduced rate brings me business that more than makes up for the reduction in her registration fee. Reciprocity and generosity show up as I graciously make an offer and allow the flow of exchange.

The second thing is that I begin a relationship with the first coach that I ever work with. He is one of the participants. We subsequently meet, and I say to him, "I know I'm getting in my own way, but I don't know how. I want to get out of my own way. I know I need help with that. Can you help me?"

He agrees. He works with me on writing out a comprehensive vision for my life that includes career, financial, and personal goals. It is the first vision board I create. Immediately for my career goal, an image of me standing at a podium enters my mind. I interpret this to mean I will be giving talks as part of my livelihood and revenue stream.

I'm having trouble coming up with words to describe all aspects of my life. The image of the podium sparks an idea to come up with images to represent all the areas of my life. Once I have collected the images and have these visual representations in hand, the words come easier.

I write out my financial goals. My coach asks me questions and gives me feedback, "Kathy, your targets are really low." He doesn't say "ridiculously low," but looking back, I know now that they were. We explore what's going on. He says, "You've fenced yourself in, created a small target area, one you have to squish yourself up to get inside of it."

I let out a sigh. My business revenue to date has been low. I reluctantly admit to him that I had to tap into my retirement savings to survive. I say to him, "What I've put here already feels like so much more than I have now. How much is too much to ask for?" A little voice inside my head is saying to me, "Really, Kathy, you think you are worthy of more? Deserving of more? Tsk, tsk."

And yet my coach is challenging me to break out of these self-limiting thoughts. This is why I've hired him, after all. "The way you have described this constrains your potential. Find a way to reword it so that it opens up your potential field of remuneration instead."

So I go back to the drawing board and rework the words so it feels good to me, making it something I can believe in that also removes, or reduces, the limits I have placed on my earning potential.

The other question I begin to seriously entertain is about whether I want a intimate relationship in my life. Would I ever want to get married again? Marriage has been a long way away from my thoughts, as I had failed so miserably at it with a person who is a good person. I blamed myself as the one who screwed everything up in my eternal search for that something "more" in my life.

I reflect on where I am in my life. I am now only in my late thirties. Would I want another committed relationship in my life? Yes. Yes, I would. Would I be willing to live with someone? Yes. Yes, I would. Well, if I'm willing to live with someone, then why wouldn't I consider getting remarried? Hmm. Decision made.

While I am doing work with my coach, the third impact of my workshop is emerging.

The consultant I met the year before who offered to have coffee and conversation about the work we each do sends me a note, out of the blue, fourteen months after we first met, to wish me luck with my workshops. I am completely surprised until I remember he is on my newsletter list. This sparks us getting together for coffee, and I later agree to participate in a pilot group mentoring program he is launching. This ultimately leads to us becoming romantically involved. We are engaged four months later and married three months after that.

I am astounded at how fast this new relationship manifests for me even as I had set an intention for it during the coaching process. Before I met him, I was carrying this question: "Who would want me? A woman with two young kids, newly divorced, freshly unemployed, starting a new consulting company, not making much money, and trying to support her kids and pay the mortgage for a house she bought assuming she would have a certain level of income?"

Who indeed? This man shows up who has never been married, who seems quite successful and full of big dreams, who talks about energy and angels and introduces me to reiki and tarot cards, who's available to meet when I'm available, and who takes my insights and observations about where he is on his path seriously. It's a whole new world. I am enamored and completely drawn in. He couldn't be more opposite the analytical, practical, down to earth focus of my first husband.

He is creative and intelligent. He has been developing facilitation processes and practices that he is using in his consulting work. He is both willing and anxious to share, wanting to grow his company and his work, wanting to share his life with someone who can share his passion and his life. The stars seem aligned.

It feels as though we have come to a very similar point in our lives via very different paths. Although I've been married before and have two children and he has never been married, his company is like his child. I have begun to accumulate personal debt, and he has accumulated company debt. Where he is a creative genius, I can bring practical components to running the business.

Early on, we decide to read together. One of our choices is *A Course in Miracles*. We love trying to understand it at a deeper level. There are a couple of times it even seems as though we are dreaming the same dream when we wake in the middle of the night; at these times, lines from *A Course In Miracles* run across a little horizontal screen in my mind. It is a sign of how connected we are, how right this relationship is. We dream of a bright future, imagine having children together. We see a future of living and working together. We imagine how we will model all the things we teach. Living purpose. Living our values. Together. I am not sure if together we imagine it will be harmonious—but I do.

My boys are eight and ten years old. They are excited about the marriage and about new things coming into their lives too. We include them in the wedding ceremony, acknowledging that this change impacts them too. It is two and a half years since I bought my house, since my first marriage disintegrated. My whole life has changed once again. I am thirty-eight years old. It is twenty years since I graduated from high school, ten since the high school reunion where my life had been mapping out on a very different track.

We decide to have our wedding ceremony and reception in our backyard. The elements of the ceremony naturally emerge through our conversations. Before long we have created a unique blend of Indian blessings, Christian traditions, our own vows, and the inclusion of my children in the ceremony, which also includes planting trees to represent our union and commitment to each other.

The day before the wedding, it rains. The rain goddess is blessing us. The ceremony is to take place at 11:00 in the morning. I planned it that way because I didn't want to wait around all day. It is early June. We are concerned about rain and blackflies. As it turns out, there was no need to worry about the blackflies. It doesn't rain, but the wind is powerful. We have a tent erected in the middle of our yard, needed now more for warmth than for protection from sun or rain. The wind is so strong that its impact on the tent over the course of the day drives the center pole a foot into the ground.

At different points in the ceremony, the wind, as if on cue, becomes stronger. We attribute good things to this—the power of the wind spirits, the power of our relationship, the power of the good we will do in the world.

It is weeks after our wedding that we take part in the drumming ceremony where the shape-shifting lion comes to greet me, waiting patiently for my "sight" to kick in. This is also a metaphor for the next decade. I feel a sense that something should be available to me—gifts and talents I do not even know I have, and my inability to see or access them—partly because I do not believe that the spiritual and energetic realms that I know to be true apply to me. True for others? Yes, for sure. True for me? I'm just an ordinary human from unassuming beginnings in a small town.

I am waiting for my sight to kick in regarding the truth of my relationship as it grows increasingly challenged as time goes by. Waiting for my sight to kick in about the stranger I've imagined compared to the truth about it. Waiting to find a voice that's been silenced—that I've silenced because I do not know how to speak my own truth. I am so far detached from my own inner knowing that I don't even know what my truth is. So I stay silent. I try to become invisible as a coping strategy. But the true stranger, the one waiting to be embraced, will not stay silent or invisible forever.

Years later, looking back, another interpretation of the dramatic winds at our wedding is the intensity of the relationship that unfolds for us, an intensity that forces—invites—a depth of personal, professional, and spiritual journey that would not otherwise unfold. For me it is a journey past the shadow to the stranger within, to soul essence, and to the fullness of openheartedness. Ironically, it begins with me shutting down more completely in the next few years, pulling protective sheathing more tightly around my heart before it is possible to meet the stranger and journey into openheartedness.

What I imagined was the beginning of an enlightened period in my life was the beginning of greater darkness, more intense shadow, and avoidance, almost at all costs, of the path that was calling me, doing what I thought was necessary for survival, retreating into myself and reinforcing walls that had been continually erected from childhood on.

What I really needed to do—though it was counterintuitive—was embrace the stranger in the shadow, the stranger in me, and open my heart more fully and completely in the riskiest journey I could possibly imagine: the road to vulnerability and the journey to openheartedness. This journey would take me past the lineage I knew, the one I grew up with, and into whole new worlds, whole new lineages—physical and spiritual—and whole new ways of being in the world.

CHAPTER 4

PROPELLANTS OF THE JOURNEY

A friend of mine offers intuition classes designed to grow capability to tap into intuitive knowing—psychic ability, really. My husband and I decide to take the classes. It works a bit on using symbols to tap into deeper knowing—symbols that spontaneously occur to us. My friend seems to think I should have capability for this. But as in the drumming ceremony, I feel stuck. I try too hard. I don't believe her when she tells me I am powerful in this way. Nothing comes to my awareness—not easily anyway.

During this program, I become pregnant for the first time in my second marriage. I feel there is something wrong in the early days of the pregnancy, but nothing is clear. One night in the class, as we are guided to ask a question or seek some answers to something of meaning in our lives, I find myself in a vision in a lush garden with white stone benches, flowers, and birds. As I'm standing there, my grandmother, who died a few years before this, appears in the garden. She comes over to me and puts her arm

around my shoulders as if to comfort me. I know, beyond
a shadow of a doubt, that my baby is lost. Later, blood
tests confirm this. Still later I discover the pregnancy was
ectopic, requiring lifesaving surgery.

My husband and I settle into life and work together. The path is far more
contentious than we imagined when we stepped into it. Unlike the eerie
calm of my first marriage, we are constantly fighting. Arguments begin
over small and not so small things that seem to take on great meaning.
Disagreements over parenting increase dramatically when our son is
born.

I do not know how to deal with the intensity of our relationship or the
intensity of our battles, which can last for up to three days, draining
me of every ounce of energy I have. This marriage, born of a vision
of enlightened journey, should not be this way. Without realizing how
much guilt and shame I still carry from divorcing, from the failure of
my first marriage, I take on a burden of responsibility for this marriage.
I find it surprising how much guilt I carry—and we carry as a society—
over marriages that don't work even given the statistics that tell us this
is predictable. Normal even. The beliefs we carry about marriage may
be outdated. What is it we carry in our collective consciousness that
still tells us marriage is "till death do us part"? What if marriage is until
completion? Does a "failed" or completed ten-year relationship have
the same stigma as a failed marriage and divorce? If I can only figure
it out, if I can only do it right, then everything will be fine. But even
twisting myself in knots does not work. Not knowing how to do it, I
try everything I can think of, most of which is designed to make me
smaller, make me invisible, hide my voice, like it doesn't count—like
I don't count.

We are in life and in work together. As business partners, we try to grow
our company. We train people, looking for alignment of values. We
bring others into our training work. For many reasons, it doesn't stick
and people don't stay in the work, in the company. We recognize that

trying to bring people on board is diverting our energy and attention from attracting the work we want to be in.

We regroup. We are advised, by an advisory "board" we have recruited, to focus. The thought is scary. We are capable of doing many things. What if we narrow our focus too much? Eventually we take their advice. It is the best advice we could have received. As we focus on one area to promote and market, people inquire about other things we might do. Focusing doesn't shut down potential; it opens it further. It seems counterintuitive, but it works.

Working with our clients, we provide good results. Working with each other is more challenging. One of the biggest challenges for me is the lack of alignment in our relationship with the principles we advocate in our work. I feel out of personal alignment and integrity, and it shuts me down. I reduce my contact with my friends. I stop making new friends without even realizing that this is a new pattern showing up in my life.

I try to find strategies to cope with the dark days I experience. Withdrawal is a strong pattern. It doesn't totally serve the situation, but it is hard for me to know what to do. There is nothing that's happening in my life I feel compelled to take a stand on—until the year I come to the Art of Hosting Conversations That Matter.

My issues of self-esteem and self-confidence are not resolved, repaired, or healed during this time—nor were they before starting a business or entering my second marriage, although I thought they were. In fairness, the journey has progressed, for sure. I just am not as far along it as I imagined—hoped—I was. In some ways, my world has become smaller and more closed in.

However, while taking part in intuition classes, I glimpse possibilities. I glimpse my spiritual lineage, although I do not know it. I glimpse what is available to me, although I am blocked by my own limiting beliefs about what I'm capable of and about what is true of me and my experience.

There is a deep unrest stirring in my soul. I am afraid it is the stranger within. This unrest is only growing stronger, more frightening, more compelling. It is a force I cannot stop, although I try.

Seven years into my path as a consultant and five years into my second marriage, things open up in unexpected and accelerated ways. That year is a turning point, the beginning of a five-year transition period during which I am invited into far more than I ever bargained for. My life is on the brink of collapse once again, much to my dismay. But it needs to happen in order to open my life up in whole new unexpected, unimaginable ways.

January 21, 2005. I am forty-three years old. I am participating in the first Envision Halifax community engagement day. I have had a small hand in supporting this new organization. One of my clients, who is on the founding steering committee, called one day with a proposition.

"Kathy," he says to me, "I'm involved in an exciting new venture that is need of some facilitation support, but we don't have any money. We could buy you lunch."

I shake my head and chuckle. "Okay, say more."

"It is an organization founded by the United Way and the Shambhala Institute, funded by the McConnell Foundation to develop a community leadership program. We want it to be about more than just a leadership program, to be guided by clear values with a compelling mission."

It's easy. I'm in. This group of people is interesting. I've not met most of them before. I have been aware of the Shambhala Institute (now Authentic Leadership in Action or ALIA) and the international summer program that they run in Halifax for some time, but I've never been to it. My excuses were that it would take too much time, it cost too much money, and it took place at a time of year that was not good for me. This joint initiative, though, is intriguing.

I volunteer a few sessions to help evolve the mission and elicit values for their work. In the end, the values are clear, compelling, and enduring. I lose track of the initiative for some months until I see the invitation for this community event. The invitation and website refer to a leadership development program. I have just begun to think about what my next personal/professional development step could be. I imagine this could be it. I could take this leadership program.

The gathering takes place a day after a big snowstorm. The organizers are not sure how many people will show up, because the roads are still slippery and not completely plowed. They are astonished as 120 people fill the meeting space in St. Matthew's Church Hall on Barrington Street in downtown Halifax.

Even as I enter the church hall I have a feeling of stepping into community. Since beginning my work as a consultant seven years before this, I have felt alone most of the time, carrying lots of expectations from my clients and more from myself. I have not felt as if I belong anywhere. But walking into this place automatically brings with it a sense of community, a sense of belonging.

This day is being "hosted" rather than facilitated. It is my first exposure to methodologies that are part of the Art of Hosting Conversations That Matter. I watch the hosting team members closely, deeply curious at how they are showing up in this space and what they are inviting.

Somewhere in the course of this day, I become aware that there is no leadership development program—yet. So I can't take the program. A crazy idea begins to take shape. *Maybe I can become part of the team that designs and delivers it.* I feel excitement bubbling up in me as I consider this notion. At the end of the day, we are asked to indicate both our interest in Envision Halifax and the commitment we are prepared to make. I proclaim my interest.

The chair of the steering committee is also interested in my background in the not-for-profit sector. The organization is in need of capacity building and fund-raising expertise. These things do not have energy for me, but the chair is persuasive. I agree to do it, but on the condition that I can also put my energy into the areas of needed work that are far more compelling to me.

Being part of Envision Halifax and the leadership development team, I realize that attending the Shambhala Institute summer program would be a good idea since at least some of what we do would be informed by the wealth of knowledge and wisdom that underlies the worldview of the Institute.

Five months later, I enter the second place where I instantly feel a connection, as though I am coming home as part of a community. I take part in an Intergenerational Village Square, which is a pre-event to the program. Not only is it intergenerational, but it is also very deliberately international, with amazing projects and learning initiatives from around the world—India, South Africa, Ohio, New Mexico, Nova Scotia. The intent is for the people involved in these initiatives to share their journey and learning and then draw on the wisdom and knowledge of the participants to understand how to move to their own next level of work in their projects.

I am completely mesmerized. By the people. By their work. By the way we have been invited to engage with them. I am meeting people who will become instrumental in my journey over the next few years in ways I can't possibly imagine at this moment.

After the first two days in this Village Square, we move into the full Institute program. With people from around the world gathered in one place who are doing interesting work with methodologies and practices I have never seen or experienced before, my world cracks open in whole new ways. Friendships sprout. My world expands in a breath, and it is just the beginning. I take part in the module on the Change Lab, which features Theory U. Theory U will be part of the Envision Halifax experience.

Witnessing the power of the methodologies, my husband / business partner and I become curious about where and how to learn more. We discover there are Art of Hosting trainings taking place in a couple of locations, but there has not yet been one in Nova Scotia, nor is there a plan for one. We begin to dream about bringing the first Art of Hosting training to Halifax.

The idea sprouts out of a conversation with one of the Art of Hosting pioneers from Denmark, whom we invite to come and do this work with us. There are several people experienced in the Art of Hosting living in Nova Scotia who can be part of the hosting team. As we explore the idea, it becomes clear that it would be helpful if one or both of us, my husband or I, could experience an Art of Hosting training before we do the one in Halifax so we could help host it.

We look around and find two possibilities. One is in England and one is in British Columbia. We would both like to attend, but it doesn't appear this will be possible, for a number of personal and logistical reasons. Only one of us will be able to go. The place is Bowen Island, British Columbia. I feel strongly, although a little bit guiltily, that I want to go. We had supported my husband in other professional development opportunities in the last couple of years so I claim this opportunity as part of my path.

A few months later, I find myself on Bowen Island, British Columbia, for my first Art of Hosting Training. This is the third place I step into in one year where I feel at home, welcome, as though I am walking into a community I already belong to. Another breath. Another cracking open in ways I cannot even begin to fathom. It is a beginning. The shape of my life is shifting, priming what will turn out to be a five-year transition. But I don't know that now. I don't know there will be times it feels interminable, exhausting, unchanging. There will be other times it feels exhilarating, breathtaking, and transforming. It will often feel both ways at the same time.

I meet people on Bowen Island whom I will develop deep, heart-based relationships with over the next few years—people I will end up journeying and working with in beautiful and unexpected ways; people who will coax, demand, cajole, and invite me to discover and embrace the stranger within and encourage the journey to openheartedness.

I come home from Bowen Island, and a few weeks later, near the end of this year, my husband and I cohost Nova Scotia's first Art of Hosting training with other more experienced practitioners. It feels mixed to me—not quite as complete as what I experienced on Bowen Island, but strong and fluid at the same time. My partner and I are experiencing challenges in our relationship, and the dynamics are flowing into my experience as part of the hosting team, even into the event itself, in subtle, energetic ways. There is shadow in my relationship and shadow in the hosting team, and it is bringing shadow into the field. It is the beginning of intense learning for me about the impact of shadow, a shimmering reflection that shows up in many places at the same time.

Envision Halifax is an intense learning field for me, both in in shadow and in setting intentions and hosting relationships. In September 2005, the first ten-month leadership program is launched. It is nothing short of a miracle. A few months previous, there were no sponsors, no program, and no participants. It is a clear example to me of something that wants to happen. It has its own energy. It would have happened no matter who was involved.

The original hosting team has six members. We are involved in all aspects of getting the program off the ground from recruitment to fundraising to hosting sponsor and participant events. In September we launch with thirty people and just enough money to run the first year. We design as we go, using Theory U as the journey and Art of Hosting as the operating system—a pattern that begins to show up in client work as well.

Overall, cool things happen in that first year. Amazing community work gets done. Strong community connections are made. Individuals experience personal growth. Many begin to work differently. As a hosting team, we learn a lot that informs the subsequent three years of the program as we continue to experiment and prototype different aspects of the program design. It is also an incredibly challenging year for my marriage. Where I have been trying to be invisible or in the background, now I am stepping in and stepping up to the call of this work. Trying to find my way invites even more argument and tension into my relationship as we each try to find our place on this team.

I continue to be inspired by the Art of Hosting. I feel within my very being that this work is an answer to the chaos in today's world. It is not about making it happen, but about opening and holding space so new possibilities can emerge. The impossible becomes possible. It calls upon us to be honest with ourselves and opens the door for us to be honest with others. I feel the draw of this call to greater honesty within myself and in my relationships. It is so compelling that it is happening in spite of me.

My marriage is in its own place of chaos. I feel particularly challenged by this because of our work together. We have so many mutual friends, personally and in the work, that I feel I have little recourse to fully explore the challenges rippling through me, not sure who to confide in and not wanting to generate rumors about the state of our marriage that might impact sustaining our business. There is, however, deep unrest in me. Deep unrest in my marriage. This is exacerbated by the challenges that grew as we worked together in Envision Halifax. These challenges stayed active in our field even as my husband stepped away from Envision Halifax to pursue a health care project he was passionate about—a project he invited me to join him in.

This project takes me to Columbus, Ohio, where there is interesting work happening in health care using Art of Hosting patterns, practices, and principles. I am here to observe and take part in some of the unfolding process. We want to see how Art of Hosting can inform the health care work we are generating in Nova Scotia. In Columbus, I am invited into the hosting team design meeting and then to dinner with the team. I am delighted and honored.

At dinner, a couple of the hosting team members pull out a deck of tarot cards. They are well practiced at readings. I ask for one.

"What is your question?" they ask me.

"What is my path?" I respond.

The two friends look at me, assessing. "That's a pretty broad question," one says. "But let's go with it. Let's see what comes up."

They do a Celtic Cross reading; this type of reading uses a very traditional pattern that has been used for centuries. The first card indicates that I should continue to do what I'm doing, that it is working for me. I take this to mean, on one hand, the work I am involved with that includes Envision Halifax, Art of Hosting, and whatever is beginning to emerge in health care. I also take it to mean that I should continue to do the deep personal work I have embarked on. My desire is to open space for myself and others and, when it closes down, to find another way to open it. It is an intense journey.

The next two cards surprise my friends; these cards represent what is visible and invisible. What's visible is calm. It is my outer veneer, what others see, how I appear, how I "influence" others. I am upset with myself when I lose this outer calm in front of others, when I show my emotions. This is the same pattern that was present in my first marriage and career; now it is showing up in a different way and context. Clearly having insight into this years ago did not make it go away. It just showed up differently, like the Trickster teaching through humor and trickery. Is this the only way I can learn?

What's not visible to others is chaos. Deep chaos. The chaos of my mind, my journey, and my life. My life is far more chaotic than I want others to know, than I am willing to admit to myself. I am aware that people who see the chaos in me and reach through it disarm me. They help me feel safe and protected. They tap into my vulnerability and draw me in. These people are mostly friends who have been showing up through the Art of Hosting world. This is the chaos that is being so deeply challenged by what being part of Art of Hosting is demanding of me—the call to self-honesty, integrity, and authenticity in a larger way than I have ever experienced before.

The cards in this reading also ask me to grow my comfort with holding paradoxes or opposites. They can both exist in the same space. It does not have to be either/or, right or wrong. This is one of the battlegrounds in my life, the battle to be "right." I resent it and resent more feeling drawn into it, but I do not really know how to step out of it.

I am called to stop living in the future, where worry and fear reside and play havoc with me, keeping me unbalanced and ungrounded. Come back to the present, to now. Live in this moment. This is how I survived the time of not knowing years before, partway through my severance after losing my job, when I could not see the path in front of me. I am called to let go of the past, which continues to haunt me, drains me of energy, and weighs down my dreams as an anchor of unworthiness and not deservingness, keeping me small.

A breath in this moment, for this moment. I am invited to continue to put myself in situations that are not entirely comfortable for me so I may continue to grow and stretch past my familiar zone, dislodging invisible barriers, self-limiting habitual patterns, and limiting beliefs.

These are hard lessons and large questions for me. The truth of them resonates deep within me. But the patterns I have lived into are hard for me to identify and then break. The coming years show me the extreme level of intensity required to jolt me out of those patterns and the craziness of the familiar zone I live in.

The universe is conspiring, though. Giving me clues, subtle and brazen. I am constantly amazed at how the right people show up at the most unexpected times in my life; how my journey navigates pathways I could never have imagined possible. This happens again and again.

I attend the Shambhala Institute for my third year in a row. I am introduced to a man who is a leadership coach and who runs an authentic leadership program. He looks intently at me, asking if we have met before. There does not seem to be any place we could have met. He looks at me but also seems to look through me or past me. I find it disconcerting and am not quite sure what to do with him.

One day, as I am walking by him on my way to lunch, he stops me, wanting to say something. It takes him a moment to consider what he wants to say or how he wants to say it. I see in his face he is hesitating. His look compels me, so I sit beside him and wait. Finally he says to me, "You are very powerful, and you are very good at cloaking your power."

I raise my eyebrows. Whatever I might have been expecting, this certainly wasn't it. "You have my attention," I tell him. He really does. He has my full attention. I completely resonate with his comment. I have felt it play out in my life over and over again.

He reveals to me that he has a gift of being able to see past lives, to see patterns across them and understand how those patterns impact in this lifetime. I have always believed in past lives. Someone telling me he has the ability to see past lives does not strike me as strange or weird in any way.

He continues. "You have been very powerful in many of your past lives. In more recent ones, it literally hasn't been safe for you. So you learned to cloak your power. You have carried that cloaking ability into this lifetime. Only now it doesn't serve you quite so well because the dangers are not literally life threatening."

This is a lot to take in. I can completely see patterns of power and then cloaking that power across my lifetime to this point. One of the ways these patterns have shown up is in my willingness to stand in the shadow of other people, not needing or wanting to stand in the spotlight, especially since I was fired from my job. This translates into my unwillingness to step into the power and full force of who I am and what is mine to do in the world. It is easier to be a shadow. Bad things show up when I get "too big for my britches," as elders in my life would have said. I had dropped over the precipice without noticing I was near it. Now I have no idea how close I am or not. Easier to stay back. Way back.

I ask my new friend about the coaching work he does. He offers a few different ways to consider working together. A one-day, in-person option where I would fly to Boston and meet him in his home for intense one-on-one work in a concentrated period of time is the one that draws me.

When I arrive late afternoon on a late August day, he asks me, "Do you want to begin now or wait till morning?"

"I am definitely ready to begin. This is why I'm here," I say, eager to get started.

He smiles; he was expecting this would be my answer. "What do you want to work on?" he asks.

I say to him, "There are two things. One is I want to work on this question of cloaking my power that you identified. The other is joy.

"About ten years ago, when I first started consulting work, as I was trying to understand how to focus my attention and energy, I sent out a note to many of my friends, asking them to share with me what they thought was my one unique ability. The responses were overwhelming, and many people talked about a certain quality I had, a 'joie de vivre.' I am certain that nobody would say that about me now. I want that back. I want joy back in my life."

It's sadly true. Somewhere along the way, in the last six or seven years, I have gotten too serious, too responsible. I have forgotten how to laugh, how to have fun, how to hold things lightly. I don't remember the last time I laughed. Really laughed. I didn't even know laughter, joy, and fun were disappearing until I looked around at my life one day and wondered what had happened to me.

As I embarked on starting a business and my second marriage, I thought I would learn to fly. Instead, more and more walls were erected around my vulnerability, shutting me down more, shutting in the stranger and damping her down without even knowing I was doing it. I have been living the human tragedy story again, still. It seems the only story I really know how to live, even though I am aware of the existence of the soul-journey perspective, believe in soul journey, touch into it occasionally, and want to dance in it. So much of my adulthood path since my late twenties has been ego-driven that even the idea of entering a more spiritual path came from ego and intellect, not from soul. I later also come to know ego as my inner judge, inner critic. "See how great I am, fixing up the mess of my life, picking up the pieces? See how spiritual I'm becoming? Aren't I good? And I'll show you how to be spiritual too."

Ego is so smooth that I don't even see the story I am telling myself. I intellectualize my experience. I don't know any other way. It is not until I can embody my experience that the soul-journey path shows up in a deeper way. No wonder I have been so challenged and so unhappy. I should be able to think my way out of it. But that is a trap.

It is the stranger within who laughs delightfully and loves freely, although I haven't figured this out yet. Where is she? Where did she go? She has been damped down by the shadows that flit across the canvas of my unfolding life. I want to know this person again. I want to breathe life into her, allow her to breathe life into me. I am fascinated to discover that in trying to protect her, I've been shutting her down. She doesn't need protection. She needs to fly free, to be able to live in the place of openheartedness, a place that feels inherently dangerous. What is the courage needed to risk dropping the protective mechanisms when it feels like doing so opens the doors to destruction instead? This is the paradox: that which I most need to do is the thing that most paralyzes me with fear.

This work I am about to embark on will open up doorways and thresholds I shut down and forgot about when I was a child, when I first began to protect the glorious stranger within. In recent years, I've seen glimpses of these doorways opened by the stranger within, but I never believed they were truly representative of me. Other people see the stranger long before I have the capacity to believe she can even exist in me.

We start. He invites a visualization, a symbol. As we begin, a nonphysical entity appears to me, a grandmother guide. I have been meeting her on and off over the last few years. She is the one who appeared in the garden when I knew I'd lost my baby. She has largely been absent in more recent times. In the chaos of my life, my ability to access her is obscured. Even when I do access her, I don't know what to do with her, how to interact with her, or how to access her wisdom and knowledge, so I don't even try. After all, those kinds of experiences are for gifted people, not for the likes of me. I mention her presence. My coach chuckles. "That's great," he says.

"It's distracting," I reply, a bit annoyed.

"Well, just ask her to step aside so you can do your work."

Really? Just ask her to step aside. It's as easy as that?

So I make the invitation. She steps aside, and five other spirit guides join her. Spirit guides. Guardian angels. Nonphysical entities or beings present, I know now, whether we are aware of them or not. They guide our path in sometimes extraordinary ways. It is surely because of them that I am finding so many amazing people—or they are finding me.

This is, of course, not the first time I've been aware of spirit guides. Other people have alerted me to them, describing them and offering tidbits on what they provide or what I can access through them. I have become aware of four in the preceding years—two I've been told about, and one (the grandmother guide) I've come to know by sensing her presence. Another dramatically appeared while in the car with my family during a wild rainstorm when I asked for support and protection from all our guides. And, of course, there is the shape-shifting lion I met during the drumming circle.

I have met them. I have been moved to tears by knowing about them. I know beyond any doubt now that I am never, ever alone. I have never been alone even in the days when I have felt completely alone. Nonphysical guides are always there, always supporting, always embracing me in deep love: love of the journey I so willingly stepped into when I agreed to take on physical form, as well as love for all the imperfections and the learning choices along the way. No matter how poor my choices, my guides will not stop loving me or supporting me. When I call them to my attention, they are strong in their capacity to help. When I let them drift out of my awareness, it is not that they aren't there; it is that I block my own access. Learning to be open to them is as much a part of the journey as embracing the stranger within and living into openheartedness. It is not a linear path.

I know it is phenomenal to have this awareness of spirit and guides. I know it is a gift. I don't know what to do with it—or them. I don't know how to be in conversation or collaboration. So they fade into the background as life's events overtake my time and attention, particularly the intensity of my relationship, which seems to demand so much of my attention on the physical plane.

Now here they are. The four I already know have been joined by two more. I share this with my coach. He is thrilled to be able to work so explicitly with spirit and energy. Often he is working with clients who do not understand the nonphysical world or how it can be such a vibrant experience that allows one to cultivate relationships with entities one cannot see with physical eyes. We are off to a powerful start.

We actively work with my guides, who represent aspects of myself. The more I relate to them, the more I step into and own these different aspects of myself. Our goal is to help me access my power and my gifts and allow the expressions of who I am to realign themselves so they don't have to compensate. My coach asks me, "Are you really willing to put it on and own it instead of wondering when someone is going to come and take it away from you?"

Powerful question. Gives me pause. Is that what I've been doing? Shrinking in fear that someone outside of me could take away my own quintessential self?

I begin to understand that the purpose of fear is to keep me safe, to protect me, and, more so, to protect my vulnerability. The reflex to protect is so strong that it is hard for me to leave the feeling of vulnerability open and exposed while I do this healing work. But then it dawns on me: power and fear both do the same job, only power does it better. Why am I defaulting to fear? When and how did this become my pattern?

I discover I have a fear of being played. This has happened to me in my past. So I try to protect my vulnerability. The very act of trying to protect it and appear strong invites attack. I cannot understand this paradox. It does not seem fair.

I am afraid of my power; afraid I will use it to hurt other people. Not that I would intentionally set out to harm another person. I fear it will happen through inattention, the lack of consciousness, awareness, awakeness. I have hurt people in the past—my first husband, people who worked for me, my parents—by my choices and/or my actions. Somehow I have ascribed this to being powerful. Being powerful becomes associated with being bad, abusive, or simply ignorant of others. It is not the same thing. It is more lack of intentionality; more being driven by ego and the need for recognition, validation, and even love.

My coach helps me see I cannot "use" or abuse my power. I can only step into my power and allow things to flow through me. When I try to "use" it, try to make things happen, I get into trouble. How to allow the energy and power to flow through me when so much has been blocked for so long is a very relevant issue for me.

The relationship with my husband needs to heal or shift in order for us to be successful. The conflict we experience is part of what has brought me here to do this work. I cannot continue to walk this path of external and internal chaos. I am afraid to voice my suspicion we are headed for divorce, although the question is alive in me. There was a strong spiritual connection when we met. We were clearly meant to be together—to bring our son into the world, if for nothing else. We have imagined we found each other so we can be together in work and life, but there is so much struggle in both of those realms that it is really hard to see the path through. Many times when I sense into the future, I do not see us together, and yet I am unwilling to give up on us and the visions and dreams that originally brought us together. I hope that by shifting enough things in me, I can contribute to shifting the space between us. My external world is a reflection of my inner world. I know shifting is possible, but I do not know if it will be enough or how long it will take. I don't have a timeline.

I am intensely curious about the gift of being able to see and connect with these nonphysical guides, which is emerging more and more for me. It is delightful and confusing at the same time. What am I supposed to do with these nonphysical guides who seem so delighted that I am now aware of them and apparently want to be in relationship with me. I don't know how to be in relationship with them yet. But this is such a rich experience that I have no doubt it is real. I have no doubt it is a gift.

I ask my coach, "Do you ever wonder why you have been called to do this work? Why you've been chosen?"

His answer: "If you believe that, on the level of soul, you made an agreement before you came into physical form, then you understand this as part of your path and not as something gifted to you by some extraneous being. It is a soul contract. And you stop asking the question."

That sinks in. I understand now that my question comes from ego. What makes me so special? Maybe this is also one of the reasons I've been in denial of the gifts—because I really am not that special. His explanation takes it out of ego and puts it back where it belongs—at the level of soul and soul journey. It invites me to lean into it in a totally different way. With curiosity. It brings freedom.

He says to me, "We are entering a time when more and more of us are awakening and being asked to walk with one foot in the physical world and one in the nonphysical world. We will be the generators of the change and transformation this world is calling for right now—all of us, through all the paths we walk. This work becomes so much easier as you access all the spiritual guidance available and allow your guides to help you."

What he says rings true for me, although what exactly it means I am not sure. How I might engage this path is even less clear to me.

He invites me again to access a symbol or image that I can work with as we continue the visualizations, the questions, the depth of healing. The image of an eagle comes to me—a magnificent white eagle with an amazing wingspan. I can see a remarkable amount of detail: the way its feathers layer on its chest, the size of its legs and claws, and even its eyes. The image sends shivers through my whole body.

Later, back at home, I look up the spiritual meaning of the eagle. It is a power animal that represents the ability to walk with one foot in the physical world and one in the world of spirit. There is no way I could have known that this symbol reflected exactly what my coach has told me. The description also talks about fear and overcoming it to step into what needs to be done.

My time in Boston is life altering. I am altered. Something in me is newly awakened and newly available. I am emotional about my connection to my guides. They are incredible, beautiful beings, just waiting to be invited to help out. I cannot believe the willingness and ease with which they are taking on my burdens and challenges. I am told my guides have so much more to say to me. I feel this to be true. I know I need to find a way to tune in to my own listening and willingness to enter into conversation, although I have no idea what that will look like or how I will do it.

I was told in the past that I am very powerful and have access to the spirit world. I never understood what that meant. I always thought the people who said this to me had it wrong, like the friend who taught the intuition class; that they were talking about someone else—not me. I felt up to this point that I surely did not possess these kinds of gifts. I was just a simple human being, awed by people who see past lives, talk with spirit, read the tarot, or possess any other gift that could possibly be termed "supernatural." This was not me.

But through this healing spiritual work, I am confronted by the possibility that this is me; that there is much I can access and certainly much I can grow into. The stranger within is sparking to life in new ways, seeing openings, speaking more clearly. I am beginning to get a sense of her, but there is much for me to learn, much for me to let go of, such as patterns that do not support the pathways that are calling to me with as much longing for me to be on them as my longing to walk in new ways and shape new patterns to live into.

As I leave to go home, I am peaceful, grounded, content, full, and supported—supported beyond my comprehension.

Such a beginning step though! How and what will manifest in my physical world when I am home as I try to walk this path? My coach is very clear. We can do a lot of healing work in the realm of spirit. But the physical situations we have attracted to ourselves over the years still need to be tended to and mended. Without attentiveness to how we walk the path in the physical world, the energetic work may not stick. Where is that magic wand? There is so much I need to tend to in the physical world. Will I even find my way? How will I find the strength for the healing needed in me with respect my marriage? I have no answers. Just questions. Many, many questions.

I continue to work with my coach by phone. We address things that come up, questions I carry, and crises that show up. I feel my way along the path. Good days and bad days. Some small improvements and some hurtling back to old patterns. More and more I am aware of the need to shift the patterns in me in order to shift the patterns around me. It is exhilarating and frustrating knowledge. It is all within me.

But what about the people around me? Do I really need to take responsibility for all of us? Why can't they meet me where I am so we can jointly navigate the way?

I give my power away when I want other people to do healing work on my behalf, when I think I can't do the work on my own behalf. I claim my power and step more fully into it each I time I acknowledge and own it.

I am not responsible for other people's journeys—not even my family members', including my husband's and my kids'. They are not responsible for my journey either.

Nobody can create in my realty unless I am attracting that to me. This is tough medicine. I want an easier way out, an easier path, but the prison I have so artfully walled myself into over the course of my lifetime requires some strategically placed dynamite to break myself out. I carry so much resistance that I do not even know the extent of it. Seems to be at least equal to the power others have identified me as having.

It begins with mini steps along the way. I discover, almost by accident, that I can see other people's guides if I take the time to sense into them.

I am in my kitchen with my husband and a friend soon after I come back from Boston. My friend asks if I can see her guides, not really expecting an answer. As I focus my attention and tune in to her energy, a sense of an essence begins to take form. I really didn't think this would happen.

I begin to describe the flashes of images that are coming to me. My friend is able to add detail. Between the two of us, we capture the essence of a few of her guides—to her delight and mine.

In the coming months, I work with her and a few other friends, helping them connect with their guides to play with and learn from them. It is beautifully crazy work.

Many of my friends have vibrant exchanges with their guides, more so than I have with mine. My most vibrant exchanges come when I'm working with my coach. He makes the nonphysical world come alive for me. I am aware I can do this work on my own—we all can—but it is amplified and accelerated when we do it with others, sensing into, building off of, and contributing to the "field" of energy.

My coach tells me that my guides have information to share with me and that it would be to my benefit to cultivate pathways for their sharing. I'm not sure what this means, but I do want to do it. I discover that running provides me with physicality and time to empty my mind and let my imagination wander with intentionality toward my guides. Different images arrive of their own accord.

A frequent image is me with my shaman guide. I see myself with him often. The "me" I see with him is a young native woman, a medicine woman. My knowing is that she is me and he is her father or a father-type figure for her. Sometimes I see us in a village. Often I see us sitting across from each other in a circle, with and without a fire. Very often there are two others with us, sitting in council.

I understand I am both in an apprenticeship and moving into mastery of what I know. Translation to the physical world of now remains the biggest challenge, but I am learning to trust it. Learning it doesn't necessarily have to be done through an exchange of words. Much can be communicated in an instant through a feeling or imagery. It does not require long explanations; just acceptance, willingness, and understanding. New worlds open up if I allow myself to surrender into what wants to make itself known.

A few months after beginning this work with my coach, I attend a conference in Halifax. Impromptu, a stranger comes up to me from across a large meeting room on the evening of the first day. He says to me, "I just have to tell you, you radiate joy!"

I radiate joy! Me! How delightful! The impact of the healing work I am doing is reflected back to me quickly. Check that goal.

A few months later, I meet a new friend who becomes an instrumental support on my path for a while. He says to me in our initial meeting, "You do know you are all about joy, don't you?"

Reflections of my journey sent to me by my guides? Who knows?

I am powerful. I am strong. I radiate joy. This is my guiding mantra from this work for the next few months.

CHAPTER 5

SOUL JOURNEY THROUGH THE CLOAK OF HUMAN TRAGEDY

My mother's breast prosthesis has broken down. She has had it now for a couple of years. She has complained to me about it, but I haven't seen it. I don't hear her through the dementia lens I've now put on her. I discredit her, although I do not know I am doing this until she proves herself.

We are sitting in one of the many medical appointments I am now attending with my parents, although this one is for my father. She reaches into her bra and pulls out the prosthesis. It has broken down and is sticky. My eyes widen in alarm, shock, and dismay. I am disappointed in myself for not seeing past the human tragedy story of dementia, for dismissing my mother, for dismissing her intelligence and her awareness. Honestly, I am ashamed. Thankfully she is persistent.

I take it from her. We agree we should just throw it in the garbage, which we do there and then, on the spot.

We decide that, rather than buy a new one, we will go bra shopping and she can stuff the left side with tissue. She has a habit, born through the increasing haze of dementia, of collecting tissue and tucking it away all over the place anyway. Why not try to be a bit more intentional about it? I want to get a front-closing bra for her because she has difficulty closing a regular bra in back. I'm not even sure she will remember how to close a new one.

We are in the dressing room at Rudolph's, a long-standing women's dress shop in Lunenburg. I am in the dressing room with her because she doesn't seem to know what she is doing here or what needs to happen next.

She takes off her blouse to try on a bra. She looks down at her chest, puzzled. She looks at the right side and then the left side, right and left again, finally focusing her gaze on her left side. She looks at me and says, "This side is kind of flat."

In spite of myself, I laugh. There aren't many choices. Laugh or cry. I say, "Yes, Mom. That's because you had your breast removed." As I watch her expression, I see her curiosity and her hesitancy. I'm not sure she understands; she just knows something is not right with her body.

There was a time before I became a patient navigator for my parents—a time they kept their medical appointments and health questions and concerns largely to themselves, when I was on the periphery. Until the day the phone rang.

"Hello there." I answer the phone knowing it is my parents but not knowing that this is one of those quiet, subtle, seemingly innocuous moments that herald the beginning of a new stage in life. Unlike those moments that have dropped in with startling alacrity, there is a barely perceptible stirring in my soul.

I engage in idle chit chat for a while with my mother. Then my father gets on the phone and says, "Your mother has an appointment with her oncologist."

My mother had a lump removed three years before, followed by radiation treatment. I was pregnant with my third child at the time. My father drove my mother the one hour trip from Lunenburg to Halifax and then one hour back again for this treatment almost every day. Occasionally one of their friends took the journey with my mother instead, giving my father a break. They came to the city and went home every day for five weeks. It had very little to do with me. They didn't visit during these trips, and I didn't attend the appointments with them. My brother, who lived in British Columbia at the time, had even less involvement and awareness. My father took care of my mother. I checked in with them from time to time, enough to know what was going on but not enough to be impacted by it.

There is something in how my father speaks in this call that has my attention. He hasn't asked anything; I sense he wants to but maybe doesn't know how.

After he mentions the time of the appointment a second time, I am moved to ask him, "Do you want me to go with you?"

"Well, yeah, that would be good if you could . . . if you're not too busy."

The appointment has been scheduled because my mother's breast cancer has returned. She already had a left-side mastectomy. I was at my first Art of Hosting training in Bowen Island, British Columbia during her surgery. There was no pressing need for me to be with my parents, although my mother and her experience were deeply in my awareness at the time. By the time I got home from the training, my mother was out of the hospital and well on the road to recovery. I do not even remember when I saw her upon my return, but she was definitely at home by then.

After the surgery, everything was fine. They believed they got all of the cancer and life could go on more or less normally. I say "more or less" because my father was already noticing signs of dementia in my mother.

This call, this appointment, marks a change in both my life and our relationship. I am about to become their patient navigator, the person who will ask questions and make calls they are not able to make for risk of offending a doctor or other medical professional, the person who is willing to impose on these people who have busy schedules.

As an occasional visitor to my parents' home who rarely stayed overnight, I had a hard time seeing the signs of the onset of dementia. My brother, Robert, would visit for a few days at a time. He became more aware of the situation and her behavior, but my dad was the one who had to deal with her gradual loss of cognitive abilities every day in big and small ways.

"I need to go behind her when she puts the laundry in because she forgets to put the lid down on the washer. The she doesn't understand why it doesn't work,." my dad said.

"She put banana bread in the oven to bake and took it out after just a few minutes. She couldn't understand why it wasn't done."

"I bought her a dishwasher, and she never uses it. She still washes the dishes by hand. Or she washes them and then puts them in the dishwasher." This was the dishwasher my mother had longed for for years that now she could not remember how to use.

Of course he is worried about her. He is gradually taking on more and more responsibility as her caregiver, as well as more and more responsibility for the household, cooking and cleaning. At the same time, he has his own health issues. He is on a waiting list for his second open-heart surgery. His first one was twenty-five years earlier, when he was just forty-five years old. He has a pacemaker, which his heart is almost totally dependent on, as well as myriad other minor and major health issues.

On Labor Day weekend I get a call. "Mother took a spill on the dock. She tripped in those goddamn shoes of hers and fell on her face. We just got home from the hospital. Our family doctor was on duty, and he was able to take care of her. She's all bruised up though."

I go for a quick visit—to see the damage and make sure she is okay. The whole side of her face is bruised, but she seems in good spirits. However, her fall on the dock sparks a range of medical appointments. She is scheduled for blood tests and a CT scan. There is some question in the doctor's mind about the cause of her fall—something which never even crossed my mind. They want to know if her breast cancer has spread to her brain. The doctor is wondering if she blacked out rather than tripped.

The day comes for Mom's appointment with the oncologist. It is just a few weeks after her fall on the dock. When they call her in, Dad and I both go in with her. I discover that it is the first time he has ever attended one of her medical appointments as more than a chauffeur. This surprises me. My brother reminds me that our mother was fiercely independent and private in some respects—her health being one of those ways.

The doctor asks Mom, "How are you doing?"

She says, "Fine." She engages in some pleasantries with the doctor. There is no mention of her fall, her trip to the emergency room, or the recent tests—from my mother, the doctor, or my father.

I'm sitting, watching, observing, and becoming more confused. I don't understand why the doctor isn't asking about or making reference to Mom's current situation. So I say, "Mom, what about your fall?"

She looks at me. "Oh, yes. I fell on the dock, coming off the boat. The tide was really low, and I tripped on something at the top of the dock. Robert was there." Her tone is the same as if she is exchanging pleasantries with someone, as though she is talking about the weather or going to the post office rather than a traumatic fall that left her so bruised.

I begin to fill in some of the details. "Her family doctor sent her for a CT scan and blood tests."

This is all news to this specialist. This is when I discover that, coincidentally, this is a regular follow-up appointment already scheduled for my mother and that it is not due to her recent fall or the suspicions about cancer having spread beyond her breast.

The doctor goes on a search for all the test results. She comes back with bad news. While there is no evidence of cancer or tumors in her brain, the CT scan shows a whole range of things.

"There are spots on her lungs. We can't be sure if they are new or the result of cancer having spread to her lungs. It is possible those spots were caused by something else and have been there for a long time. We won't know for sure until we do a follow-up.

"We're seeing some arthritis, but it's nothing we need to be concerned about.

"There is fluid showing in her uterus. We don't know what it is. It is not a large amount. It may have been there for some time, but we need to check it out."

The most troubling thing is the spots on her lungs. They may have been there for a long time, caused by some infection somewhere along the way or they may be a sign that cancer has spread to her lungs. While my parents have always talked about not ever doing chemotherapy, now, all of a sudden, we are being referred to a chemotherapist for consultation. Something that seemed not to be on the agenda suddenly is.

I can't help entertaining the difficult and troubling question of what to do about my mother's care. She has dementia that has not yet been diagnosed, although she is being tested every few months because it is clearly progressing. There is a standard set of ten questions that people suspected of having dementia or Alzheimer's are asked. She passes with flying colors every time. But her growing incapacity is becoming more apparent all the time. Now we're talking about compounding her confusion with chemotherapy. It is a difficult time with difficult questions that go unasked. Die of breast cancer or languish, maybe for years, with dementia?

Nobody in health care asks us these kinds of questions. Head down. Symptoms identified. Treat them all, one at a time, independently. Does anyone even know how to create openings for and to engage in these kinds of big, difficult questions—the ones that look at the whole person?

We wait.

We do the rounds of medical appointments. One is with a gynecologist to examine her and her uterus. My dad and I attend the appointment with her. We begin in the office, going through medical history.

The doctor says to us, "The fluid on Mary's uterus is probably nothing. In all likelihood it's probably been there since her last period without bothering her at all. But now that we know about it, we need to do something about it." Hmm. Now that we know, we can't just let this be? Even though it has not caused any problems in how many years?

My mother goes into an examining room off of the office we are in. The doctor goes in to examine her. The room is not soundproof. I can hear the conversation.

The doctor asks Mom, "What's that scar on your abdomen from?"

My mother, sounding a bit puzzled, says, "I don't know. Maybe my daughter can tell you."

When asked, I say, "Mom, that's your appendectomy scar—from when you had your appendix out when you were sixteen."

While I shake my head with some consternation and some amusement, I am also aware that dementia is not just causing my mother to forget recent events and to have trouble expressing her thoughts, it is also causing her to forget events from when she was young. Her memories are disappearing. She is becoming lost—to herself, her experiences, and the stories she has used to make meaning of her life. She is becoming lost to my father, who lives with her and her situation every day. And she is becoming lost to my brother and me.

Mom has a bone scan, another CT scan, and more blood tests. It is just before Christmas. We go back to see the oncologist we have been referred to, expecting to be told that Mom will be starting chemotherapy in the New Year. I am still wondering where the room is for the difficult conversations, and I am not sure how to broach them myself now that chemotherapy has been presented to my parents as the only option forward and my parents are accepting the authority of the specialists. There is only so much I can do to be helpful and not interfering.

We almost cannot believe what we are told now by the oncologist.

"Her blood tests all came back good without the markers in it that point to cancer. The bone scan is clear. The little dots in her lungs that we were concerned about haven't changed at all. If it was cancer, we would have expected to see changes. It probably means they were caused by something else, likely a long time ago."

A little dazed, not quite comprehending, we wonder, *What does all this mean?*

"The cancer has not spread. You are free to go."

Free to go. It's like dodging a bullet. We do not need to ask the tough questions about cancer versus dementia. Now we just need to live with dementia. Or, more accurately, Mom and Dad need to live with dementia with my mother's increasing dependence—and strain—on my father.

While this is going on with my mother, my father's heart situation is getting worse. He is regularly using his nitro puffer to calm his heart so he can breathe. All the time. Nights are the worst for him. I am less hopeful and more worried about him. He goes for an angiogram to track his blood vessels and veins to pinpoint the exact problem areas and map out a strategy for surgery.

We have many conversations on the topic. "I hope they don't send me home too soon," he says.

We meet with his heart surgeon to look at the mass of arteries and veins around his heart and to try to understand how his bypass twenty-five years ago was done. Because the arteries and veins are not in good condition, there are many risks involved no matter what we do—in waiting, in operating, in doing angioplasty. He could die on the operating table. He could die before he ever gets there. They could decide not to operate because the risks are too great.

I call the hospital to find out what they are deciding to do and to stress the urgency of his situation. He is put on the waiting list. If my father dies, I do not know what we will do with my mother, but it is clear that she cannot live on her own.

And so we wait. Day by day goes by. My dad is getting by. He's still taking care of my mother, and he is in an increasing amount of distress.

At four o'clock one morning in November, the phone rings. My husband answers, talks for a few minutes, and hangs up. He tells me it was my mother. She called to say that Dad was in the emergency room in Lunenburg.

I ask him where my mother is now. He doesn't know. It is four o'clock in the morning, after all. No one is very coherent.

I call my parents' home, and Mom answers. She sounds cheerful and unconcerned. "I couldn't figure out how to get out of the parking lot," she says. This is what has her attention, not my father, not his situation. I am beginning to understand the inappropriateness of her responses as an impact of her dementia. I ask her where Dad is. "I left him at emergency," she tells me, as she once again describes her challenge in getting out of the parking lot.

I call the emergency department in Lunenburg. "Yes, your father's here. We have him hooked up to IVs and monitors. The doctor is trying to figure out what to do with him—whether to send him to Bridgewater or to Halifax."

I ask the obvious questions. "Why wouldn't he be sent directly to Halifax, which is where he would need to be for surgery?" They don't know. They're waiting, trying to understand the severity of the situation. I know how severe it is. We have been waiting for a long time.

I have as much information as I am going to get at this moment. I call my mother back. I call Robert and fill him in.

I lie back down, but sleep is now impossible. I am waiting to hear back from the hospital. No matter what they tell me, I need to go get my mother. She cannot stay on her own. I head out at 6:00 a.m., before the sun is up and after several conversations with the Lunenburg hospital—the last one with the paramedic who will be transporting Dad by ambulance. I find out they have decided to send him directly to

Halifax. Not that I am a medical expert, but this makes the most sense to me, and it is a relief.

As I drive the sixty miles to Lunenburg at this early hour of the day, my thoughts are filled with what is ahead, my mother, my father, and the uncertainty of the future that is looming. There is little I can do. I stay focused on the immediate. Staying present. I prevent myself from making up stories about a future that has yet to reveal itself. I become aware that I will probably pass my father's ambulance going in the opposite direction. Then I wonder if I have already passed it and somehow missed it. That is a ludicrous thought. There are hardly any vehicles on the road, and as I am about to discover, the ambulance is impossible to miss.

The sun is coming up over the horizon, and miles away in front of me, I suddenly spot it coming over the horizon. The lights of the ambulance are flashing, the siren is sounding. It is one of the most surreal moments of my life—driving on the highway toward Lunenburg, passing the ambulance with my father lying in the back going in the opposite direction. It plays out in the slow-motion picture show of my mind: the ambulance and I driving toward each other on an otherwise barren highway; my father going in one direction, I going in the opposite direction. Two vehicles passing in the early dawn. My father is being taken care of. It is my mother who needs tending now. I continue to drive into the dawn, toward my mother.

I arrive at my parents' home. My mother is lying on her bed, under the covers, fully dressed. She is cheerful. Her main story is still about being stuck in the parking lot. Dad drove the two of them to the hospital, and Mom drove herself home. The very fact that she did not stay with him is evidence of the progression of her dementia. Inappropriate choices. This is something she would never have done pre-dementia.

I pack a bag for her and for my father, not knowing what is in front of us, what they'll need, or even how many days to plan for. I find all their medications and tuck them into the bag. We head out—back to Halifax and directly to the hospital. The only good thing is that now we know when he is going to have surgery. They can no longer send him home to wait. He is about to bump somebody else, a non-emergency patient, off of a scheduled surgery date.

We arrive at the hospital, and I have to track Dad down. He was admitted through the emergency department but was sent directly to the cardiac unit. His surgeon is not in this day. His heart is laboring with so much difficulty that the medical team needs to take the pressure off. They insert a balloon pump to take over the functioning of his heart. This means he has to lie completely flat and still on his back until his surgery. They decide they will wait for twenty-four hours for his surgeon, who has mapped out his veins and arteries and has a plan for this complicated surgery, to be back on duty. Nothing more is going to happen this day.

I bring my mother home with me, where she is going to stay for a couple of days until my brother can come from Prince Edward Island.

My mother now usually goes to bed early—around six or seven o'clock in the evening. We get her set up in the bedroom in our basement. She gets ready for bed and goes to sleep. We have to get an early start in the morning because Dad will be in surgery first thing.

Around ten thirty, as I am getting ready for bed, I hear a noise downstairs. My mother is up, completely dressed, including her shoes—lying on the sofa in my family room. She has no interest in going back downstairs to bed. She's ready to go—somewhere, anywhere. I get a blanket and cover her up, shoes and all. She sleeps fine for the rest of the night on the couch, and I sleep with one ear open, listening for her. We have an alarm system in the house, so if by chance she does try to go outside, I'll know.

We head to the hospital around five o'clock in the morning. I want to be there before Dad goes into surgery. He will be reassured knowing we are there. My mother goes along with however I guide her, as though she is just along for the ride and has no comprehension of the seriousness of what is before us on this day. We see Dad into surgery. We are shown into the family waiting lounge and introduced to the helpful woman who will keep us updated from time to time on how my dad is doing. We know we are here for the long haul. His surgery will take hours.

I take my mother down to the Tim Hortons coffee shop in the hospital. We grab a coffee and a bite to eat. She enjoys the coffee shop and enjoys being social. We look at shoes in a little shop, putter around for a bit, and head back up to the lounge. We have magazines with us, but even now my mother no longer really reads. She looks at things, but I'm not sure whether she can read anymore.

While we wait at the hospital, my brother is getting ready to leave Prince Edward Island and come over, a five-hour drive. He is preparing to stay for a while because he will be taking care of Mom while Dad is in the hospital and will stay with them both for a bit when Dad comes home. I am grateful for this because there is only so much I can do with three kids and a business. However, as often happens, there is enough spaciousness in my calendar that I can be present for my parents. My husband is taking care of the home front.

Hours go by. The woman comes in to give us an update. So far, so good. There is not really any news to share. She updates other people also waiting for their loved ones. We wait. We go to the hospital cafeteria for lunch. We come back to the lounge.

The woman comes back at three o'clock in the afternoon. She tells us the surgery is complete. It has gone well. Someone will let us know when he is in recovery so we can go see him. Other families are led out of the lounge to visit with their loved ones. Still we wait.

Robert arrives at four. We still have not heard the final word on the surgery. The room is empty of other families, and the wonderful woman who delivers the updates has gone home for the day. We are told that the surgeon will come and find us.

At 5:00, my mother stands up, puts on her coat, and gets ready to leave. It is like an internal alarm clock has gone off. She is done. Time to go. I marvel at this and chuckle a little to myself as I gently get her to sit back down again. She does, but she keeps her coat on, ready to go at any time.

"No, Mom, we're not going anywhere until we hear about Dad and get to see him. We haven't seen him yet." She stays seated, with her coat on, restless.

We bump into another surgeon we know. He asks us if we have had word on Dad. When we say no, he tells us a little bit and promises to send someone to us. Finally, Dad's surgeon comes in.

"The surgery went well," he says. "We had to do a fair bit of bypass because of the previous surgery. When we finished, there was a bit of bleeding. We left him open on the table for a couple of hours because we wanted to be sure that everything was working properly and that there were no bleeders before we closed him up. It would be far worse if we closed him up and then had to go back and reopen him to fix problems. He's in ICU now, and his vitals are all good. He's responding well."

Relief! He had been in surgery and open on the operating table for eleven hours. In the ICU, doctors are adjusting things to try to find the right combination of meds and oxygen and who knows what all to keep my father comfortable and begin the recovery process. Later we find out they are making adjustments until midnight. We visit with him for a few minutes before heading out for the night. My brother is taking my mother back to Lunenburg so she will be home in her own environment. We will all be back the next day.

They keep Dad sedated the whole next day, although they have woken him up long enough to know he is okay and responding as they would like. The balloon pump is still attached to him. When they remove it, he needs to lie flat for another six hours. Given postsurgery confusion, they decide it is better to keep him sedated during that time.

When they finally stop the sedation, it takes him a while to regain consciousness. Even as he regains consciousness, he seems fuzzy, out of it. He can't speak. He makes some eye contact and seems to know we are there, but then he fades back into unconsciousness. The nurses assure us that this kind of thing happens. Sometimes it takes a while to recover from the anesthetic and the trauma of surgery. And in my dad's case, it was emergency surgery, so his system was already weakened and traumatized and his system was reliant on a balloon pump for the twenty-four hours preceding his surgery and for quite a few hours after surgery. There are many factors in the mix.

On day three, I check in with the hospital. Still no real change in my father. He is on a ventilator with a breathing tube down his throat. They are feeding him intravenously, and he is on fluids. He has periods of seeming consciousness during which he becomes distressed and tries to pull out his tubes. He is not really aware.

I call home to Lunenburg to update my brother and my mother. My mother answers the phone. She fills the conversation space with what's happening in her world—my brother making breakfast, going to the post office, and the other minutiae of life. She is as cheerful as always and doesn't even ask about my father. I begin to tell her what news I have. She brushes it off and hands the phone over to my brother.

I can only suppose that her dementia is shifting her awareness and focus. My mother—the mother I knew—would not gloss over this.

Four days into this situation with no change, I ask a nurse, "When should I be worried?" The nurse looks at me and says, after a thoughtful pause, "When the doctors are?" Okay. When the doctors are. Good. So I don't worry. I stay present with my dad where he is, visiting daily, often more than once, and checking in with the nurses by phone when I'm not there at least twice a day. My brother brings my mother up from Lunenburg almost every day to visit. We confer. We wait.

The days go by. Daily, other patients come from surgery and go to the step down unit. Except for my father. He is the only constant in the ICU—the only one who has yet not regained full consciousness. I send out e-mails to my friends, describing the situation and asking them for healing prayers. I get so many beautiful messages back from my friends; I am hopeful and encouraged. I send updates from time to time.

Dad's friends and family begin calling. They have noticed the absence of my parents in their small town or they have noticed the presence of my brother. "How is Hector? How is Mary? Is there anything I can do? Let us know how he is." Robert and I create a list of people we should be in touch with. It hadn't occurred to us that we should be calling people. Dad was only supposed to be in the hospital a few days.

Because he is vulnerable, being in a hospital and on a ventilator, he gets sicker. He gets several infections. The pump and the drugs for sedation, pain relief, and clearing infection create a chemical soup that keeps him foggy and out of it. We have to gown up to see him. This is disorienting for my mother. My brother tries to keep her occupied in order to extend our visits, but it does not always work.

When Dad finally starts coming around, he does so slowly—one step forward and a half step back. He is able to move all his body parts, and his organs are working well. He still needs assistance with his breathing, although at some point they have to start weaning him off the ventilator. It is a judgment call. He becomes more and more lucid; his eyes don't seem quite so cloudy anymore, and this is making him cantankerous. He is uncooperative with the nurses, and he is not happy about being in bed.

The nurses put him in restraints because he is pulling his tubes out. The more he fights, the longer this takes. When my brother or I are visiting, they will take the restraints off, but we need to be vigilant as he tries to grab the ventilator tube. If he pulls it out, it will be worse for him, because they will need to reinsert it. As my father lies in this state, and as I hold him back from ripping out his tubes, I pray that he does not remember any of this when he finally wakes up, because I'm sure he will be angry at me.

It is challenging to go visit him, because he is trying to communicate and I can't understand him. He gets frustrated, and I get discouraged. I want to help, and I want to understand him, but I can't. And, more than that, I want him off the ventilator and clearly on the road to recovery. Sometimes when I visit he gets more agitated, and he can't talk with the tube in his mouth.

Nobody told us about this kind of postsurgical possibility. We hear it is not common, but not uncommon either. The doctors aren't worried yet, but the longer he stays in the ICU, the greater his risk of infection.

Around day ten I bump into his surgeon in the hallway. "Doctor," I ask as I look him directly in the eyes to see his full response, "Are you worried about my father?"

There is a pause. He returns my look. Finally he says, "I'm not happy. I won't be happy until he is out of ICU and down on the step down unit like he should be. In every other way he is responding as he should." Okay, not happy. He didn't actually say whether he is worried. But it is good enough for me. I won't worry. I will hold space, consciousness, and awareness for healing. I will keep praying and asking my friends for their prayers and healing energy. We know prayer works, even when people do not know they are being prayed for. And, thanks to research on the impact of prayer there is proof too.

Day thirteen dawns. This day is different. Susan is Dad's nurse today. I have gotten to know all the nurses. I have praised many of them. One I asked to not have assigned to my father again because of the nurse's abrasive attitude. Even if my dad is not fully aware, I am certain that his healing will be energetically impacted by that attitude. This is the first time I meet Susan. My first introduction to her takes place in my morning call to the ICU.

"Your father is in a catch-22 situation," she tells me. "He needs to get off the ventilator soon, but his agitation serves to create the conditions where he requires it. Whenever he is aware enough of his circumstances, his agitation increases. It essentially makes finding good conditions to remove the ventilator almost impossible."

Speaking to me about this situation, Susan says, "I know it doesn't sound good, but I have a plan." Her proposal: "I've asked for a special chair to be brought into this space so I can sit him up, take him off the ventilator and put him on an oxygen tube. If we can alternate for periods of time with him sitting and on oxygen but off the ventilator, and then maybe back on the ventilator, we just may be able to get him off the ventilator altogether."

Excitement and fear ripple through me at the same time. Progress. Maybe. If it goes well. We won't know till we try.

During the medical team's morning rounds, Susan advocates her care plan with the doctors and residents. This becomes her personal mission. When I visit my father later in the day, he is sitting in a chair without the ventilator. Her plan was successful and he never goes back on it. He shows the greatest level of consciousness and awareness that I have seen since before his surgery and he rapidly grows more aware.

A day or so later, Dad asks me, "Why did I suddenly wake up?"

I say to him, "You had an angel of a nurse that day."

Another nurse on duty overhears me say this. She interjects, saying "You have no idea. Susan made it her mission to get your father off the ventilator. We all left her alone so she could do what she needed to do. Nobody asked her to fill in during their breaks or lunch because we all wanted her to succeed."

And succeed she did. My father never looks back. We never see Susan again. Mom and Robert discovered in conversation with her that she had, like Dad, refinished an old wooden boat. It had been commissioned by the same people who had commissioned Dad's boat, the *Bluefin*, and it was from the same era. She had an affinity with my father that must have been evident, even at an unconscious level.

The next day, I am back visiting my father again. He is increasingly conscious and aware. He is now beginning to remember things, although it is all fuzzy. He begins by asking about his surgery—when he will have it?

"Dad, you've already had your surgery, and it went well," I say to him.

"Yesterday?" he asks.

"A few more yesterdays ago than that," I say, smiling.

He gradually begins to grasp the extent of his situation, but it takes him a while to fully realize he has lost eleven days. He remembers very little, thankfully! He does remember, from time to time, being on a gorgeous, large yacht sailing the ocean. Years later he tells me that he went "above" and was told that it was not his time to go yet and that he had to come back.

He is aware that he needed to be restrained.

He asks me, "Why was I so crazy?"

I don't have an answer for him. I try to explain about the ventilator and the drugs and the general confusion of his state.

He asks me, somewhat irritated, "Why did you have me on life support when we talked about that?"

I am floored. It takes me a moment to respond as I consider and begin to comprehend this unexpected question. He was on a ventilator, receiving oxygen, nutrients, vitamins, and fluids intravenously with all of his vital functions being monitored twenty-four hours a day. Of course he would think it was life support. It was. Just not in the context of our conversations.

"Well, Dad, it wasn't like that. There was never a question of you not waking up or of anything being seriously wrong with you. It was just a question of when you would wake up."

Dad rapidly goes from not even being able to swallow water, to feeding himself; and from not being able to stand, to walking with assistance to walking with a cane.

He is released from the ICU to the step-down unit, where they treat him as fragilely as if he had just had surgery. His long period of unconsciousness means that his incision is pretty much healed by the time he goes to the step-down unit, and his fear before surgery of being sent home too early is no longer a concern. (Be careful what you wish for. You never know how it will manifest.)

One week after he wakes up, he is released from the hospital and is back home. His legs are weak. The long period of unconsciousness has taken its toll. It takes a little while for him to build his strength back up, but he does. He is persistent and he has a lot of things to do around the house, in his shop in the garage, in the boat shed, and on his boat. And, of course, the boat is launched come June. Getting it ready is probably one of Dad's best motivations to regain his health.

During this journey with my father and these beginning days of my mother's dementia, I shift into a stage of my life, entering full-force into the sandwich generation. My kids need tending, and my parents now require support. I am still building my business. My business partner (who is my husband) and I are having significant challenges in our relationship and our communication.

I am aware that I have a relationship with spirit guides, although I lack intentionality in cultivating it. I know I am able to navigate the health challenges of both my parents in so calm a manner most of the time because I know that I am supported by spirit, as are they. We are in a soul journey together, and this will play itself out however it is meant to. I have learned to stay present in the moment-by-moment unfolding and not to worry about a future that has not yet appeared, but it is a practice to be leaned into over and over again, every day, many times a day.

This is how life continues even as issues and challenges show up; spiritual journey unfolds, and the path stretches ahead, beyond where the eye can see.

CHAPTER 6

MY WORLD IS ROCKED

We are visiting Nanny Hanson in Digby. She is not my real nanny. She is a dear friend of the family, and we visit her often, along with other friends in this town. I am maybe five or six years old. There is an older girl visiting. I don't really know who she is, and it doesn't really matter. We have fun together. We go upstairs to play in one of the bedrooms. There is a big, soft bed. We jump on it. This girl encourages me. I am not sure why—maybe we were getting ready for bed—but I remember being naked while jumping on the bed. Eventually one of the adults comes up to check on us and we get in trouble. We crawl into bed, pajamas on, laughing together.

It is early one January evening. I am sitting in my kitchen, scanning my e-mail after a full day of teaching. It is the last day of a three-day program. My family and I have had supper and cleaned up the kitchen. Now I am catching up on what I've missed during the day. One e-mail catches my eye. I read it, blink, and reread it. I shake my head with disbelief, peering at the screen, not trusting my very own eyes. It reads, "You don't know me, and I don't want to upset you, but I have reason to believe you might be my sister." My chest tightens.

"You don't know me." It echoes in my brain. *You don't know me . . .*

"I don't want to upset you." Time stands still. My heart stops. Everything else is frozen out of my awareness.

I have reason to believe you might be my sister? Surely I misread that. I have reason to believe you might be my sister?

The outer world of my kitchen and family room disappear, lost in a haze. Blood rushes into my head. My ears roar. My face flushes. Nothing has changed, but suddenly something is radically amiss.

You might be my sister? How is that even possible? A few days earlier, I turned forty-six years old. We are about to celebrate my parents fiftieth wedding anniversary. *You might be my sister.* Really?

I shake my head as if that will correct my eyesight. I turn back to the screen.

"My father and his first wife had two children—you and Debbie, who is three years older than you. His wife (your mother) left him when Debbie was three and you were just a baby. Debbie went to live with your grandmother, and you were adopted by Mary and Hector Jourdain, who were family friends. I was born eight years later when my—our—father remarried."

I was adopted? *Adopted!?* No. Not possible. There were times when I was growing up as a teenager when I wished I'd been adopted—but didn't everyone? I never actually believed it really possible; nor did I give that idea any more thought as an adult. It couldn't be true. Could it?

I read the e-mail again. I minimize the e-mail screen and stare off into space for a long moment before popping up the screen again, expecting that maybe the e-mail has disappeared because it wasn't really there. Nope. Still there. I read it again.

I forward it to my brother. "Be prepared for something weird" is how I preface the e-mail. I wait for him to call, but the phone is silent. The minutes tick by. I get up off the stool I've been sitting on at the edge of the center counter in my kitchen and walk around the island, my elbow cupped in one hand, rubbing my chin with my other hand, thinking and not thinking at the same time.

My husband, who has been putting our five-year-old son to bed, calls to me to say it is my turn. I go upstairs to say good-night, sing my son some songs, and tuck him in. I go through normal evening routines and actions, but I am distracted as this e-mail tugs at the peripheries of my imagination.

I come back down the stairs to the computer and reread the e-mail. I take a deep breath. I know these people. I don't know the woman who wrote the e-mail. But I know the grandmother. And I know the little girl. I remember them from when I was little.

Nanny Hanson was a kindly older woman, a friend of the family we visited often. I remember her yellow house just back behind the yacht club in Digby. The kitchen was just inside the door—a large kitchen in an older house. A wood cooking stove stood in the kitchen, from which emanated warmth and good cooking smells. Wood for the stove was stacked nearby. A wooden rocking chair—I remember people sitting in it, rocking. I remember Nanny Hanson sitting in her rocking chair, rocking. I remember always being warmly welcomed in this kitchen, in this house.

Through a door was the living room, which had an easy chair in it, the kind with a footstool that pops out when you pull the lever; it was a brown cloth chair. A television sat across the room from it. I don't remember the other furniture in this room. There must have been a couch.

A big, soft bed stood in a bedroom upstairs. I vividly remember jumping on the bed with a little girl. We used to sleep there too. This little girl was bigger than me, with light-colored hair. We jumped on that bed until we got in trouble. But it took a while for anyone to notice. The grown-ups were all visiting downstairs, enjoying drinks, telling stories. I remember her, but I don't remember her name. I don't really know who she is. I just know she was there, sometimes, when I visited—like a cousin or something. Like Nanny's actual granddaughter.

It never before occurred to me that this woman and this little girl were related to me, that this actually was my grandmother and not just a woman I called Nanny, or that this little friend, who encouraged me to get in trouble, was my sister.

But as I read and reread the e-mail, the possibility of this truth is fighting with the sweeping waves of incomprehension that muddle my thinking.

Instantly, there are two other little bits of information that pop into my mind the moment I read the e-mail. They also hint at truth. They have both been in my awareness at different points in my life, but not so much so that I question them or have any inkling of their significance.

The first is that there are no stories of my birth. The one time I asked my mother what time of day I was born, she couldn't remember. I simply attributed this to my mother being who she is—not a stickler for details.

The other is that I had always believed I was born in Digby, a small fishing town in Nova Scotia, where my family was living at the time I was born, but my birth certificate says I was born in Halifax. When I first noticed it, I thought it must be a clerical error. It didn't even occur to me it might be right. I just assumed it was wrong. And I decided it probably wasn't very important and never pursued it—never asked my parents about it, never called the Registry of Births. It was, however, enough in my awareness that when I applied for my passport, I thought about what place of birth to put on the application. I opted to use Halifax, the city stated on my birth certificate. This is the story about my birth certificate that I lived into. It is a small story, or so I thought.

It takes a while for incomprehensible news to sink in. I read and reread that e-mail, trying to understand the words that appear on the screen. Yes, of course I can read them, but what do they mean?

There is a second e-mail as well, a brief one from the girl I remember, but she is not a child anymore. She simply acknowledges her presence and what she anticipates will be my shock.

Finally I say to my husband, "There's an e-mail open on my computer. You should go read it."

He does. He looks at the computer screen and looks at me. The e-mails have come from Facebook, so he goes into Facebook and looks at the pictures. I tell him about my birth certificate and there being no stories of my birth—still not comprehending this news. I have this information, but I'm not sure what it has to do with anything.

He says to me, "Why would these two people make this up?"

"I don't know," I reply. "I don't know them. Maybe they're delusional. I remember Deb. Maybe she made this story up, convinced her sister it was true, and then they colluded in contacting me." What other explanation was there for this strange note and story?

It is amazing how far the mind will reach to try to reconcile seemingly irreconcilable information. I know as I say it, it is ridiculous, but the other possibility is even more ridiculous—too ridiculous for me to think it could be true.

I curl up on the couch, waiting for my brother to call. Even though he is younger, because his memory is always better than mine, maybe he remembers or knows something I don't. I need his help. I need to sort this out with someone who can understand.

I give up on waiting for him to call me, and I call him. Voice mail. I leave a message for him: "Clearly you are not home. When you get home, read your e-mail and then give me a call."

He calls a bit later. With a nervous little laugh, he says, "I was home." I hear the disbelief in his voice. He is reeling in his own shock. Of course he is. It is in this moment that I understand this is his story too. It isn't just about me. We have grown up together and lived many of the same stories. Of course he would be shocked. Of course this would displace him as much as it displaces me.

We sort through what is before us. Is it true? Is it lies? What might be true? What might not be true? What else isn't true for us and our life stories? What do we remember? Were there hints along the way? What does it mean? Why didn't anyone say anything all these years? Was he adopted too? No, he was clearly of Jourdain blood. But wasn't I? Don't I look like the family too? How come nobody ever questioned that?

How is it possible that this story line of my life is completely unknown to me, and that I am, in some ways, a stranger in my own life? In an instant, many of the stories I have used to interpret and understand my life and, essentially, my identity, are shown to be just that—stories. These are stories I made up and lived into; stories used to make sense of my life and to know who I am.

My immediate family members are all tall. I'm short. Story: both my grandmothers were short. My hair started going gray when I was a teenager, but my mother has less gray hair in her seventies than I do. Story: my mother's mother had beautiful gray hair from a young age, so that explained that. I was born in Digby . . . er, Halifax. Did anyone ever tell me I was born in Digby, or did I just make that up and no one ever contradicted it? I'm not even sure my parents were ever around when the subject came up. It's not the kind of subject that comes up often. Why would it? I thought my heritage a mix of French Canadian, First Nations, Irish, Scottish, German . . . but what now? When my youngest son was born with notably large hands, everyone looked at them and said he had Hector's hands. Not true. Simply not true.

What do I know now? That everything has changed. Things I have understood about myself are maybe just stories that I have made up to explain things—stories that fit with my understanding of my life, helping me make meaning. And yet nothing has changed. I look in the mirror and I am still the same person. I look the same. I feel the same, shock and incomprehension aside. I have the same relationships, and my journey to this point is the same as it was before. But I will discover whole new layers of meaning and interpretation over the next year or so as I settle into this new story and it settles into me.

Yes, everything has changed . . . and yet nothing has changed.

The stranger in me is being revealed in a dramatic, startling new way. Will I be able to embrace this new face of the stranger in me? And will I be able to embrace the hidden strangers now being revealed in my loved ones—particularly my parents—as this deeply held family secret comes to light? And what about those strangers who are showing up, declaring themselves as my family? Who exactly are they? What do they want? Why are they contacting me now, after more than forty years of living with this secret? How will I reconcile all of this?

In order to process this, I need more information. I write to Deb because I remember her. At least she feels real, like someone or something I can grasp onto as I am drowning in a lack of understanding.

I write an e-mail to her: "I remember you. I remember Nanny Hanson. But the rest of this is a bit incomprehensible. Is there more you can share with me?"

She writes back with more details. They all make sense. At the end of her e-mail, she says, "If I were you, right about now I'd be looking for concrete information. You were born in Halifax and can probably verify that information."

Yep. I can verify it all right. I don't need to go far. All I need to do is walk over to my desk, open my desk drawer, and look at my birth certificate.

I now have enough information that resonates truth to me that my next step is to talk to my father. I know this is a step I have to take and that I need to do it before I can communicate further with these two women who are telling me they are my sisters.

My mother's dementia has advanced to the point that her needs are growing beyond my father's capacity to care for her. We are about to initiate the process for long-term care. It is difficult to know how much of this she could comprehend. More importantly, what might the impact on her be if I try to explore this with her? I decide I will only talk to my father.

Fortunately, my life is full of support systems, and I do not go into this conversation unprepared. I was in correspondence with my good friend and "storycatcher" Christina Baldwin. She gave me the following advice: "It is very important how you talk to your father—what frame you set to receive his story. The fullness and candor of his story will depend on the basket of receptivity he senses in you, how you are emotionally.

"I would suggest you ask yourself, what is different if this is true? What is unchangeable in my relationship with my parents? What if it's not true? You hold as steady in yourself as you can and just keep space for what unfolds."

This is the journey I am already on—finding my steady point, center, or ground in the midst of conflict that characterizes my marriage and some of my working relationships; in the midst of financial scarcity that challenges my aspirations for abundance.

I have been journaling. I have been seeing people and circumstances as a reflection of my journey, a guide to where I am and where I need to go. I have been in an inquiry about what I have attracted, am attracting, into my life and why I have attracted it. I am reconciling myself to the notion that everything that is in my life is here by my invitation—the pleasant and the unpleasant; that it is part of my soul journey, what I've come to explore in this physical manifestation.

I am working with my coach, who accesses the nonphysical to heal energetically in connection with my guides, through the use of imagery and symbolism. I am learning how that translates into the physical path. Still, I am not even aware of all the pain, grief, and suffering I carry. Much of it is deeply buried, and the rest of it I am trying to shove into boxes in my being so I can be calm and professional on the surface.

I am learning to hold this space Christina speaks of. In the work I do, the Art of Hosting work, I know I hold a depth of space. I know I can hold this for my father. I do not want to confront him or accuse him. I intend to invite him to share with me what he knows, what has been hidden for so many years.

My coach suggests I print out the e-mails I have received and take them with me so I have something to give my dad and he has something to focus on as he receives this information. I am glad I do.

The night of my parents' fiftieth wedding anniversary in early January is the night I intend to have the conversation with my father, simply because it is in the days immediately following this news in my life. My husband, my three sons, and I are in Lunenburg to take my parents out for dinner. I am staying on for a few days to prepare for an open house at their home a couple of days later, at which we will celebrate their fifty years together with many of their long-term friends.

My brother, Robert, and I had hopes of bigger plans. We wanted them to be able to renew their vows on their fiftieth wedding anniversary, as my father's parents had done in their turn. There was a time when this was what my parents wanted. Robert had called the Boscawen Inn where they had had their wedding reception fifty years earlier. The Inn is now a seasonal hotel, like so many places in Lunenburg. Robert got them to agree to open in January for this occasion. We expected that some of Dad's family would come from Quebec and that we would be able to fill a certain number of rooms.

As we got closer and closer to the anniversary date, it became clear that my mother would not be capable of participating in such a significant celebration. Disappointed, we knew we would need to scale back the celebration plans. We were unsure if we would even be able to do anything at all.

Closer to the date, we knew we could plan a small open house at my parents' home, inviting a few close friends. This is why I am staying in Lunenburg now for a few days, to prepare for this event. Usually if I stay, it is only for a night. Usually I am there just a few hours. Now I am planning to stay a few days, marveling at how the timing of things naturally works out. Here I am, on the night of their fifty years together, preparing to ask questions about things I never remember being spoken about or even whispered just within earshot.

In her current state, my mom usually goes to bed early in the evening— around 6:00 or 7:00 p.m. This night, partly because we went out to dinner for their anniversary and maybe partly because she can sense something in the air, she stays up later. I am waiting for her to go to bed so I can talk to my dad alone since I am not sure how this news will impact her or what, with her dementia, she could reasonably contribute to it.

I watch the clock. Half hours go by. Eight-thirty. Nine o'clock. Nine-thirty. At ten o'clock, I call my husband and tell him this conversation is not happening this night. At ten-thirty my mother finally goes to bed. I cannot wait another day to begin.

I turn to my father. "Dad," I say, taking a deep breath to steady myself even as I plunge in. He turns to me. I have his attention. I go on. "I received information this week that I am having some trouble digesting.

127

I just need to know the truth." I can see in his face that he already knows where I am going with this. He's been waiting for this conversation for decades, afraid of it, relieved it hasn't happened, and feeling guilty at the same time. "I have received e-mails from Robyn and Deb Hanson, and they seem to believe I might be their sister." There is silence as I hand him the e-mails.

I might be their sister . . .

Seconds tick by. The pause goes on forever. Dad takes the e-mails but doesn't look at them. He doesn't need to.

Finally he says to me, "Well, that's another long story."

Another long story . . .

He confirms the information in the e-mails he hasn't even looked at. I am not surprised. At this point, I do not see how it can be any other way. He tells me they—he and Mom—wanted to adopt both Deb and me, but Deb wanted to stay with her father. He says he doesn't know why they didn't tell me, but that they, and my mom in particular, were worried about how I might react when I found out. One day slips into the next, and the next thing you know, forty-six years have gone by and you have lived with a secret for a lifetime, my lifetime. You even trick yourself into believing the truth you want to believe, rather than the "facts." To my mom and dad, I was their child as surely as if I had been their own flesh and blood.

This night, in this first conversation, Dad and I speak about this for thirty minutes. Dad says to me, "If you want to change your name . . ."

I reply, "I didn't change my name when I got married; I don't see any reason to now."

He wonders how my brother will receive the news. I tell him Robert already knows and is good. He wonders about our relationship—his and mine—and I tell him, "We have forty-six years of history together; I think we're good."

We talk about whether I will bring this up with my mother, but we both agree there might not be much point in doing so and that it could potentially cause harm.

He speaks about relief; he is glad that it is now out in the open. He speaks about guilt—for not having revealed this information to me earlier in my life. He speaks about fear.

He tells me it was "love at first sight." I know this is true. I remember the stories told of when I was sick with a cold or the flu as a baby. Dad would lie down with me on his chest for hours.

He took me everywhere with him. There used to be a booklet of pictures in our house of me when I was little. The booklet disappeared years ago, and although I have searched for it periodically, I am unable to locate it. I particularly remember the last picture—me at about two years of age, standing in a booth at a restaurant in Digby where my dad regularly took me for ice cream.

After my mom goes into long-term care six months later, the booklet of pictures resurfaces. She had hidden it away in some obscure place where my dad eventually found it. He gave it back to me. What I had not remembered was that most of the pictures in that booklet were of me and the little girl I used to play with at Nanny Hanson's house. Now when I look at the pictures, I see the two little girls look a lot alike. They are clearly sisters. It never occurred to me before. I was not looking for deeper meaning. I was not looking for connection or for secrets. I just enjoyed seeing those pictures of me as a toddler.

When Dad and I finish talking, we are done for a time. The subject does not come up between us the rest of the weekend. It is not brought up between my dad and my brother when my brother arrives from PEI the next day, although Robert and I talk about it. Because I am there a few nights, a rarity these days, Dad is able to experience in these days that he and I are, just as I had said, good.

Everything has changed, and nothing has changed.

It is some weeks before my dad raises this conversation with my brother. Robert waits until Dad is ready to speak about it. He needs to sort through his own experience and his own response to having this family secret revealed. When he is ready, he brings it up to Robert.

I also wait to have more conversations with him. I tell him when I am going to Alberta to visit my sister and let his own curiosity guide the unfolding conversations. We are eventually able to speak openly, honestly, and without awkwardness about the situation. And while my adoption story is unfolding, we are also dealing with the increasing impact of dementia on my mom and her eventual admittance in July of that year into long-term care.

When I come back from Lunenburg and celebrating my parents' fiftieth wedding anniversary, I tell my two teenage sons the news of my adoption. They are, of course, surprised. Not as shocked as me as they are a step or even two removed from the situation. They feel more vaguely connected to it, but they are surprised nonetheless.

They handle the news well. My oldest son completely echoes my own sense of things: "Wow, it's like everything's changed, but nothing's changed." At one point in the conversation I looked at both of them and say, "In case there is any doubt, you guys are both mine!" They laugh. They'd had no doubt of that.

My youngest son, who is only five, is introduced to all of this in a more subtle but also deliberate way. As this unfolds for him, one day he asks me, "Who's my birth father?" This is a peek into the reasoning of a five-year-old as he makes sense of an emerging story, wondering how he relates to it and it relates to him.

Now it is up to me to make choices about relationships—existing relationships and new ones. I have a new point of reference for the idea that it is not what happens to me that is important or life-determining—it is my interpretation of what happens to me. I have a whole new practice field, whether I wanted it or not!

I know that as I am receiving this information and trying to comprehend it and what it means to me, there are at least two other people out there who have taken a risk and are waiting anxiously for some kind of response. I recognize their need via from my own sense of awareness of other people and my long-entrenched pattern of taking care of other people's needs. Now I also recognize my own need, the need to deal with my own emotional responses before I can hold space for someone else's. I see the steps in front of me.

The saving grace is the perspective within which I choose to receive and interpret all this information. I have, at times in my life, been a keeper of secrets. Who hasn't? I know what it is like to keep secrets, and there are many, many reasons we do so: because we don't want other people to be hurt, because we don't want to burst what we believe to be other people's perceptions of us, because we are fearful and do not know where to turn or even how to begin. I do not believe my parents intentionally meant to keep me in the dark about this. They have always been people who want to do the right thing.

It wasn't always easy when I was growing up, but I always knew my parents loved me. Unconditionally. They had demonstrated that unconditional acceptance many times over the years—of me, my situation, my friends. When my first marriage ended, they showed up to help me move. They were there whenever I needed them—no questions asked, no judgments, no explanations required, despite my knowing they must have felt deeply disappointed by some of the events in my life.

Without having thought about it, I considered my parents as friends. I invited them to every occasion—birthday celebrations, seasonal gatherings at my home, holiday occasions—and they always came.

In preparation for their fiftieth wedding anniversary, I had already been thinking of the gifts I had received from my parents—the things that truly resonated for me over this lifetime. When I learned they had adopted me, these gifts of unconditional love, generosity, and acceptance were instantly amplified.

I believe my parents, and everyone else who held a piece of this story, made the choices they made out of love and caring, not out of ill intent. Later I also understand the role that fear played in keeping the secret; it was maybe as strong as, or even stronger than, love.

I do not feel betrayed. I do not feel angry. I do not feel the need to demand an explanation. I certainly feel stunned, but curious too—cautious, but curious.

I can clearly see the two paths of my experience—the emotional path and the intellectual path. The wild ride of shock and incomprehension gave way to cautious curiosity. The emotional path was about making sure I was taking care of myself. The intellectual path informed my own knowledge and created the awareness for me of what other people were likely experiencing throughout this. I want to take care of other people's experiences. It is what I do, after all. This is a pattern in my life. The gift that is emerging in my relationships and my work is to discern the balance in holding space compared to doing the work of taking care of someone else—work that is theirs to do, not mine. I know I need to take care of my own needs too; that I need to do that first. I need to host myself so I can host others well.

Taking care of my needs means making sure I am well and that my dad is well, and that this secret that has been between us all these years is released in a well way. Once I have confirmed with my dad that what I have been told is true, I feel more ready to respond to my sisters.

I have had one e-mail exchange with Deb. I have not yet found it in me to respond to Robyn. Robyn is, to me, an unknown person making wild (and, as it turns out, true) claims. I am aware that Robyn might be anxious for a response, and I want to respond, but I also need to respond in my own time, juggling my intellectual awareness with my own emotional needs.

1. Mary and Hector Jourdain, Wedding Photo, at the
Boscowen Inn in Lunenburg January 1958

2. Fred and Joanne July 1960: My birth parents, Fred Hanson and Joanne Saulnier before a dance in Digby July 1960

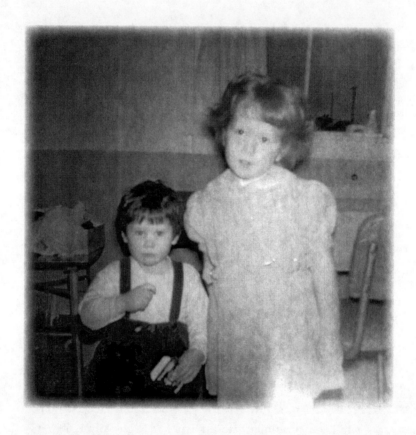

3. Deb and Kathy 1964: Kathy (2 years old) and Deb (5 years old) visiting in 1964 at Nanny and Grampy Hanson's house in Digby

4. Bluefin: The Bluefin—Hector's pride and joy for over 30 years, docked in its regular spot in Sunnybrook near Lunenburg

5. Shasta, Jacob, Kathy and Spencer January 2008: Shasta (6 years old), Jacob (18 years old), Kathy and Spencer (16 years old) in the restaurant where we took my parents, Mary and Hector, for dinner the night of their fiftieth wedding anniversary, days after I found out I was adopted and the same evening I asked my father about the news I had received.

6. Mary, Kathy, Hector and Robert at mom and dad's 50th wedding anniversary, January 2008: Celebrating the fiftieth wedding anniversary with friends—Mary, Kathy, Hector and Robert—my mother is already experiencing and advanced state of dementia and six months later she is admitted into long term care.

7. Robyn Hanson and Kathy Jourdain meeting for
the first time in coffee shop, March 2008

8. Fred and Kathy meeting now for the second time, March 2008. There is a wall of pictures behind them and if you look closely you can see my baby picture on display for the first time in forty-six years, tucked into the wooden framing on the wall.

9. Kathy and Deb enjoying a beer on the steps of Chichen Itza in Mexico in January 2009, one year after we connected. This is the trip where people keeping asking if we are sisters because we act like sisters.

10. My vision quest circle in Gold Lake where I met the ancestors.

11. A depiction of the medicine woman guide who is one of the guardians of my path, who I met in Gold Lake but drew in an Art of Hosting retreat near Sao Paulo my first time in Brazil in 2010.

12. Floor teaching at an Art of Hosting retreat near Rio
de Janeiro, Brazil in April 2012—an example of the work
I get to do all over the world with good friends.

Chapter 7

First Contact

I am driving on Highway 103 to Yarmouth, a small community three hours southwest of where I live, at the westernmost tip of Nova Scotia. It might as well be at the end of the earth. It is not just a trip; it is a journey—a journey to a past and a life track I do not know but is surely as much a part of me as anything I do know.

I am going to meet my birth father. I only just found out he exists, that there is such a thing in my life. He is still just a concept to me. Yet he has known about me all my life, made decisions that have impacted the course of my life, and followed some of my life story.

Who is this man, and what the hell happened to me?

Having cleared the path for next steps by initiating the conversation with my father, I begin to ponder the situation more. Why did my sisters decide to contact me now, after all of these years had gone by, having known about me all my life? The answer to that question comes in a note from my sister, Deb.

"Over the years I often wanted to try to contact you, but I was always afraid that you didn't know the situation. Our mother passed away last May (which I only found out about at Christmas, but that is another strange story). So after that happened, I talked with Robyn, and we decided that none of us is getting any younger. If we wanted to find you, we should do more than just talk about it."

Based on this, their timing made sense. Since going to Boston, my healing work and work with my guides has been continuing. I can connect with my guides on my own, but it is in working with my coach, by phone now, that the connection is amplified and a vibrant exchange takes place. The exchange with my guides is more placid on my own.

The nature of our sessions responds to whatever is alive for me in any given moment, prompted by my guides. I see each of my guides as offering or holding a piece of my whole. A master guide—a wizard, who is powerful and strong—takes my fear, and it dissipates in a ball of flame. A stunningly beautiful woman with long, flowing hair and flowing robes offers me grace, serenity, and strength.

I am trying to hold the conflict and dynamics between my husband and me with greater compassion—for each of us. We came together in a strong spiritual connection that was later obscured by tension, misunderstandings, and communication challenges.

Something was awakened in me from a deep slumber. I am disoriented, not quite remembering where I am. I want to go back to sleep to hang on to the dream world, not fully understanding that the dream world can be just as vibrant, and maybe more so, from an awake state. Walking in a foreign land with beings who want to connect. I do not quite know which knobs will dial in a clearer connection; I believe, even, that those knobs, those channels, are not available to me. But it is all within. There is no "out there."

I feel the love, support, and willingness to help of each of my guides, but really understanding this and its potential remains elusive.

I have so much fear to work through. Fear of money. Fear of lack of money. Fear of failure. Fear of contributing my own voice to my work and the world. Fear of loss. Fear of taking up too much space.

Running is one of the ways I connect with my guides. It is an opportunity I have a few days a week to be intentional about the connection, to let my mind and imagination wander, knowing that images and symbols that arise hold meaning. I experience it in a halting way. I do not trust myself to be able to access spirit. I still do not believe it true of me. How many times I wonder if I am making it up!

One morning, while checking in with my guides, a black woman appears. I don't know why she is there. I cannot access any other information about her. I ask my coach about her. As so often happens, a simple comment from him unlocks so much. He says to me, "Use her voice to sing 'Amazing Grace.'" The words are not out of his mouth, and the impact is immediate and powerful. Information floods into my mind about a past life as a slave. It leads me to an awareness of sorrow in my soul. Deep sorrow. I am looking for release. Is this why there is so much angst in my marriage—to help me tap into and release the well of sorrow?

Now that I've discovered it, I work with my coach to explore it, understand it, release it. As we settle into the session, sorrow is sparring with blackness. There is a message I cannot access. My coach helps me. He says to me, "You were born very gifted, with easy access to your gifts. You were able to recall and recount past lives. It put fear of the unknown in your parents and their fear took hold. The need to cloak this power took hold. The sorrow began to take root."

As he says this, my whole life flashes before my eyes. I know what he is telling me is true. Energy flows in and around my body, growing stronger, sending shivers through me. It is like an energetic orgasm.

My coach says, "Pull certain threads on the cloak, and the whole thing will fall away." I feel like someone just blasted away the bricks and mortar of a wall that has been holding me captive. I am free. Freer, anyway. Freer than I have ever been.

I am in an emergent phase. And I am still waiting. For what, I do not know.

When I am focused on me and trying to make things happen, I am disconnected from spirit. That disconnect contributes to a sense of irritation. The irritation gets in the way of connection to spirit. When I focus more on the work and less on me being powerful, or on what I should or should not be able to do, I am connected. The less I try, the more I surrender, the more successful I am. It is counterintuitive.

I reconnect to an image or visualization from a decade before—of people lying down, asleep. A wave of energy floats over them, and they wake up in response.

As I continue to work on the issues in my marriage, my coach asks me, "Are you willing to let go of the story to find out who that other person really is? Can you be curious instead of judgmental?" I do not know the answer to this. I have been hurt in the relationship, hurt by my husband's actions toward me. I am holding onto it, carrying a grudge. I want someone else to be responsible for making it better and yet, in wanting this, I am giving my power away.

"You need to stop worrying about your relationship," my coach says to me. "Worrying about it disconnects you from yourself and from spirit." Despite all this, feelings of inadequacy still arise. My internal critic is alive and well. It is at this point that I say to my coach, "I feel like something is still blocking my growth and my ability to connect more deeply to my intuitive side, to spirit and to spirit guides."

Then the e-mails from my sisters show up. This just may be the block I've been sensing! It is a particularly significant part of my heritage I have been totally oblivious to. How much has it influenced my path in ways unknown to me? How much is it responsible for my blocked memories, for the strangely transient life I've been living while never moving from Nova Scotia, for my not maintaining childhood friendships, for my not staying married, for my creating a number of different companies under which to do the same consulting work, for my moving more times than I would have imagined? How much has it contributed to my understanding life choices, life paths, in whole new ways, or to the fact that while others identified me as powerful, I couldn't see it, as it was too deeply cloaked by secrets only now being revealed. Having this new knowledge of a birth family suddenly revealed to me makes sense. If there is to be a perfect time to receive this information, maybe this is it. The subsequent journey just might be easier for me because it blends into the path I am already traveling—not that I have any real idea of what the implications are or could be.

As I continue to digest the news and the implications in my life, a path of contact begins to naturally emerge. I already know in my heart that I will explore this strange turn of events in my life. I will meet these people as I am ready. I can not imagine taking any other course of action—or inaction. These people have reached out to me in their own fear, anxiety, and vulnerability. Of course I am going to respond; I don't think it is in my nature not to, and my curiosity is too great. So I sense into what it is I think I am ready for and allow the path to open up to me and for me in its own timing.

E-mail is the first step. I am mindful to include my brother in as much of this as possible since I understand it is his story too, even though his relationship to it is different from mine. After a few e-mail exchanges, I feel more ready to make a phone call. It is a methodical, natural approach that allows me to put my toe in the water and test it before I jump into the deep end. But, truth be known, I am already, automatically, in the deep end. I am just figuring out how to swim.

At first it is hard for me to speak this news to friends. Although I essentially feel the same—still like me—there is something earth-shattering, life-altering, about this news. I find myself trembling deeply, and it is hard to say it out loud. Emotionally I am in it, and I feel it physically too.

When people hear the story of me receiving an e-mail through Facebook, they express surprise at how the first contact was made. I am glad it was e-mail. It gave me time to process and adjust, to be more gracious—how I want to show up in life and in my relationships. I have no idea how I would have reacted if these people had called or shown up on my doorstep, given I had no awareness of their existence.

I choose to respond to Deb first. In a later note, I apologize to Robyn for the delay in my response to her. "As long as I don't respond and as long as I don't talk to anyone, I can almost pretend 'these people'— you guys—don't exist or aren't quite real, despite all the pictures on Facebook. But, even with my confusion, I would not have wanted to not know." It would be incongruent for me to be any other way, given my path.

While my sisters initiated this contact, they did so, and continue to do so, with grace and spaciousness. They leave me in control of when and how to contact them. At no time do I feel any pressure from them although I am aware of the expectation inherent in their desire to connect with me, meet me, and maybe get to know me. They make it as easy as possible for me. There is beauty in this for me. Robyn later says to me, "After we found you on Facebook, I went into my account and labeled all my pictures so you would know who people were." It was a thoughtful gesture, and it was appreciated.

After each contact I take a deep breath and get ready for the next. Looking back, I have the impression that months passed during this time. The e-mails, however, show it was just a matter of days and weeks. After establishing e-mail contact, I feel ready to make phone calls.

Again, I approach Deb first, because of my memory of her. It is about two weeks after she first contacted me. It seems like a lifetime. It is a remarkably easy call, partly because of a sense of connection between the two of us, partly because of the amount of information to be shared—the stories and experience of my adoption; the stories of Deb's life and my life, the stories of our birth mother, Joanne; the stories of her finding me on Facebook and the decision to make contact—and also partly because of deep curiosity on both sides. My curiosity was still partly formed out of disbelief, and Deb's was formed out of wanting to know about me and wanting to share with me, wanting to catch up on a forty-year gap in time and relationship.

Through the stories we are discovering that although we have grown up in completely different environments with completely different life stories, we process information the same way and we have a similar approach or philosophy toward life. Despite having very different starting places and careers, we have had remarkably similar career trajectories. Later we discover we are pretty much the same height and body build and many of our preferences are the same.

A few days after first making contact, Deb sends me a note: "I just want to let you know that I can appreciate how life-changing this is for you. Two nights after we first 'spoke' on Facebook, I was getting ready for bed and talking this over with my husband. I said to him, 'Here I am all excited and pleased and going to have a good night's sleep, and I am sure that Kathy is going to bed staring at the ceiling, wondering what all this means.'"

When I initiate the conversation with Robyn, the shape of the stories is different because Robyn's and Deb's experiences are different—both their experiences of me and my adoption, as well as their life experiences. Where Deb had firsthand experience and memories of me, Robyn mostly knew about me through her mother, Fred's second wife. There is an eleven-year difference between Deb and Robyn, and by the time Deb was seventeen, she was pregnant with her first child and married while Robyn was a six-year-old growing up with her parents.

Deb lives in Alberta and has for all her adult life—first in Fort McMurray and then in a smaller community a couple of hours north of Edmonton.

She is in her third marriage and has two daughters of her own, eight stepchildren, and some grandchildren.

Robyn, recently separated from her husband, is living back in Digby, Nova Scotia, with her three children and going to school. For years she lived in the next community over from where I lived and worked at a local pharmacy—where we went for all our prescriptions and drugstore shopping.

Through my conversations with Deb and Robyn, I begin to piece together the story of first contact. Deb, at some point in her life, had the same realization with Robyn that I had with Robert. Even though Robyn had never met me, I was her half-sister and she knew about me. I was part of the fabric of her life as an absentee sister. Deb's knowledge, though from childhood, was firsthand. It had not occurred to her that I was also part of Robyn's story. When it dawned on her that this was the case, they would have the occasional conversation about finding me, wondering about me, who I was and where I was. But they never acted on it.

All that changed when Deb found out our birth mother had died. The relationship with our birth mother had demanded a lot from Deb. Overall, it was not very satisfying. She really could only handle one disappointment at a time. While she was deeply curious, she was not really sure she had it in her to make another contact.

One night in January 2008, Robyn and Deb were in a conversation across the miles, about me. Robyn's boyfriend was on the computer. He decided to put my name in Facebook to see what would happen. It took three tries with different spellings of my last name before my profile popped up.

A little shiver of excitement went through all three of them. He said, "It's her!" Robyn asked, "How do you know?" He replied, "Because she looks like Deb."

Well, that might be so, but they had a need for confirmation. So Robyn sent me a quick note from her boyfriend's Facebook account that I almost missed because I did not recognize his name or picture. But Robyn's last name caught my attention—Hanson. I knew the name but could not place it. So I read the note. It said, "Looking for old family friends. Do you know Mary and Hector Jourdain?"

I sent back an equally brief note. "Yes, they're my parents." I didn't ask the question that leapt into my mind: "Who are you?" I figured my brother was going to get a similar note, given that they were looking for old family friends. He would probably be the better resource, given the clarity of his memories.

The next day, as I was driving home from a day of instructing, this thought flashed into my mind: *Oh! Hanson? Nanny Hanson!* Shivers ran up and down my spine as I remembered this kindly friend of the family from Digby. But I had no idea of the note that was awaiting me on this night or the flurry of excitement my simple response had sparked in my two sisters as they then burned up the phone line between Alberta and Nova Scotia trying to figure out how to write a note and what to say to me, now that they had found me.

Together they drafted and redrafted the note. Deb was sure I did not know I was adopted. They wanted to find some wording that would work whether I knew or not. When they finally hung up the phone, Robyn spent another hour refining it, going over it in detail.

Finally, it was as ready as it was ever going to be. Robyn pressed the send button. It was off, not to be taken back. An irreversible chain of events were set in motion—possibly. I could always have chosen to ignore the e-mail instead.

In addition to Facebook, they Googled me. As a consultant and writer, I want to be found on Google, for professional reasons. I had never given a thought to any other reasons someone might want to Google me. I have to say that in the early days of my incomprehension, I was a little creeped out by this. Can't have it both ways, though.

It is a good week or more after Robyn and Deb first contacted me that I asked about my birth father, Fred Hanson. Deb made reference to the death of my birth mother, so that much I knew. There were pictures of Fred on Facebook that looked pretty recent, so I assumed he was probably alive, but I cannot even ask the question for a while. I had more than enough information to gnaw on and digest for a time.

Finally I sent a note to Deb asking about him. She told me he was living in Yarmouth, Nova Scotia, a community three hours from where I lived—with his third wife, Doris. (Fred's second wife, Robyn's mother, died of cancer quite a few years before.) He is turning sixty-nine on his next birthday in March. He has survived a bout of colon cancer and is now living cancer-free.

At first he doesn't know that Robyn and Deb have contacted me. They wait until after they know that I am at least receptive to meeting my birth family before they tell him. They don't want to disturb or disappoint if I decide to ignore the contact or rudely reject them all. Robyn calls him and tells him the news. He is a man who rarely displays a lot of emotion. She reports back that he was so excited she wasn't sure she had the right phone number.

Deb gave me all his contact information but I needed to wait until I felt ready to make first contact. While it seems now, looking back, that a lot of time passed—it was only a week between the first contact I received from Robyn and Deb and when I made first contact with Fred.

On an evening I was feeling both tired and restless, I went to bed early but could not sleep. I knew it was time to compose an e-mail. I got up, turned my computer back on, and began. It was important to me that he knew I did not hold this against him and I did not have any regrets.

I write the following message:

Hello there,

I've been told that, numerologically speaking, 2008 is a year of new beginnings. How apt. I guess I can fully attest to that—and in ways that I couldn't possibly have imagined just one week ago. I really had no idea I was adopted. This news is so large it is taking my brain and my heart a little while to comprehend it all—and I'm not fully there yet. This is why e-mail contact is easier for me at the moment—even though writing to my birth father still feels surreal—like it is someone else's story.

I have seen your picture on Facebook. I have attached a picture of me and my family.

Through Deb, Robyn, and my dad I have heard some or most of our story. I look forward to the time when you and I will meet and I will hear whatever you would like and need to share. I believe this will not be too far in the future. I do want to say to you, as a daughter and a parent, that I can appreciate and understand the difficulty of the decision you had to make all those years ago. For what it's worth, I think you made a wise decision considering the circumstances, and I think it took courage to accept, honor, and live with that decision for the last forty-six years.

I have no idea how hard it has been for you in wondering where I am, how I am, and being in the tension of wanting to make contact, not knowing where to begin and not wanting to disturb my life.

As much as this is a lot to take in, I did say to Robyn that this is information I would have wanted to have, and as my shock wears off I will be able to embrace it more, and then I'll be ready for a conversation and/or a meeting—given that you only live three hours away from me. This is probably enough for now. Kathy.

Fred's response back:

Hi Kathy, sounds like we are both taken back by events of the past few weeks. I am happy to know that you now know about your sisters. What happened forty-five years ago (right or wrong, but like you, I think it was right) is over. I thought about you often and hoped everything was okay. I hope to hear much more from you, and I will leave the time frame up to you. Just decide how you'd like to go about things and let me know. Hope to hear soon. Fred.

Another deep breath.

I would have gone to meet Deb first for the same reason she received the first e-mail and the first call—because I remember her and also because I now feel a sense of connection with her through our phone conversations and discoveries of similarities. However, she and her husband are traveling and visiting his family in January, and my schedule is crazy for most of February and March, not allowing the time for a trip out west.

So, probably fittingly, Fred is the one I visit first. Originally we set a date in February, but as I look at my calendar one day, I discover it is possible to visit in January, a mere twenty days after receiving that first e-mail.

I tell Fred I will drive to Yarmouth in the morning, stay for a while, and drive back later in the day. He tells me that that is a long day and I am welcome to stay. *Thank you but no thank you*, I think. I know a few hours will be about the extent of what I can take in for one trip. I find a way to politely decline the offer; my own boundaries in this are clear to me.

I have several offers from friends to travel with me, but I know I need to go alone. It is a pilgrimage, not a tourist trip. I will be changed by the experience—not as an observer, but as a participant. The time on the way there lets me continue to sit with and digest all that has been unfolding and allow the opportunity bring myself to a place of presence. I know I will need the time on the way back to process. I am honoring my need for solitude.

On the way there, it occurs to me that I am going to meet a man who, intellectually, I know is my birth father, but who I have only found out even exists just three weeks before. I am still feeling a bit stupefied by it all. It is still an intellectual concept. He, on the other hand, has known about me all my life. He has been curious about me. He has been aware of my whereabouts and some of my activities throughout my life; he lost track about ten years before—right at the time I lost my job and my first marriage fell apart. I cannot imagine what it would be like to be in his shoes, the level of anticipation that must be rising up in him. For me it is like going through the motions of someone else's story. This is the kind of thing that happens to other people you hear about or read about, not something that happens in your own life journey.

Two-thirds of the way there, I pull into the parking lot of a coffee shop. I am exhausted. It is hard to keep my eyes open. I recline my seat and close my eyes for ten to fifteen minutes before heading back out for the final leg of this journey.

When I arrive at Fred's home, it is clear he has been waiting for me. He's been watching for me, pacing between the living room window, the kitchen window, and the door. The door opens as soon as I pull into the driveway, before I am even ready really.

I look more intently at him than I mean to, looking for any sense or feeling of resemblance or remembering—and maybe also to discern truth. Unlike many adoptees, I have not grown up wondering where I came from or whom I look like. Part of me is still wondering if this is really true. Is this man really my birth father? I have not yet come to terms with this. In some ways, maybe I never really will.

Nothing comes flooding in. No memories. No recognition. This could be any other older man I happened to meet somewhere along the way, except that he has pictures of me as a baby.

Fred's wife, Doris, is also there. For a while the three of us sit in quiet tension and uncertainty, fumbling our way through conversation. Then Doris gets up, politely excuses herself, and goes downstairs—probably with a great sense of relief. I don't even know what's downstairs, whether it is a comfortable space or a storage area.

It is just Fred and me. *My birth father and me.* Who the hell is this man, and what am I supposed to do now?

The first thing Fred does when I arrive is hug me. It feels awkward to me. After all, I do not know this man. I have not imagined him over the years. The second thing he does is bring out five pictures of me from when I was a toddler—pictures that show that he and Deb were in my life when I was little; pictures he had tucked away for safekeeping. There is a picture of Deb and me with Fred, one of me with my parents, one of my grandmother, one of just Deb and me, and one of me that had been professionally taken that has also been hanging in my parents' home for as long as I can remember. I am touched by the pictures and the offering of them.

We begin to talk. I don't remember the specifics of the conversation, but it is clearly about the story of me and my adoption; Fred and my birth mother, Joanne; and some of life's stories—mine and his. We come to know each other a bit through this.

Greater ease flows into the space. Doris is invited to rejoin us, reprieved from the basement. Fred grabs old photo albums and shows me pictures of the family—*my family*—from over the years. I see my sisters when they were little, grandparents, weddings, nieces and nephews, and Fred's second wife, Robyn's mother.

I take a few pictures of Fred and Doris. Doris takes one of Fred and me sitting on the couch with Fred putting his arm around me.

I stay for three hours. Then it feels like time to go. I have taken in as much as I can. I am really glad I did not make a commitment to stay and that I did not bring anyone with me. I will have a deep breath of another three hours to sit with it all, without having to speak to anyone. I can just drive and be, going through the motions of a story—one that I still feel is surely not really mine.

Later friends ask me if I liked him. I think about the question. *Did I like him?* How do you answer that question about a man you have only just met and have only known about for three weeks, who happens to be your birth father? *Did I like him?* Finally my response is, "I didn't not like him." When looking at the picture of Fred with his arm around me, someone asks me if that was comfortable. Again, I consider my response, "It wasn't uncomfortable." What is a person supposed to feel and experience under these kinds of circumstances? I surely don't know, and I'm living it.

Overall, it is a good visit—a good beginning, or maybe a beginning again. When I take my family down for a visit later, I notice that the professional baby picture of me—the only one I left with Fred of those offered—is now on display on a family wall of pictures in Fred and Doris's home, tucked into one of the frames already there. I am deeply touched. It speaks to a level of caring and love that might not be so obvious on the surface.

Months later, after our family visit, the wall of pictures has been rearranged and now includes me, my husband, and my children. It seeps into my awareness that healing is taking place because a family secret has been revealed.

About three weeks after meeting Fred for the first time, I meet Robyn. I am delivering an afternoon workshop for a client about an hour from where Robyn lives. I decide that since I am going to be that close, I will make a visit possible. We agree to meet at a coffee shop in the community where my workshop is taking place.

One hour turns into the next, and before we know it, a lively three hours has passed. We share stories about our families and our lives. I learn about Robyn, her children, and how they came to live in Digby.

I am told the story of how she and Deb came to the decision to search for me and of their finding me on Facebook. I relate my experience in receiving the news.

Robyn tells me she knows about me through her mother, who died when Robyn was eighteen years old.

It is clear we could have talked for days, but at this point we only have three hours. We start to talk about when we will have our families meet. Naturally, Robyn's children are curious about mine. Mine are also curious about Robyn and her children in their own way, because as it is for me, this is all new to them. I have intentionally opted to meet my birth family first on my own, but now it is beginning to feel like time to bring my husband and children into this.

We decide that, if Fred and Doris are willing, we will all go to their home on Easter weekend, which coincides, as it turns out, with Fred's sixty-ninth birthday. My family will book a hotel—with a swimming pool for all the kids—and Robyn and her family will stay with Fred and Doris.

Robyn offers to call Fred to work out the details. Of course I take her up on her offer.

Two and a half months after the first note I received from Robyn, four adults and eight children, ranging in age from five to seventeen, descend upon Fred and Doris's cozy little home in Yarmouth. There is a lot of curiosity all around. My kids are interested to meet these new people and well aware of the oddity that they are cousins. I am just curious to see how it will all work out. I am curious about these people to whom I am connected, whom I have been connected to all my life in the weave of life that is invisible and unknown to me.

One of Robyn's kids brings a gaming console. This makes my youngest very happy, and he spends most of his time playing or watching, developing a bond with Robyn's middle child.

We spend some time at the house. We go to the hotel to take all the kids swimming, then out for ice cream, and then back to Fred's for supper. At some point we call Deb to bring her into this circle. That night the kids go for a walk in the neighborhood—basically doing what kids do; it is surprisingly normal in strange circumstances. The next morning, my family has breakfast in the hotel, and we head back to Fred's for a few more hours before heading home again. A day and a half seems like just enough.

It is a whirlwind trip.

In the crazy juxtapositions that now seem to be my life, the next day, Easter Sunday, I have my mom and dad and my in-laws in for Easter dinner—blending experiences of the new and the old in a span of days. It is bittersweet in many ways because we initiated the process for long-term care for my mother in January. We carry the awareness that during the following year, our family circumstances will be much different again.

Early Easter Monday, I head out to Alberta for my first in-person visit with my sister, Deb.

While my first visits with Fred and Robyn were both just three hours, Alberta is a long way to go for a three-hour visit. It was looking more like three or four days.

When booking my flight, I was on the phone with Deb at the same time, looking at flight options. I said to her, "I could arrive Monday around noon and leave early Thursday morning. Is that too long?" She laughed and said it probably isn't long enough. As it turns out, she was right. It is a beginning.

In many ways, this is the visit and person I have been most curious about because of my memories of her. Even in our phone conversations I feel a sense of connection that is different from the other two new family members. Deb, more than any other person, was a guardian angel of my soul. She held the memory of me, loved me, and cared for me from the place of spirit. Her spirit watched over me even as her physical self could not. She was the weaver between worlds: hers growing up, the intersections with mine, and the connecting thread between us—and our birth mother and Fred.

Deb picks me up at the Edmonton airport, and our visit starts with a two-hour drive to her home. Her husband is there when we arrive. He is leaving the next morning for Fort McMurray to do contract work (where they had lived and worked before retiring), and he is, naturally enough, curious to meet me too.

It is comfortable from the start. We fall into easy conversation—mostly getting-to-know-you kind of stuff. We go over the story of searching for me and my response once again. Deb shares with me the story of our birth mother, Joanne, as she knows it. We have forty years of life to cover and lots of time to do it in. There is never any shortage of conversation.

At one point I think of our time together as being like the flow of a three-day retreat, with one big difference: during a three-day retreat, the first day is about getting to know each other, the second is about going deeper, and the third is about getting ready to go back out into the world. For us, this is true of day one and two, but day three just keeps going deeper. By the end of the three days, there isn't a topic we have not covered or any significant details of our lives that have been left out. We have only just met, and there are no secrets. We are very comfortable with each other and develop a rhythm to our time together.

Because I am flying out early on Thursday, we drive into Edmonton the night before to stay in a hotel. We have dinner with Deb's two daughters. It's a lot of fun. They regale me with stories of their lives with their mom and their dad. I ask them what they think of this whole thing—of Deb finding me and reconnecting. One of them shrugs and says, "Oh, we're used to adding new family members. About every ten years or so, Mom goes out and adds a whole bunch more—only this time she didn't have to get divorced to do it!"

I am struck by the relationship that Deb's daughters have with each other. It reminds me of the relationship my older sons have with each other, despite the gender and age difference. (Deb's daughters are more than ten years older than my sons.)

Deb and I spend our last night in Alberta together in a hotel room in Edmonton. We talk about Joanne, our birth mother. Deb says to me, "If I had tried to find you ten years earlier, you would have had the chance to meet Joanne."

I say to Deb, "For me, the idea of a birth mother is just a concept, not someone I have been searching for or waiting for all those years. I had no idea she even existed. You, on the other hand, have always known you had a birth mother. Of course you would be wondering. Me? There was nothing to wonder about."

She shares with me her deep disappointment that Joanne never was able to acknowledge her publicly as a daughter. It was so obvious that in the few rare times they were together in public, other people, strangers they came across while shopping, commented on their resemblance. Joanne denied it, claiming they were just friends.

It is an emotional night for Deb and me. As we talk over the points of connection and speak about Joanne and Nanny Hanson, we both strongly feel their presence with us.

In these early days, there is no end to the exploration we are in. By the time I leave, it feels as though something special has been regenerated between the two of us. It is like someone plucked us out of the 1960s and dropped us back into 2008 and we just picked up where we left off. The only disturbing question for Deb is, where are the memories that should be there?

It is a strange thing to have a whole life history unfold in front of your eyes. A life history that coexisted in the space of your life, though you had no conscious knowledge of it. I am the wanderer in William Stafford's poem "Who are you really, wanderer?" I am wandering, perhaps. In search of something, it would seem. In search of family? That had never occurred to me. In search of someone who looked like me? Also, that had not occurred to me. For sure I am in search of the deeper meaning of my life, my life's purpose, what it is that is mine to do. In search of connection? Yes. In search of community? Yes. In search of family? Can't say it ever occurred to me. In search of healing? Yes, but I wasn't consciously aware of this dimension of it at the time or of the healing potential that emerged from discovering, being made aware of, this stranger in my own life—the stranger in me, the threads of my life woven with the threads of other people's lives, invisible to me but visible to them.

A couple of months after I leave Alberta, Deb comes to Nova Scotia for an extended visit. She spends time with me and my family, along with Robyn and with Fred, and we all spend some time together. My brother comes over from Prince Edward Island for one night of her visit, and we have a few close friends over for dinner. We pull out pictures—ones that Fred has given me and some of my family photos. We have pictures of Joanne and recent and old pictures of Fred and my dad.

Looking at the pictures, some things are startling obvious. My dad and Fred, from back in the 1960s and now, look as though they could be brothers (and we're pretty sure they're not!). It is likely one reason nobody ever looked at me and thought I didn't fit in with my family. Young Fred and my oldest son are almost identical. There is no question of the lineage there. There is also family resemblance to Joanne, particularly for Deb but also for me.

It is hard for me to see my resemblance to my birth family, even with the pictures. It is surprisingly easy for me to see my resemblance to my family—the family I grew up in, even without a physical lineage. I consider my family of origin as the family I grew up in, even though I now know I was birthed into a different family. My loyalty is to the family I grew up in.

I experience moments of confusion along the way. I can no longer think of my family without the awareness that I was adopted. You cannot forget something as impactful as this once you know it. It now always runs in the background. Something is forever different now, yet the depth of connection and relationship that exists between the members of my family I grew up in is strong.

While Deb is in Nova Scotia, we go to Digby. Digby is the birthplace of this whole story. It is where Fred and Joanne started, where our grandmother lived, and where my parents happened to be located for a few brief but significant years. Both the yacht club and Nanny and Grampy Hanson's house, which was just up from the yacht club, played pivotal roles in the stories and in my own memories. I have almost never been to Digby as an adult. There was no reason to go.

We stay a night at Robyn's place. It is the first time we three sisters have ever been together in one place. It gives us an opportunity to connect more and to do joint storytelling, going over the same stories all over again, but for the first time all together, so the stories take on different flavors and nuances, occasionally allowing us to look at them in new lights. Storytelling is what binds us together and allows us to share our experience and identify the threads that have the greatest meaning for us, allowing us to continually draw new meaning from the same circumstances and experiences. It is one late night! There are so many stories to share.

The next day, we visit a friend of the family, a woman who was Joanne's best friend while she was growing up. Deb and Robyn both have connections with her. Although I don't remember knowing her, she greets me warmly and is so very pleased to have the opportunity to meet me now.

She shares with us stories about Joanne from when they were growing up. She comments on how much Joanne loved Deb and how she took Deb everywhere with her. Her stories of Joanne and Joanne's mother fill in some blanks and contribute to a deepening of our own knowledge and understanding. She also has pictures for us. It is an interesting, informative, and touching visit with a lovely, caring woman.

Later this day we travel to Yarmouth—three of us in three different cars. How symbolic of our lives is that? We meet up with Fred at the Red Knight, a local community tavern he frequents. For the first time ever, he is out in public with his three daughters—something he never dreamed would be possible. He shakes his head in wonderment every so often. The rest of the time, we keep returning the zingers he sends flying—especially to me, since there is lost time to catch up on.

We stay with Fred and Doris for two nights. Doris is working late the first night, so Fred is playing host on his own; he is in his element, from what I can see.

The next day, we go for a drive, the parents in the front seat and the three kids in the back. When I was a child, going for a "Sunday drive" used to be a nice, leisurely family thing to do; the drive usually ended up somewhere where we could get an ice-cream cone. We three sisters have a bit of fun with this by pretending to be children, having missed out on those great adventures when we were growing up. "Are we there yet?" "I'm bored." "I'm hungry." "Stop touching me!"

Instead of going for ice cream, we end up at the tavern for late afternoon snacks and a beverage or two.

Reflecting on my experience of that weekend, I still feel like a bit of a voyeur peeking in on someone else's story. It is only five months after I have had the biggest shock of my life. The news is still settling in. I am still coming to terms with this information, with this expansion in understanding my life, my life story, my parents, and my journey.

I leave Yarmouth and head home. Robyn goes back to Digby. Deb stays for a couple more days in Yarmouth before heading back for another visit with Robyn, which this time includes a visit to Nanny Hanson's grave—a visit Deb has made every time she has gone to Digby. She tells me later that it is the first time she does not cry.

Upon hearing this little story, the impact of the healing that is taking place hits me. In the world I live and work in, we talk about the fragmentation that is occurring in the world, that this is a time of great healing. I can suddenly see my own experience and my family's experience as a microcosm of this fragmentation. Healing in our family is taking place, bringing some wholeness to the fragmentation that existed. If it is happening all around me in my family members, I know it is also happening within me even if I cannot see it or understand how it is happening in this moment. It is hard to see your own healing when you did not know you were fragmented in a certain way.

Deb stays with me for another day or so before heading home to Alberta. Our time together is filled with ease and continued storytelling. It is not hard to see her go because of the depth of connection and the knowledge that we will stay in touch and that we will find a time to connect in person once again before too long.

Later in the year, I travel to Yarmouth to give a talk for a client. Being in Yarmouth, I take an extra night to visit with Fred. My plan is to interview him to capture his story for this book. Doris is working this evening, so other than a quick visit with Doris at the store, Fred and I spend the evening together—just the two of us.

We begin our time together by visiting the tavern that has become a place of community for Fred and Doris. Fred introduces me to his buddies as we sit at the bar. The conversation follows many different threads and at some point turns to family. I interject a comment: "Yeah, I only just found out I'm related to Fred." The comment seems to get lost in the conversation. A few minutes pass. I notice that some of his buddies are staring at me. When I return the look, I am asked, "Is that true? That you just found out?" When I acknowledge this is true, the next question is "Did Fred know?" That possible perspective never occurred to me! There is a dramatic pause followed by gales of laughter.

After a couple of hours, we head back to Fred's home and settle ourselves in for storytelling.

I have prepared an interview guide before visiting to make sure I capture all the main categories of his story. This kind of interview is intended to set the stage and get the interviewee into a space where recollection of past events becomes thoughtful, clear, and easy. I know the interview space we have created is a success when he references "the kids" in one of his stories and then looks at me, embarrassed because he has forgotten who he is talking to. He says, "Well . . . you guys," meaning Deb and me.

There is a richness to his story as he begins to remember things long forgotten, as he reflects on things, events, and people in new ways, inspired by the questions I ask. As he reflects on his life and the choices he has made, patterns that have emerged over time, I learn things I had not yet heard and walk away with a more comprehensive understanding of some of the story surrounding my birth, adoption, and life.

During our conversation, Fred asks me what I do. I tell him about one project I am involved in that is particularly compelling to me. He says, "It's clear you love what you do."

His observation touches me deeply. I say, "It is not always easy for people to understand what I do."

He says, "When people ask, I tell them you are a motivational speaker." That certainly captures one aspect of what I do.

In this night, this encounter, as storytelling about the past turns into conversation about the here and now, Fred and I bond in a new way.

A few weeks later, I interview my dad. Again, I have questions prepared. I am interested in the story that started even before I arrived in his life. My dad's responses contain vivid detail, including things like the kind of car he was driving when I came into his life. He says to me again, "It was love at first sight when I saw you."

He goes into detail about certain aspects of my life. He tells me he had to confront my grandfather, Lee. Lee used to come by and take me for drives. He was often intoxicated, and my father feared for my safety. He said to Lee, "It's okay for you to come and take Kathy out. But you need to be sober. Otherwise, we will not let her go with you." Lee took it to heart. He still came by to take me out and he was sober.

It is hard for me to imagine the quality and texture of this weave of relationship—the camaraderie, the tension. The families stayed connected as long as my grandmother was alive. She was the glue, the social fabric of connection. In the mix was the not knowing of what do with the "secret" of my adoption. Had my grandmother lived longer, this secret likely would have been revealed to me much sooner in my life. Shared history would have continued.

As it is, eleven months after we reconnect, Deb calls to tell me her oldest daughter has just gotten engaged. She and her fiancé plan to marry in Mexico in January. They will be staying at an all-inclusive resort, and Deb is the only one on her side of the family who is attending, partly because Deb's husband is terrified of flying, partly because of the swiftness and timing of the wedding. It is also the first time Deb will be meeting her son-in-law's family.

I have a cancelled airline ticket for a work trip that did not happen in the fall. I tell Deb I might be able to use that ticket to go to Mexico with her. In the end, it all works out. I attend the wedding, and Deb and I spend another week in each other's company—literally twenty-four hours a day, since we share a room.

We regale the groom's family with our stories of my adoption and hear, not for the first time, that we should write a book.

We are asked a couple of times by random strangers if we are sisters. I ask one person, "Why? Do we look like sisters?"

We are told "No, you act like sisters." I wonder how that is possible after knowing each other for only one year. And yet it is exactly true.

In one of her visits to Nova Scotia, we go to Lunenburg so Deb and my dad can meet. They hold deep curiosity about each other, having come really close to being family and having me and my early beginnings in common. They are also bonded in soul journey even if they have not walked much of the physical path together.

Most of the time we are together at my dad's house is spent in storytelling around life in general. Toward the end of the visit, our attention turns, ever so briefly, to the story of my adoption. In some ways it is like coming full circle.

I do not know what my life would have been like growing up in my birth family—or their life either, for that matter—other than that it would have been a different journey. For starters, I would have been first the youngest sibling and then the middle child when Robyn came along instead of the oldest, as I was in the family I grew up in.

As this new story of my life—new to me—unfolds, I am, at many points, able to see the gifts emerging: the gift of healing for so many of us, and the gift of meeting each other and getting to know each other.

Deb gained the gift of meeting a sister she knew and knew about all her life, was curious about, and, at some level, yearned to meet. Robyn was gifted with meeting a person she had heard about and asked questions about many times but had never known, someone she knew she was related to and desired to meet, though she didn't feel it was her place to initiate a search.

Fred was able to meet the daughter he gifted to another family and to have all three of his daughters together a couple of times—a dream of his that had died at least a decade before. He has had the opportunity to get to know this daughter (me) a bit, learn about my life, and meet my family.

I have a deeper appreciation for life's choices and how their impacts can be far greater than we know. I have a deep appreciation for being loved by more people than I could possibly have known otherwise.

My dad has received the gift of releasing a long-held secret and the guilt that went with that, finding out in the process that the history between us and our love continues to hold our relationship together.

My children get to understand a more comprehensive picture of their heritage.

I probably have the greatest gifts of all: a gift of healing things I didn't even know needed healing, a level of insight into things that impact our lives—even things that happened before we have conscious memory. I see this as an opportunity to know and understand all parts of my heritage and to be able to integrate them in ways that bring a greater level of depth and wholeness to me. I have sisters. I still have the family constellation I grew up in. It remains a strong reference point for me, and now I have a larger family constellation as well.

I have gotten to know myself in ways most people never will, and I have had the opportunity to discover my response when incomprehensible information comes my way. In doing so, I have learned that I can deal with this kind of information with grace and compassion.

I have a story to share with others that is part of my reason for being in this lifetime.

For all these things, I am grateful to my sisters for the conversations they had that brought them courage enough to reach out to me, despite their uncertainty of my response. This is something I would have wanted to know. As it turns out, I needed to know it!

I'm not particularly close to Fred. This is, in part, because we have little shared history and none that I remember. Our life paths were very different, creating little common ground. My children do not know him, and he lives far enough away that it is a bit of a journey to visit at a time in my life when there is much that has my attention: being a focal point for my parents, still providing stewardship for my children, and continuing to pursue an avocation that has me in deep work at home and on the road, although I continue to look for occasions to visit. Fred does not like to travel anymore, so he has yet to venture back to Halifax to visit me. All of that is okay.

I am glad I have had the opportunity to meet my birth father and get to know him. His life and his choices have had a tremendous impact on my own journey, even though I did not know he existed until a few years ago. He gave me—and my parents—a gift when he entrusted my care to them at a time when he did not have the resources or support to care for me himself. I grew up loved and supported. And while I missed the opportunity to have relationships with my sisters growing up, we also passed all those sibling rivalry stages without incident.

CHAPTER 8

PARALLEL TRACKS OF LIFE—PART 1

Mommy is in the front hallway of our home, putting on her coat. She is getting ready to leave. Not just to leave for now. Not just to run an errand. But to really leave. Leave me. Leave my baby sister. Leave our family.

I am three years old. I don't know how I know this, that this is an important moment, but I do. I don't know how I know I will never see her again, but I do.

And then she disappears. Like she no longer exists. Because nobody talks about her—at least not in front of me, and not to me.

I don't know how I know I'm not supposed to ask questions, not supposed to talk about her, but I do.

—Deb van Soest

Digby is a small town on the northwest coast of Nova Scotia. Like most small towns in Nova Scotia, it is on the water. At the time my birth parents were growing up, it had a thriving fishing industry. It is a place where ordinary, everyday stories come alive, where people live day to day, season to season, year to year. The landscape changes slowly like the landscape of people's lives.

This small town I lived in for just a few short years in the beginning of my days is the backdrop for the themes and patterns that influence the stories of my life without me ever knowing it. Without my awareness, there was a whole other element of who I am that lived and breathed almost independently from me and yet was sacredly connected to me as well—a stranger alive and well in my very midst, invisible and within me.

I imagine, as I make sense of my own stories, that this is simply living. It is what we do. One day rolls into the next. Stories of our lives fade in and out, depending on recency, vibrancy, and how alive particular themes are, no matter how recent, no matter how much time has passed. Some things recede; others take their place. Some things never seem far from our thoughts or awareness: the stories we weave, human tragedy woven into soul journey, soul journey woven into human tragedy.

In the ordinary living of life in a small town, many stories play themselves out disguised as the movement of days, weeks, and seasons. Human tragedy perspective is what seems to hold our attention. Soul journey is like a musical score woven into, around, and underneath the stories of our lives. We have become adept at tuning it out most of time and are often taken by surprise when we tune in by accident. It takes silence, reflection, and intentionality to tune back in more consistently, to see larger patterns, and to lift ourselves out of the human tragedy perspective.

The Hanson family home was just behind the Digby yacht club. As young boys, my birth father, Fred, and his older brother spent a lot of time beachcombing. Being on the beach was one of Fred's favorite things to do. That and running away from home, which he did probably four or five times a week. He would go down to the beach, round the corner where you couldn't really see anything else, and hide there with his dog until suppertime. Then he would get hungry and he'd go home to eat.

His father, Leander Hanson, contracted tuberculosis when Fred was just a boy. For many years, he was in treatment in a sanitarium a few hours away. In those days, living in a different community was the same as living halfway around the world. Travel was difficult. Communication technology as we know it today did not exist. Fred's mother, Pauline, was left to the task of raising two young boys on her own while also traveling to spend time with her husband, leaving Fred and his brother with their grandparents for days and weeks at a time.

Because of Lee's extended illness and later alcoholism, Fred never knew his father well. He didn't have a relationship with him even after Fred came home from the sanitarium. Rather than a father figure, Fred's experience was that it was more like having a boarder living in their home.

While Fred was still young, his brother who was five years older than he was left to go to Toronto to find work, and Fred was left alone with his mother. They were close, and they spent a lot of time together, laughing and playing games. She took good care of him and loved him deeply.

Fred kept his own company well, but he also had a strong social side. He was popular in school, a good basketball player, and captain of the basketball team. With his sense of reckless adventure, sportsmanship, and striking good looks, he was particularly enchanting to a young girl who had no sense of family or rootedness and who was deeply impacted by family secrets—Joanne Saulnier, my birth mother.

When Fred was in the eleventh grade, he landed a job in Halifax, over two hundred miles and many hours of travel away. He had successfully completed the Civil Service exam, so he left school to go to Halifax to work. In that day, an eleventh-grade education was pretty good, and a Civil Service job was even better. For Fred, it was the way to go. His job was electrical drafting; he worked in the dockyard. Looking back, after I met him, Fred said, "If I had stayed, the pay was getting real good, but I never stayed in one place long enough to do anything."

Joanne followed Fred to Halifax even though he just had a room at a boarding house. The lure of the city was powerful, especially to a teenager who felt trapped.

In a story typical of the day, Joanne got pregnant and Fred married her. Maybe they were in love; maybe they weren't. Getting married was the right thing to do. They welcomed Deb into the world in January of 1959. They were happy to have her, although money was a problem. Fred was not making enough money to support his young family. He arranged for Joanne to take Deb back to Digby to live with his parents. Deb grew close to her grandmother even as Joanne doted on her, taking her everywhere she went. However, Joanne was trapped back in the town she had tried to escape from, and now she had a baby girl to take care of too. There was no question she loved Deb and no question life was now even harder for her.

After a couple of years, Joanne moved back to Halifax with Fred. They lived as a little family for a while, but Fred and Joanne were still very young. They partied hard on weekends with friends. There was a friend of Fred's in particular that they used to hang around and party with a lot. In the midst of all of this, I was born in January 1962.

One day, soon after I was born, Fred came home from work to an empty apartment. No Joanne. No kids. Just a note. "The girls are across the hall with our neighbors. I'm going away. Don't try to find me. Love, Joanne." The closing "Love, Joanne," because it was so incongruous to the situation, stuck in Fred's memory. She had left town with Fred's friend. She had escaped again, although one never truly escapes the human tragedy story of one's life by trying to run from it.

Fred called his employer and found out he had plenty of vacation time available for him to take. He did not have to go back for a while. He was angry. Really angry. "The thing is, she left me. Fine. That didn't bother me in the least. That she left you two, that's what got me. You know, how can a mother walk out on her kids? I couldn't figure it out." He was in such a state of shock and disbelief that he did not leave his apartment for a week. He was sure Joanne would come back.

He talked to friends, talked to a lawyer, and worked out his finances. All his money was going toward the apartment where we lived. He could not see how it was possible to go to work and take care of his two little daughters. He couldn't hire anyone to do it because he did not have enough money. That's when he knew he had to bring us back to his mother in Digby. We would stay with our grandparents until he figured out what else to do.

Fred was twenty-three years old, alone with two young children, and unprepared for what he now faced. A mother taking off and leaving her children was practically unheard of in the early 1960s. Divorce was not common either. This was considered scandalous in a sleepy little town, as scandalous as being pregnant without being married.

Fred packed us up for the train ride to Digby, a journey already quite familiar to him because he had made it so many times before while Joanne and Deb stayed in Digby and he worked in Halifax. But this trip was different. During this trip, he was on his own with two little girls, trying hard to understand how this had happened and wondering what had happened to Joanne. Deb remembers being on the train. "It was fun. A really cool adventure. Not at all sad."

Once again, Fred began to travel back and forth between Digby and Halifax. He was back in a boarding house during the week and living with his ailing parents and two small children on the weekends.

The physical, mental, and emotional exertion it took to take care of two small children (and especially a baby) was more than Fred's mother, Pauline, could handle. She had been sick for years. As far back as Fred can remember, she had vertigo due to a brain tumor. She lived with it for many years, but the stress of caring for two young girls was exhausting. Fred's father, Lee, was already well on his way to alcoholism. Something had to shift.

Fred knew Mary and Hector Jourdain through the Digby Yacht Club and through his father, Lee. It was Lee who began the conversation with Hector, likely over a drink or two, at the yacht club, where Hector both worked on other people's boats and kept his own boat. The story of Joanne taking off and leaving her family behind was good gossip in a small town. Because it directly affected Lee, it naturally showed up in conversation. Who better to have this conversation with than a hardworking friend who was also a drinking buddy and who, as it turned out, was having problems having babies with his wife. The possibility of a mutually agreeable arrangement emerged, and the conversation broadened to include Fred, Pauline, and Mary until an agreement was reached. Fred had few choices available to him, and this opportunity was too good to pass up.

The arrangement began with Fred dropping Deb and me off at Mary and Hector's home at the end of every weekend and picking us up at the beginning. Deb used to cry inconsolably when it was time to go back to Mary and Hector's house. It became harder for Fred to leave her with them, so Deb began staying more and more often with our grandmother. He began leaving me alone with Mary and Hector more and more often, even on the weekends, just picking me up for an afternoon drive or visit.

Around this time, Fred started dating the woman who would become his second wife. She had recently moved back to Digby with her young son and was living with her mother and father because she was also going through a divorce. They had mutual circumstances and a lot in common. They began spending more and more time together. They became a couple, and Deb began staying more often with Fred's girlfriend during the week when he was working in Halifax.

Deb had a fear of Fred leaving. He left us in Digby on Sundays to go back to Halifax, where he worked during the week, and he would come back every Friday. "I was fine in between his visits," says Deb, "but if he was supposed to be home Friday at ten o'clock, and wasn't there at 10:02, I was afraid he was not coming. After having Joanne simply disappear with no explanation, there was no guarantee he wouldn't just disappear too." Even though she was just three years old, she clearly remembers the day Joanne left. Even the recollection of it has as surreal feel to decades later as when Joanne left.

Eventually the question of what to do about me came to the forefront. Initially, no one talked about it. When it finally was brought up, they all agreed that Mary and Hector should officially adopt me. It was hard for Fred to reach this decision. It meant letting go. But it was the decision that made the most sense at the time because of the deep bonding that had been occurring between me and my parents. And it was the most honorable decision that could be made. It was made for all the right reasons.

This necessitated tracking Joanne down for two reasons—one was to have her sign the adoption papers for me, and the other was so Fred could divorce her. He was still angry enough that she had abandoned her children and left him with the responsibility that he wanted to be sure she would have no claim to us. He could have left it to chance that she would not come back, but with everything he and we had been through, it was not worth the risk.

Fred discovered that Joanne had moved to Montreal with his best friend. Because Joanne was in Quebec at the time, Fred was told the divorce would cost him a lot of money, as it had to go through two provincial jurisdictions. The laws in Quebec are substantially different than those in Nova Scotia. Fred wanted that loop closed and felt he had to do it no matter what the cost.

Then Fred's lawyer did something unexpected. He called Fred to say he had business in Toronto and that he would be willing to do a stopover in Montreal, take a taxi, serve Joanne with the divorce papers and get her signature, and take the cab back to the airport. He said he would only charge Fred the cost of the taxi—an unusual and generous offer sparked partly because, like Fred, he could not believe that Joanne had taken off and abandoned her children in that way.

For a while, we all lived in Digby. On weekends, Deb and I would be dropped off at Nanny Hanson's house while the adults went to the dance at the yacht club. Deb and I played together. After the dance, everyone would head up to my parents' house and sit around talking and partying for the rest of the night. They had worked out a comfortable and easy pattern of interaction for a few years. Soon after adopting me, my mother became pregnant with my brother Robert. He was born in December 1963. Now my parents had what they called the "million-dollar family"—two children, a boy and a girl.

Then Fred got a job in Quebec and moved there with his family. That is when the visits between Deb and me stopped for a while. They went to Quebec when Deb was five and came back when she was eight. By this time, I was living in Lunenburg with my family, after a short spell in Shelburne. I was barely a memory for Deb until she moved back and Nanny Hanson jogged that memory for her.

Deb was eight when the family moved back to Nova Scotia. That's when she was reminded she had a sister. Both families were visiting in Digby at Nanny Hanson's house. Deb was indignant to find this other girl already at her grandmother's house—*her* grandmother, whom she cherished and who loved her best. She demanded to know who I was and why I was there. Nanny Hanson said to her, "She's your sister." And then Deb remembered that she did have a sister.

In fact, she was overjoyed with this news. She was sure I would find this really exciting too. Arrangements had been made for Deb to go to my house in Lunenburg for a visit with me.

I was already in the car when Deb raced up, got in the backseat beside me, and said, "Guess what? Nanny says we're sisters!" Apparently I did think this was exciting news, although I have no memory of it now. I called my mother over and said, "Guess what? Nanny says we're sisters." A very stern look crossed my mother's face. She looked Deb directly in the eye and said, "You mean for the weekend, right?"

Oh . . . right . . . for the weekend.

This reaction seared itself into Deb's memory. She never brought it up again, although at that age, she did not understand why it was a problem or what the big deal was; she just understood she was not to speak about it. It was the stuff of family secrets; those family secrets that comprise the fabric of small and large towns everywhere; half-whispered, half-spoken-about things. Half-truths in families are sometimes discovered by accident, sometimes shared at critical points in life journeys, and sometimes never made explicit, leaving people with a sense of something out of place, maybe even patterns in their life that do not make sense. People in such a situation never have the opportunity to meet this aspect of the stranger within. But for now, for Deb, it was still okay. This was enough. No matter what my mother said, Deb knew the truth. She knew she had a sister.

Deb visited with us several times over the following few years. I have a vague recollection of someone coming to stay with us but no specific memories. I just knew she was older. When I was old enough to really pay attention, she stopped visiting. The visits stopped when I was seven, primarily because Nanny Hanson finally succumbed to brain cancer.

Her death in late 1969 changed everything. It was the beginning of the end for Lee. He continued to work on the wharf and continued to drink. Finally, he lost his job at the wharf because of his drinking. He didn't pay his bills, and he crashed his car.

Fred and his brother were both living and working in Halifax at the time Lee was spiraling downward. There was little they could do to stop or influence his descent.

Lee sank more fully into alcoholism and ended up on the streets of Halifax. Although he was picked up a few times by Fred and brought home to sober up and get cleaned up, he always made his way back to the streets. It is assumed he died derelict on the streets, as there is no record of his death and no chance he is still alive today.

I received a jewelry box containing costume jewelry when Nanny Hanson died. Of course, I had no idea of the significance of this gift, although I appreciated it. I played with that box and the jewelry in it over and over again for many years. I still have it, although much of the costume jewelry is long gone. When I mention this jewelry box to Fred, he also remembers it. He describes the size, color, and decoration on the box.

With Nanny Hanson's death came the end of our family contact. She was the glue that had held us together. Between her passing, Lee's alcoholism and detachment from the family, and Fred's somewhat nomadic life style, contact dwindled.

The last time Deb saw me, she was about fifteen. It was a random, impromptu visit as far as she knew. One day Fred suggested they go for a drive. They were living in Halifax at the time and ended up in Lunenburg. Deb recalls the trip: "I remember being surprised when we got there. We certainly hadn't talked about it—about you or who you were. I don't really know why we went there."

They sat in the front living room of our house on Dufferin Street. It felt really formal. I can only imagine the tension that must have been in the room. I don't know if my parents expected Fred and Deb or if they just showed up. The family secret would have loomed large in that space. I was completely oblivious—at least I imagine I was, because I have no memory of this visit. I was buzzing around, getting ready to go to figure skating. I left. They left. Deb didn't really know what that visit was for—a bit of a check-in to see me and see if I was okay. Apparently I was going about my life as a normal twelve-year-old, blissfully unaware of who, exactly, these people were or why they were visiting.

Robyn was born early in 1970, not too long after Nanny Hanson's death. Fred and her mother were married a month before Robyn's birth. Deb was eleven. For the next six or seven years, the family lived in Halifax.

As Deb got older, she started to hear stories about Joanne, although nobody mentioned her name and Deb still didn't ask questions. "It seemed like you weren't supposed to ask," she said. "It was Robyn's mother who told me about Joanne. There were some things she was adamant about, and this was one of them. She thought I should know about my mother and my sister."

The year after Robyn was born, a family moved in across the street that influenced the course of Deb's life. There were five children in this family. The middle son was a year and a half older than she was. Deb became friends with his younger sister and was always at their house. She developed a crush on her friend's brother. When she was fifteen, he took her to her first high school dance and a young romance was born.

At seventeen, Deb became pregnant. She had been using the rhythm method of birth control. Standing at the bus stop one morning someone mentioned the date. It flashed in Deb's mind that her period was late and she knew she was pregnant, even knew the exact moment she became pregnant. This discovery way made in the summer between grades eleven and twelve. It was a stressful summer for her. "I didn't know how my father and step-mother would react to the news. They were talking about moving. I didn't want to start grade twelve at a new high school pregnant. Just being pregnant was about as much as I could take. I tried to hide it as long as possible, but of course, you reach a point you can't hide it anymore."

Deb and her boyfriend told his mother first. She was very supportive. She had a pregnancy test done for Deb. At the time, home pregnancy tests did not exist. Instead, one had to take a urine sample to the drug store, and the pharmacist checked for results.

When the father-to-be called in for the results, the pharmacist congratulated him. "Not sure if congratulations were what we had in mind," Deb said to me, "but it's what we got." Deb had no idea what she was going to do, as she was still in high school, living with her parents. Her boyfriend was an unemployed high school dropout who was living with his parents. "The only thing I knew for sure was that I was keeping this baby!"

When they did break the news to Deb's parents, under threat of a deadline from Deb's future mother-in-law, Fred and his wife took it pretty well, although Fred turned pale, shook, and broke out in a cold sweat. "I think he was flashing back to his own past and flashing forward to a future potentially full of broken promises and hardship," Deb said to me.

Deb went back to school in September 1976, a couple of months into her pregnancy. She got married in October, surrounded by friends and family. She had worked throughout the summer to help pay for the wedding, and by then, her fiancé had a full-time job. They got their own apartment and were in love, as happy as two expectant teenagers can be.

Deb's first daughter was born in February 1977. The pregnancy was difficult and landed Deb in the hospital for three months prior to the birth. "I tried to go back to school in March. For a variety of reasons, it didn't work out, so I pretty much left school. The school contacted me, asking me to write a few exams. They actually awarded me a high school diploma. They knew that if I'd have been able to stay in school, I would have graduated, and they wanted me to at least have that to draw on. I don't think that could happen today."

Her husband wanted to go back to school to further his education so he could better support his family. To make this possible, they ended up moving in with his parents in cramped quarters. His two brothers and two sisters already lived with his parents, and now there were three more in a four-bedroom apartment.

Meanwhile, wanderlust took Fred out to Fort McMurray with his wife and their daughter. At the time, Fort McMurray was a transient town that was very different from the East Coast culture and landscape. Fort McMurray is located in Northern Alberta and became a town because of oil. People went out to the oil sands to work, made some money, and often drifted back home to wherever it was they had come from. This meant that well-paying jobs were plentiful there. People were encouraged to recruit their family members. The idea was that if more family showed up, more people would put down roots and stay longer. The strategy worked, as there are now several generations of families living and working in this booming town.

Fred kept calling back home, telling Deb and her husband of the many opportunities in Alberta and how good the pay was. Finally Deb's husband put his name in and quickly got a call to move to Fort McMurray. As he was on the phone, all Deb could hear was "How much? Can you say that again? How much? Yeah, okay, I need about a week."

When Deb, her husband, and their daughter moved to Fort McMurray, the two families began a tradition of Sunday afternoon gatherings. Deb's second daughter was born soon after they moved there. Robyn was old enough to help look after Deb's two children. They played board and card games all afternoon and had dinner together. They were as close to one big, happy family as they had ever been. Everyone has good memories from that period of time.

Some of Robyn's fondest memories come from that time. As a family of three, they traveled, camped, went to the mountains, and drove across Canada three times. Some summers Robyn and her mother would fly back to Nova Scotia for two or three weeks to visit family, and then in August, the three of them would go on road trips through the mountains and to British Columbia. Other summers they would take the whole summer off and drive across the country.

Back in Nova Scotia, I was finishing high school in Lunenburg, getting ready to go to university in Halifax, completely unaware of this parallel track of life where, even if I wasn't talked about, my absence was present in their midst.

After six years, in 1983, the year of my first University graduation, Fred had enough of the oil sands and, like so many Atlantic Canadians, found his way back home to Halifax for the next few years. Deb and her husband and their children stayed in Alberta.

While her husband worked, Deb stayed home and raised their girls for a few years, babysitting other children. "It had always been on my mind to go back to school. When the right opportunity presented itself, I did. My husband gave me his blessing, despite the fact I now would not be generating any revenue of my own and we needed to put our children in daycare. It wasn't easy doing all the juggling, but it was worth it. I graduated with a certificate in business administration."

When she was twenty-seven, Deb and her husband separated after ten years of marriage. (I was only getting married for the first time when I was twenty-seven.) It was a traumatic event in Deb's life. "I'd been sure this love would last forever. Now that it was clearly gone, I was sure I was never going to fall in love again. It was heartbreaking and devastating."

However, like so many of us, she married a second time. She married a man who had three girls similar in age to her two daughters. They worked for the same company, and he liked the outdoors: skiing, camping, fishing—everything she also liked to do. "It was all great, except that I wasn't in love with him. When things started to go wrong, there was no glue to bind us together. It was impossible to get through the bad times. Five teenage girls living in the same space didn't help the situation. Five years down the road, we separated. When we did, we sat all the kids down and talked to them about their choices, reinforcing that we both loved them all." The result of this is that Deb still has good relationships with all three of her second husband's daughters.

As Deb was moving into her own apartment, she sought help from a friend, someone she knew through work. He was also moving and divorcing at the same time, so she knew he had boxes. He was shocked to find out her marriage wasn't the happy situation it appeared to be. The timing was fortuitous for them both; they began to date.

This man had five kids, three of whom he and his second wife had adopted. There were many challenges for Deb and him to sort through. Sorting through them contributed to the development of a strong relationship as they fell in love. Deb's third marriage with the love of her life, Rob, brought her to a total of ten kids altogether: her two girls and eight stepchildren!

With distance, age difference, and different stages in life creating little common ground, Robyn and Deb naturally drifted apart and out of any kind of regular communication.

During this time, Robyn's mother, who had been back in Halifax a few years, became ill with colorectal cancer. It was quite a battle in a short period of time with many highs and lows. She was given the news she was in remission just days before she died of massive organ failure. Robyn was just eighteen.

It was a tough time for Robyn. "Because your mom is not supposed to get sick," she said to me. "Your parents are not supposed to get sick. Your parents are not supposed to get old. They are not supposed to die." Especially when you are only eighteen.

Robyn was determined to see her mom in the hospital, despite repeated attempts by family members to keep her away, especially in the last few days of her life. Robyn was shocked by her mother's appearance. She had changed drastically in a short period of time. She was in a lot of pain and heavily sedated. She could not talk and did not know anybody. Robyn and Fred were with her when she died.

The next period of time was difficult for Robyn. "I had been sheltered and protected by my mother. She and Dad had different parenting styles, and now I felt like I was all alone in the world."

Robyn was nineteen when she first met her husband. She worked in a business center in Halifax. Her office was just off the main reception area near the office manager. He worked for a courier company and used to make deliveries into the office. When Robyn met him, he was going through a divorce. Initially he irritated Robyn, but then she found herself thinking about him more than she cared to admit.

Despite a disastrous first date, they continued to date for a year and a half, and then they moved in together. They got married in Jamaica in 1994, and a few months later Robyn's first child, a daughter, was born. Two years later, her first son was born; and her third child, also a son, came along five years after that.

Issues and challenges got the better of Robyn's marriage, and she and her husband separated. Encouraged by her aunt, Robyn rented a U-Haul and, with her three children, moved back to Digby.

"I decided to go back to school, to do my adult education to complete grade twelve and get a graduation diploma. I went to vocational school after grade eleven, but I really wanted to show my children the importance of a grade-twelve education," she said. "After that I started a business program online through Nova Scotia Community College. I worked hard and did well." She graduated from this program the year after I met her.

Deb felt a loyalty to her stepmother, so it was only after she died that Deb felt she could search for her own mother. Deb initiated the search thirty years after Joanne had left.

She asked Fred about Joanne. "He doesn't talk much about stuff like that," she said to me, "so he didn't have much to offer. That was partly because he also didn't know much about what had happened to Joanne over the years, although he had a pretty good idea where you were." Deb did not have it in her to look for both of us at the same time. She decided to focus on Joanne because, from the exchange she'd had with my mother years before, she was pretty sure I did not know I was adopted, and she did not want to rock my world.

She started her search in Digby during one of her visits there. After talking to Fred, she went to talk to Robyn's aunt, who put her in touch with a high school friend of Joanne's, someone who knew everybody from that time in the early sixties.

Deb went to visit Joanne's high school friend. She said to Deb, "It's like Joanne has fallen off the face of the earth. Nobody has heard from her. Nothing. I received one Christmas card with no return address and a request asking me not to try to find her."

This high school friend found it really surprising that Joanne had left us. She knew Joanne as a loving mother. Deb and I were always with her, especially Deb.

She talked about Joanne's childhood and told Deb that Joanne had sworn she would never abandon her own children the way she had been abandoned.

"I wanted to be able to put a face to a name. I wanted to see where I came from. I didn't look like Robyn or Fred or that side of the family," Deb said. "I felt like I didn't belong anywhere. I told this family friend, with no expectation of this actually happening, 'If she ever comes around, give her my phone number.'"

Having turned fifty that year, Joanne started having thoughts about going back to visit the aunt and uncle who had raised her after her grandfather had died. Then as she got back to Digby, she went to see her friend who gave her Deb's phone number.

Soon after Deb's visit to Digby, her phone at home in Alberta rang. Deb felt it before she even picked up the phone. It was Joanne. After thirty years of no contact, Joanne had decided to go back to Digby—just a short while after Deb had started asking questions about her.

Deb picked up the phone and heard, "This is Joanne."

In yet another surreal moment, Deb said, "I know."

"Joanne, your mother."

"Yes, I know. I recognize your voice."

It was true. After thirty years, her mother's voice still resonated in her being, calling her back to a distant childhood.

When Deb asked her where she lived, Joanne told her she was in British Columbia. She was reluctant to elaborate any more than that. She told Deb she was married and had an adopted daughter who was the same age as Deb's oldest daughter.

For Deb, "it was the weirdest phone call ever. She didn't tell me anything. She didn't tell me where she lived. She didn't give out her phone number. She didn't even tell me her last name. It was one of the most confusing calls ever!"

Deb asked her, "What do you look like?" When Joanne gave her description, Deb recognized her mother's features in herself. "Finally I felt like I belonged to someone, at least biologically if not emotionally," Deb said to me.

Joanne said to Deb, "I need time to think. I'll call you back." Deb hung up, not convinced she would ever hear from Joanne again. Surprisingly, she did. Joanne asked Deb to go to Vancouver, where she would be staying for a conference, to meet her.

Deb arranged vacation time for this trip. Her second husband drove her to the airport, wishing her luck. As she got on the plane, she started having second thoughts. "Maybe I should have left well enough alone. What if she's fat and ugly? What if we don't like each other? What if? What if? What if?"

Joanne had asked Deb to call from the lobby before going up to the hotel room. Deb recalls this: "I sat in the hotel lobby for the longest time. I almost turned around and went right back to the airport." She wrestled with her own fears, doubts, and what-ifs. Finally she summoned her courage and used the house phone to call. Joanne invited her up.

It was a long elevator ride and longer walk down the hall. Deb's heart was in her throat, beating erratically. She knocked on the door. When Joanne opened the door, Deb had no doubt the woman she was staring at was her mother. No doubt at all. They looked that alike. They even dressed in a similar way. They stood and regarded each other for a long few moments. Then Joanne reached out and hugged Deb.

Now Deb knew where she had come from.

Joanne suggested they go to the bar for a drink. They ordered the same drink—not a commonplace drink, such as a glass of wine, but a whisky sour. Later, when they ordered dinner, they chose the same meal. Yes, this was definitely Deb's mother.

This was when Deb discovered the reason Joanne had been so vague when she first called. Joanne was married. She had never told her third husband that she had been married the first time or that she had children.

She had never told anyone about us.

She had lived with this secret all her life. She was scared to death that the secret would come out and the life she had so precariously built for herself over all those years would come crumbling down. She lived in fear of her past and the stories she could not bring herself to tell—the human tragedy perspective of her life, her choices, and her path. These stories comprised some of the fabric of who she was that she had put in metaphorical boxes and tucked away, never to be opened. Not even now. Not even with ghosts from the past literally knocking on the door. But, it was turning fifty that that caused Joanne to start having thoughts about going back to visit the aunt and uncle who had raised her after her grandfather had died. Then as she got back to Digby, she went to see her friend who gave her Deb's phone number.

During this first visit, Deb and Joanne got along well. As Deb left to go home, Joanne said she was going to try to figure out a way to make the relationship work. She wanted to, but it was creating dissonance between the stories she had told herself her entire life and what might be possible now. Stories of loss, rejection, and being a bad person. Stories of no one from her past wanting to know her anymore. Stories of it being better to let well enough alone.

Joanne called again in a few months and asked Deb to meet her again, this time in another city in British Columbia. She was attending another conference. Deb went again. Again they had a great time. Joanne introduced her to her friends as a friend of the family.

They went out shopping. Twice Deb was referred to by complete strangers as her daughter and Joanne denied it, claiming they were just friends. "Even in a city where nobody knew us," Deb said to me, "she could not bring herself to acknowledge me as her daughter, even though it was obvious. The questions made her nervous and she seemed afraid." For Deb it brought such crushing disappointment that she did not even want to admit to herself the depth of the disappointment.

Joanne called a third time on very short notice, asking Deb if she would meet her again. Deb challenged her. "I told her I already had plans. I told her that, because of the secretive nature of this relationship, I was starting to feel like I was having an affair—with my mother! I told her I couldn't always just drop everything to meet her when she called like this. I told her that she and her family were welcome to visit any time they wanted, but something different needed to happen here. Joanne told me she was working on it, that she had written a letter to her husband explaining the whole story. She just needed to find the courage to give it to him." The fear of his response, in the end, was an insurmountable barrier.

After being challenged in this way, Joanne never again asked Deb to meet her, although she continued to call her. "I didn't see her enough or know her enough to feel a real bond. I did understand her as my mother, but without any depth of relationship."

And the relationship was causing Joanne so much stress that it became a role reversal. "I felt like I was the strong person, like I was looking after my mother and looking after her interests, like I was parenting my mother instead of the other way around. Joanne would be the one phoning me when she had a problem."

Deb always held on to the hope that Joanne would somehow turn it all around and they would have a more normal mother-and-daughter relationship. She always hoped Joanne would acknowledge her as her daughter. While hope springs eternal, it never happened.

What surprised and hurt Deb the most about Joanne was that she did not remember her birthday. She was shocked when Joanne asked her when it was.

"It was hard enough for me to imagine how a mother can leave a child, knowing there are a thousand reasons it happens. But not remembering when you gave birth to either one of your children? I had always imagined that on my birthday my mother would be thinking about me. If she never thought about me the other 364 days of the year, surely she would think of me on my birthday." Deb's tone was quizzical and sad as she recounted these thoughts—an illusion shattered.

In their conversations, Joanne always talked to Deb so singularly, as if she were the only one, the only child. Deb was surprised that she never asked about me or tried to find out anything about me now that she and Deb had met. "But she didn't ask probing questions to other people any more than she wanted them asked of herself. She wanted to leave well enough alone."

The relationship eventually leveled out with a yearly letter from Deb to Joanne enclosed in a Christmas card, in which Deb updated her on all that had happened in the past year, and she received the occasional phone call from Joanne. "I would have liked more, but Joanne was unable to give any more."

Deb sent her last Christmas card to Joanne in December of 2007. As she prepared the card, she thought, *I haven't received a call from Joanne in quite a while.*

Later that month, Deb came in one day after walking her dogs and checked the phone for calls, and Joanne's phone number showed up. There was a voice message, but it was not from Joanne. It was from Joanne's husband.

He had received the Christmas card Deb sent to Joanne. In his message he said, "I don't know who you are, but you wrote such a nice note, I thought you would want to know that Joanne died last May."

Joanne died last May . . .

Last May?

Deb stared at the phone for the longest time. "I often wondered how I would find out if something happened to Joanne, since no one close to her even knew I existed." Well . . . now she knew.

She wondered whether she should call Joanne's husband back and whether she should tell him the story. But she also wondered what that would accomplish. This man was already grieving.

195

Deb finally decided that if this secret was important enough for Joanne to take to her grave, it was not up to Deb to share it with Joanne's husband now that she had died. Deb put the phone down, thinking, *But if he calls back . . .*

When Deb first shared this story with me, I was completely struck by her response because I knew this is also how I would have responded if I'd found myself in the same situation.

Three months later, he called Deb back. When she answered the phone, he said, "If I had known there were children, I would have accepted them as my own."

Nine months after Joanne died, the truth came out. Life has a strange way of working and of revealing things.

He was preparing to go on a winter holiday and was searching for his passport. He came across a stack of cards and letters Deb had sent to Joanne over the years—about sixteen years since the time they first met. He began to read them, and at the bottom of the stack was the letter Joanne had written to him, telling him the whole story. If she had not died suddenly, would she have told him? If she had had any warning she was going to die, would she have destroyed the letters? We will never know.

Deb's first reaction when she found out Joanne had died was anger. "I was angry that Joanne had died without fixing things. It was the first time I realized how second-class I felt to Joanne, like everybody else was so much more important to her than I was."

Deb realized she had probably always felt that way, but she had been giving Joanne time to fix the situation. She hadn't fixed it. "She didn't fix it because we had ceased to exist for her when she left us. She couldn't face bringing us back into being by acknowledging our existence. That part of her life was over, and she desperately needed it to stay that way."

Not only was Deb rejected when Joanne had left two unsuspecting children all those years before, but she had also been rejected when Joanne refused to acknowledge her later in life. The searing disappointment of this resonated in the depths of Deb's being.

In the end, the only person Deb could really speak to about this, who understood despite having a very different experience of it, was me.

Over the years, Deb had drawn two conclusions about me. "One was you didn't know you were adopted, which was the one I was pretty sure was correct because of my memory of the exchange with your mother. The other scenario is that you did know, and knew that all of us were out there, and none of us even bothered contacting you, so why would you care? We didn't seem to; why should you?"

Joanne's death—along with the realization that none of us was getting any younger—sparked a flurry of conversations between Deb and Robyn about finding me.

Deb was torn. She wanted to find me, but she was afraid of the possible result. Deb's experience with Joanne caused her to think this was not really meant to be. And she really did believe I didn't know. So she chose to just leave it be.

Robyn's boyfriend was the one most able to act on his curiosity, because he was less attached to the outcome and because this was all new to him. For Deb and Robyn, my silent presence in the family story was just status quo.

About a decade before Deb and Robyn found me, Fred had lost track of me. That was during the time I was going through job loss and my first divorce. I was no longer showing up in the media from time to time, as I had left the not-for-profit sector and begun a consulting career. For a while, I was pretty low-profile.

By this time, Fred thought I knew I was adopted. As the years went by, he wondered if he should try to get a hold of me, but he decided that if I wanted contact, I would get a hold of him. Robyn and Deb asked him on occasion what he thought about finding me and if it would be okay to do so. He said he was all for it, and he felt it really would not be difficult to find me. But he left it in their hands. It took a while for them to pursue it.

After Robyn called him with the news that they had found me, he began to wonder how soon I would show up. He waited for contact. He was deeply moved that he was the first person in my birth family I chose to meet. While he was waiting for me to arrive, he walked from window to window wondering, *When the hell will she get here?*

Later, when I asked him about that moment, Fred said, "I was kind of excited, really. I don't know how I looked when you got out of the car or anything, but I think I had your picture, so I knew who to look for. All I knew was that I was looking for a gray-haired old woman to come."

CHAPTER 9

PARALLEL TRACKS
OF LIFE—PART 2

I imagine what it must have been like to be my birth mother, to be born into her life, to live the human tragedy perspective from even before she was born, to feel that thread throughout all her life, and to move in the world through threads of fear, worry, and anxiety, not just because what she did might be discovered, but also because she might be judged into eternity for her choices, dismissed as a bad person, and cast out of society to atone for her sins. I don't know for sure if this is true. It is one of the stories I make up about her.

I am also curious about her mother, my grandmother. Her I imagine as an ephemeral being floating on the edges between ordinary and non-ordinary reality, lost and alone in the land of physicality, gifted in the ways of spirit, not knowing how to land fully on the earth. I do not know if this is true. But if stories are the stuff by which we understand our world and make sense of our lives and our lineages, and if I do not have more solid information, then I am choosing the story that plays out at the edges of my imagination when I think of her, fairylike in the land of the living.

I was not meant to know my birth mother in this lifetime. She left in 1962, soon after I was born. I only found out I was adopted in 2008, eight months after she died. And yet she had a profound impact on my life. For starters, without her, I would not exist, and neither would my sister. Without her choice to leave, my life would have been different, although I do not know how. Would I have found my way down some of the same pathways? This seems likely, since the path seems to call me. However, it is impossible to know anything for sure.

Joanne's life was such a mystery. She feared her stranger within and could never imagine embracing it. She lived in intense fear throughout most of her life.

Her disappearance was a contributing factor, and maybe the first big incident in my life, that led to the creation of the protective and survival mechanisms I used to keep me safe, to hide the stranger in me. Even as a baby, something in me was aware that something big had just happened; that my life had changed. I would not have thought it possible, but examples of how my life was affected come out at the most unexpected times. And it has nothing to do with how my life was because I was adopted. It is beyond my physical journey in this world; beyond the human tragedy lens.

I was not meant to know I was adopted until after Joanne died and a depth of personal journey readied me for this incomprehensible shock to my understanding of who I am.

It was finding out about Joanne's death that prompted my sisters to search for me, and it was because of their search that I found out I was adopted. When I first found out, I imagined that hardly anyone must have known. My parents moved back to Lunenburg in 1967 with two small children. They would not have had to explain that I was adopted. I figured that in order for such a big thing to stay secret for forty-six years, it was necessary that only a few people knew, and certainly not people who were close to me. I caught no whiff of it in my interactions with people—not that I tuned in to, anyway.

As it turns out, there were all kinds of opportunities and clues along the way that could have led me to this information—for instance, the city on my birth certificate, which I mentioned earlier. I also found out that one of my best friends in high school had discovered by accident that I was adopted and never breathed a word of it to me. When I bumped into her at the long-term care facility both our mothers were in, I thought I would surprise her when I mentioned my sister. Instead, she surprised me. "Oh, you know," she said.

How on earth did she know? She had found out as a teenager through a crazy, unintentional set of circumstances. She bumped into someone visiting Lunenburg from Digby who knew the families and spilled the beans. When my friend asked her mother what she should do with this information, her mother said to her, "It's not yours to tell." So she kept it to herself for thirty years.

My older cousins knew. Odd references had been made to my brother asking if I was in touch with my sister. He, of course, dismissed the comment since we did not have a sister, and the subject was quickly dropped. Pictures of me and my sister existed, but I never clued in, never noticed the resemblance. I was not looking for it. I was living into the stories that helped me make sense of my world. Competing data was ignored or eliminated when it did not fit with the sense-making. My mother did the same thing. She kept filtering out data that did not fit with me not being born to her.

I never clued in that there was a whole other track of life separate from my own that also influenced my life. The stories fascinate me now. They illustrate how life paths are shaped and shifted by things beyond our control, by things that happen before we are born, by things that are in our lineage, by invisible threads that bind us to people, places, and events. My birth family is such a story. My birth mother has such a story.

Joanne's story starts with her mother—and likely her mother's mother, although I am not privy to that story. Even the "facts" regarding Joanne's mother are limited.

I was told Joanne's mother had multiple children all by different fathers. I have no idea what "multiple" means. Two, five, ten? All of the children were given over to somebody else for care and upbringing. This in and of itself would have been considered aberrant behavior in the late 1930s and early 1940s. Her children carried the stigma and shame of having been born out of wedlock, illegitimate—as though it were somehow their fault. It would have been a whispered secret in the family and in the small community in which Joanne was raised. Even if they didn't know their own circumstances, there would be an energetic impact on them and their lives—the result of family secrets, whispered perhaps, while just within earshot.

Who was Joanne's mother? What was she like? Deb and I had conversations about her as some mysterious woman, like a character in a story, until Deb pointed out the obvious fact we had both missed in that conversation—Joanne's mother was our grandmother! The realization was a jolting piece of information in a space it did not quite fit in. It was as though in knowing it, something needed to shift in my being in order for me to make sense of it. It was as though I had been hearing a make-believe story only to discover it was not make believe at all, but that it was real and was part of my own history, my own lineage. My lineage was already unfamiliar to me, and this was one step further back in time.

Who was this woman? My image of her, the story I make up, is of her as a child woman. Was she a war child? A free spirit? Did she have a mental illness? Did she live more in a spirit world than the physical world? Was she the town slut? I have no way of knowing. I can only imagine stories, and I prefer to believe the ones that are gentler and kinder to her. She is my grandmother, after all.

When Joanne was born, she was given over to her grandfather and an aunt to be raised. They cared for her until she was in her early teens. Her grandfather died, and her aunt got married. Her aunt's new husband didn't want Joanne in their life.

Joanne had been abandoned by her mother, her grandfather through his death, and her aunt through her marriage, and she was now given over to another aunt and uncle who were in their fifties who had never had children of their own. I can only imagine it was hard for them to become the custodians of a young teenager and it was hard for her to fit in with her new caregivers. Maybe the pattern of abandonment started in this family lineage before Joanne, but it was alive in her lineage backward and forward. I know men were involved, and it feels like a female lineage. It is how I feel the story in me, and I have identified patterns of abandonment in my own life since I became aware of the story of my birth: my mother abandoned me as a baby, my grandmother "abandoned" me by being too sick to care for me and then by dying, my sister abandoned me by choosing to stay with the birth family, and my mother eventually abandoned me through dementia. These things are stories. They are not logical. They don't have to make sense. And they form the fabric of life, my life, in ways that are difficult to really know.

For Joanne, she carried the heritage of her birth and upbringing like it was a deep, dark secret of her soul. She was unhappy and troubled. She walked around like she carried the weight of the world on her shoulders. She had an aura of being haunted even as a young girl.

Consciously or unconsciously, she was looking for a way to escape the life that she had been born into—she thought she was looking for happiness, and understandably so, but really she was looking for escape.

While she was still in her early teens, she met Fred. He was a handsome, dashing, daring young man—the captain of the basketball team. He had also had his share of challenges growing up, so they could relate to each other in a number of ways.

They met in school. She was a couple of grades behind him. She worked in the cafeteria after school doing the dishes from lunch. He stayed after school all the time for basketball. They bumped into each other regularly. Eventually they started to go out together. In a small town with few options, that meant hanging out with a few friends, drinking and smoking, and making out in the backseat of a car.

When Fred got his job in Halifax, Joanne followed him. They were finally free of the small town and the suffocating air of secrets lived, particularly for Joanne. It was just an illusion of freedom though. They partied a lot, and then Joanne became pregnant with their first child. After Deb was born, Joanne ironically found herself back in the same small town she had been trying to escape from. Fred's job did not pay enough for him to support his young family in Halifax. The solution was to send Joanne and Deb back to Digby to live with Fred's parents, while Fred continued to live and work in Halifax—traveling home each weekend by train to be with his family. After her dramatic escape to Halifax, Joanne was now more trapped than ever.

She doted on Deb, taking her everywhere, loving and adoring her. She often said she would never do to her children what was done to her, as she had been abandoned by her mother and forced to move around from place to place, which left her feeling unloved and unlovable. But she wrestled with guilt and disillusionment in addition to the sense of disgrace that comes from embodying the secrets of her own family heritage. She didn't know how to cope with the circumstances of her own life.

After a couple of years of living in Digby, Joanne took Deb back to Halifax to live with Fred. The parties continued. Not only were they young, but the drinking and partying was another means of escape from the life they now found themselves in, considerably farther away from a fairy-tale romance than Joanne might have hoped.

In the midst of this, I was born. On New Year's Eve, they were at a party and Joanne began to feel unwell. They went to the hospital, and in the middle of New Year's Day, Joanne gave birth to me. The addition of another big responsibility was difficult for Joanne. If it is true that she followed Fred to escape her past and the drudgery of a small town, replacing that with the responsibility of children at a young age and a tight budget was not a romanticized version of life in the big city. Having an infant added to this small family was too much for Joanne. Maybe she had postpartum depression, but we will never know for sure.

Because postpartum depression was not well known or documented in the 1960s, Joanne would not have had any information or support to help her deal with the challenges she was facing. Support to families was not available either. And she was still just a young girl at the time. She had no family of her own to turn to, and Fred's mother was coping with her own illness and with her husband's alcoholism.

Options were limited. Choices were suffocating. Joanne must have felt her only recourse was to run away. She must have thought her children would be better off without her in their lives.

Soon after I was born, Joanne left town and never looked back—at least she tried hard to never look back. The air of being haunted that she carried as a child followed her throughout her life, now compounded by her choices—not just the choices of her mother or the people who had taken over her upbringing, but her own choices and an inability to confront the bleakness and hopelessness of her young life.

Joanne repeated the pattern from her own mother's life, despite declarations to her best friend that she would never do that to her children. She could see no other choices. She abandoned her husband. She abandoned her children. She abandoned the path her life was moving on and ran away as fast and as far as she could. She was barely twenty years old.

She disappeared. Nobody who knew her knew what happened to her. Even thirty years later, they said it was like she disappeared off the face of the earth—no one had heard anything from her. Early on, she was tracked down in Montreal, where she lived for a time, for two reasons: to sign divorce papers and to sign adoption release papers.

Eventually Joanne moved all the way across the country to British Columbia, where she again lived in a small town. She rebuilt her life, and along with her third husband, she became an upstanding member of her community. Her indomitable spirit and ability to survive shone through in the way she rebuilt her life despite her past. She was amazingly resilient. And noticeably silent on some subjects.

Throughout the years, she carried the secret of her two children without ever telling a soul, including her third husband. When Joanne and her husband decided that they wanted to have children, they were not able to conceive. Joanne sent her husband for all kinds of tests because she knew she could have children. She already had two that nobody knew about.

Finally, one day, he came home and told her that it was not him, so it must be her. She went for tests, and they confirmed that she could no longer have children—the ultimate irony.

They decided to adopt and adopted a little girl. That little girl grew up knowing that she was adopted but not knowing that her mother already had two children whom she had left behind and who haunted her very existence whether she acknowledged it or not. Joanne was a good mother to her daughter, although there were oddities in her behavior. Understandably, she was much more ready to be a mother in her thirties than in her late teens and she lived most of her adult life trying hard to forget what had happened in her late teens.

It took her thirty years to go back to Digby to visit friends. Her visit was inspired by her fiftieth birthday. In the oddly ironic and synchronistic way that things work, Joanne's visit occurred shortly after Deb's visit on which she asked questions about Joanne. Deb had left her phone number with a few people, and it was passed on to Joanne.

Joanne took Deb's number and made what had to be an exceptionally difficult call for her. I can only assume how much courage she had to muster up to even make this call. Even during the call she was evasive because this was a big secret in her life—a secret she feared might be exposed. She must have wondered why she was even making the call, but the draw of calling her daughter was too strong for her to resist.

She lived with the torment of her secret all of her adult life. She lived in deep fear that she would be found out. She told Deb that she tried not to watch the TV show *Unsolved Mysteries*; she turned it off whenever it happened to come on. She was afraid she would see her picture with two little girls wondering what had happened to their mommy.

When Joanne did reconnect with Deb, she found that Deb held no animosity toward her anymore, and neither did Fred, because so many years had gone by, their time together had been very short, and so much life had been lived since then. The fear she had lived with all her life was for naught. This would have completely challenged her perception of her own world and the stories she had created to make sense of her life and her decisions, which were partially built on how awful other people would think she was. She thought nearly everyone hated her and that those who did not hate her liked her only because they did not know the whole story; she thought that if they found out, she might be abandoned again. And, at an unconscious level, she felt that if she were not an intrinsically bad person, the trick of shadow silencing the voice of the beloved stranger within, her mother and others responsible for her upbringing would not have abandoned her. There had to be something wrong with her, in her estimation. How could a good person take off and leave two little children behind? Only a bad person could do such a thing. Maybe worse than bad. Maybe even evil.

Even when she discovered that Deb did not hate her, she could not find the courage to tell her husband or adopted daughter about her past—fear had too much of a grip on her. After living all those years with this secret, it was so much a part of her she could not let it go. She tried. She wanted to. She wrote a letter to her husband that told the story, intending to give it to him, but she died suddenly in May 2007 before she summoned the courage to do so.

Fast forward to December 2007 and her husband's call to Deb—a message that went without a response: "I don't know who you are, but you wrote such a nice note, I thought you'd like to know that Joanne passed away last May." A secret left sacred. Deb did not return the call. She decided to search for me instead. But the letter Joanne had written was still there—lurking in a drawer to be discovered by her husband nine months after she died.

Once he read it—and all the cards and letters Deb had sent over the years, which Joanne had saved—he called Deb to say, "Had I known there were children, I would have accepted them as if they were my own."

Joanne lived in fear of the unknown. She created her own stories, like we all do, to make sense of her choices, her world, and her expectations of how others would feel about her or treat her. She imagined they would mirror back to her how she secretly internally viewed herself and her actions, and she could not face it. She was fully in the human tragedy perspective, unable to completely embrace who she was or the choices she had made.

Fear and worry are the interest paid on trouble that never comes. They shut the door on what more is possible—love, forgiveness, ease, and the rewriting of stories of our lives that could instead be lived with grace and empowerment.

Now, ironically, my sister Deb; my half-sister, Robyn; Joanne's adopted daughter; and I are all "friends" on Facebook. Deb has spoken with Joanne's daughter. She told Deb that Joanne was a good mom. There were, however, quirks to her behavior that make a lot more sense to her now that she knows her mother's secret.

So I never had the opportunity to know my birth mother. She left when I was an infant, and I did not even find out I was adopted until after her death. I was clearly not meant to know her in this lifetime. And yet she and her story have had a significant impact on my life. Her leaving made it difficult for Fred to care for me, leading to my adoption, causing me to be raised in a different family, in a different community, without knowing my sisters as I grew up.

It is hard for me to know exactly the impact of this because my older sister, Deb, and I have discovered how alike we are despite having gone through very different life experiences. Ultimately Joanne's departure changed the nature of the decisions that needed to be made in my birth family. They also changed the nature of the decisions made in my family, changing the course of my parents' lives forever. All of these choices and decisions wove a web of connections, both visible and invisible that shaped the lives of many people in different ways.

In some ways, I do know Joanne. I have lived aspects of her life in my own life without ever knowing she existed. Some of my early behavioral patterns make more sense to me now that I know her story.

I can see that familial patterns and ancestral lineages will make themselves known until they are healed. Healing takes place by leaning into the stories and patterns with courage, compassion, strength, and love for all concerned, including—and maybe especially—ourselves. We all have these qualities within us, the beauty of the stranger within.

The tragic sadness in Joanne's story is how fear, shame, and denial led to a deeply held secret. This secret shut down the opportunity for Joanne to know her two biological children, for her husband to also know us, and for relationships to emerge between her adopted and biological daughters during Joanne's lifetime.

When the story finally did come out, after the initial shock, there was mostly sadness and disappointment that Joanne did not trust the people who loved her enough to share her story. This ultimately means she did not trust herself enough to share the deepest, darkest secrets of her life.

I remember this fear from when I lost my job and divorced at the same time. I feared that if people knew the whole story, they would think less of me and abandon me too. At that time I was not aware of this pattern of abandonment in my life until this parallel story was unearthed. The conscious awareness of this pattern of abandonment emerged when I could piece together the lineage. Then I understood that some of my own fears stemmed from things within me I could not have known about. I could even see a story of abandonment by my own mother as she slipped away into dementia.

It is not the reality of these stories that is important. It is the interpretation of them. It is how they are received in the soul journey and how they reside in the cellular memory.

It is no wonder I constructed so many walls around my heart and my vulnerability, even as my path was showing me how protected and loved I was in this journey, demonstrated first by my birth family wanting the best for me and by my parents receiving me into their lives when I was just a baby. Later by discovering how supported I am in the non-physical realm with spirit guides and power animals.

It is in the surfacing of these stories and how we tell them that we create the space for the healing necessary for the journey to openheartedness, by changing the story, rewriting it in progress, and imagining the new endings we can choose to live into. Our lives are shifted and shaped by the choices of others, but they can also be intentionally shaped and shifted by our own choices. We are not simply at the mercy of others, the mercy of our past, or the mercy of already lived experiences. As we increase our awareness of the stories we use to make sense of our lives, the way we tell those stories and the things we choose to emphasize can and do shift. Is my story one of abandonment or resilience? Loss or love? What is the pattern I want to choose, given that both of these themes are prevalent in my lineage?

The stranger within wants to shine the light so we can see through the shadow, yet we develop the shadow through stories filled with fear and self-loathing that shape the walls we build to protect ourselves (from ourselves, as it turns out). We do not so much keep others out with these protective mechanisms as we lock ourselves in.

Without my birth mother's choices and actions, my journey in this lifetime would have been shaped differently. I might not have been able to realize the soul connection I have with my father, Hector, or my mother, Mary. I would not have been gifted with the collective journey of the family I grew up in. I would not have had the same vehicle to understand the depth of soul journey and soul commitments, nor would I have fully understood how the shape of a person's life can shift relationships and experiences in both subtle and dramatic ways.

Through knowing about Joanne and her journey, I have come to understand the depth of cellular memory and connection. In some ways the early part of my life was shaped in the pattern of my birth mother—restlessness, the desire to escape living in a small town, the search for affection or validation through relationships with men. The moment of revelation shook me to the core, given I'd had no idea she even existed when I traveled this part of my life.

Joanne went on to live a full life. She was resilient, a survivor. She met a man and entered a lasting marriage with him, and she was a loving mother to her adopted daughter.

Just as I was oblivious to a whole portion of my existence because I did not know about it, Joanne was oblivious to a whole portion of her existence because she worked hard to shut it out. To be curious might have broken her heart and to break her silence might have caused her world to collapse around her—something she had experienced many times already. How could she risk it?

We can only deal with what is in our awareness. To understand the depth of impact on our path of things that are not in our awareness is both stunning and often almost too much to take in.

CHAPTER 10

ROADMARKS ON THE JOURNEY TO OPENHEARTEDNESS

September 2008. Much to my own surprise, I am in Switzerland, working with the Geneva Trade and Development Forum, bringing World Café to this audience for the first time. When I got the call, it was all I could do to bite my tongue and not refer the work to European friends and colleagues.

This trip is a hero's journey for me. I have experienced warring within myself, feeling not worthy of the work, not knowledgeable about international trade and development, and not of the ilk of trade ministers from around the world.

I do a lot of grounding work before I leave and continue to work on me while on the plane there. I know that by the time I arrive I will be ready. The trip and the experience are successful beyond my wildest expectations. The people I need show up when I need them—and then some.

The first café is with the ministerial caucus. After a near crisis when one of the ministers gets up to leave but is stopped by the program advisor, the process goes well with good results, insights, and themes they can work with. Later we are told that four of the ministers who went directly from the café to a plenary spoke with more openness and candor than usual.

The second café is for a broader audience in the main plenary room. Despite the room being too big and the tables too large, with fewer people than we might have hoped, those who do show up are fully engaged.

The cafés become the buzz of the conference. People who have not been part of the cafés start asking questions, wishing they had been there. The buzz grows as the days go by. In the closing plenary, all five of the speakers reference the cafés, even though not all of them have participated in one. I can hardly take it all in.

A few weeks later, I am back in Nova Scotia, working with a local client in Cape Breton. We are hosting a stakeholder engagement process and a board retreat. The work goes well, but I find myself back in my hotel room, antsy and at odds with myself. What is wrong?

I journal, and the voice of my internal judge surfaces. "Sure," it says. "Sure you did well. But you didn't do as well as you did in Switzerland. Remember? There you had everyone talking about the work you did, even people who didn't participate in the cafés. In comparison, this work here isn't even on the radar. You need to shine all the time, like you did in Switzerland."

This is the voice of my internal judge or critic—the one I mistake for the stranger within, though this voice in fact loudly covers over the voice of the stranger within. Insidious. Chameleonlike. I hardly know where or how it will show up, but it will not let me rest.

As I journal and see its words unfolding on my page, I have to chuckle. It has somehow created a new performance bar for me to measure all my performance by, even though most circumstances will be nowhere close to the conditions I encountered in Switzerland.

Just realizing the craziness of this internal process allows me to release it into humor, thereby loosening its grip on me and my journey, making it silent, and creating openings to embrace those parts of me that still lurk in the shadow, inviting me into openheartedness.

In April 2009 I am part of a hosting team in Ontario with friends I met when I did my first Art of Hosting training on Bowen Island. It has taken four years for this long-held intention to work with these friends to manifest itself. The work is beautiful.

My awareness of how easy being with this hosting team is—on so many levels—reverberates in my being. Three members of our team have worked together many times over those years. I do not feel like I am becoming part of their team. I feel like we are all showing up as equals, bringing what we have to offer to this work; truly co-creating it together. I feel invited to step in, in any way I choose. I offer to hold a thread of Theory U throughout the training, since I have accumulated quite a bit of experience with it over the last few years, combined with Art of Hosting. My offering is warmly received.

About midway through the training, I feel my own restlessness stirring in my soul. I am not sure what it is about. I am aware of the need for movement, to get out for a walk. Several of us head out. The pace is not fast enough for me to physically release this restlessness I feel, but I stay with friends on the way down to the park.

On the way back, I apologize to my friends and indicate my need to walk briskly. One friend offers to walk at that pace with me. The walk feels good; the conversation, delightful. I tell my friend, with his permission, about a guide of his that I have awareness of. Some of the detail blows him, and me, away.

Later that evening, I reflect on the edginess I had experienced within me. I realize there was a time I would have looked for someone to rescue me. The lack of that would have driven me deeper into my own restlessness. I would have had to invite someone into that conversation with me, to rescue me. This time I found my own way out. Such beauty. It wasn't that I could not talk to someone; it was that I did not have to rely on it. I could be aware of my own experience, be in it, and tend to what my body, my emotions and my soul seemed to be calling for—in this case some grounding work through rigorous physical movement—and do for myself what needed doing.

As our team checks out at the end of our time together, I feel my emotions welling up in me. I have had such an amazing experience in myself, in the larger group, and as a part of this hosting team. I have experienced so much ease. It is almost a new experience for me. So much of my hosting work has happened in the context of hosting teams that have experienced significant challenges. Hosting the hosting team required attention and energy and detracted from the attention and energy that could be devoted to the hosting work. Those kinds of experiences are deeply draining, and they are what I've been attracting to myself since I started hosting, reflecting what has been my internal experience. There are no accidents. This does not happen by chance. It happens because it is in my vibrational field, attracting that which resonates with it, pulling experiences to me like a magnet. I am aware of it and am deep in the inquiry of why I am attracting these new circumstances of my life to me.

As part of my checkout with this team, with this experience of ease as contrast to many prior experiences, I say, "I am saying *yes* to ease." I shout to myself, "*Yes!* Yes to ease."

I continue. "I do not know what I will face when I go home. I am at a point of transition in my life and on the verge of entering some difficult conversations in my marriage." The courage to speak this to this team also puts it out there. It is now a stated intention, strengthened by the mere act of speaking it aloud, even as I am in the tremble of what is in front of me.

At the Ottawa airport, I sit with one of my friends from the hosting team. We talk about two things. One is this book. The original conceptualization of it is as the story of finding out I was adopted from various perspectives—mine, my sisters', my dad's, and my birth father's, as well as what we can piece together of my birth mother's story.

My friend says to me, "You could create a companion guide. Something like 'hosting the stranger when the stranger is you.'" This resonates for me. It brings me to the title of this book: *Embracing the Stranger in Me.* Something has stirred. We speak about my marriage, the challenges in the relationship. I share some of the depth of conflict, the preparation I have been in through my self-journey, my inquiry into who I am. I share the patterns in my life, the knowledge I have that it is time to be intentional in what happens next, in opening up space in me and between me and my husband for the conversations we need to have that maybe we have been avoiding. I know it is time. I feel the fear of it too.

My friend says to me, "You know, Kathy, I'm going to be in Halifax in six weeks' time. When I see you, I will not pretend that everything is all right with you and your husband." These words are offered in a kind, loving, and yet matter-of-fact way.

I feel as though I have been put on notice in a beautiful and nondramatic way. It is exactly what I need to support my stated intention to begin a conversation with my husband when I get home. If nothing has changed in six weeks' time, my friend will not allow me to live in my own complacency. I have been warned, challenged to step up to my own path.

I have been preparing for these conversations for a long time—longer even than I have been aware. The preparation for this has been an intense personal journey for me over a period of time, years even. It did not start as an intention to separate. We had such dreams for our life and work together when we met. The ghost of this dream is still in me, despite the enormous challenges we have faced in our path together. Challenges that have shown up in deep conflict, crazy tension, resentment, and competition. It has gone on for so long and with such intensity that it has obscured the love, excitement, joy, and connection that brought us together. We try often to clear our path and renew our connection. We go to couples' counseling and couples' retreats. We each do our own individual healing work. While there is some reprieve periodically, the patterns of intensity, tension, and competition, along with deep hurt and resentment, reassert themselves over and over again.

It is in me. It is in him. It is in both of us. We are stuck in a pattern that seems bigger than us. It is entrenched. It is proving impossible to shift, no matter what way we come at it, individually or together.

I reached a point at which I knew I could not do this anymore. I did not like myself. When I was really honest with myself, I knew at times I even hated myself. I could not live like this anymore. There was poison running through my veins, seeping into my soul, overflowing in my field of being. I walked on eggshells every day, never knowing what to say or do to improve things. I was joyless. Again. Still. The weight of responsibility and failure was seated so deeply in me I did not remember how to walk any other path. I was drowning in a life pattern that was suffocating me. I had a heightened awareness of and was more challenged in hosting work because I was so far out of personal integrity. I had lost my way—again, or still. I could not find my voice.

I did not know where my boundaries were; they had been so blurred the last few years.

One day, standing in my laundry room, I threw down the gauntlet to myself. I declared, "I am not doing this anymore. And I will never do it again. So I better figure out why I have attracted this to myself so I stop repeating the pattern." I had no comprehension of the challenge of personal journey I had just placed in front of myself, but the path unfolded—slowly, crazily, intensely, and, later, more gracefully.

I was supported by a coach who challenged me to go to deeper and deeper levels of self-honesty and to more fully connect with my emotions. Early in the coaching process, she said to me, "Kathy, you think your emotions make you weak."

"Yes," I replied with some confusion. This seemed self-evident. "Yes, of course." I do think this. They do make me weak.

"You're wrong," she told me. "If you learn how to work with your emotions, they will make you stronger and more powerful. You can be vulnerable without being open to attack or ridicule. And because your emotions are the doorway into your experience, if you understand what you are experiencing, you will be able to work with it and be in the truth of your experience. It will give you more options and more flexibility."

I am challenged by what she proposes. I do not understand how this can work, but I trust her. And she embodies all the things she is telling me could also be true for me. She is strong and gentle, vulnerable and courageous.

Still I am leery. This does not seem possible. I could not see how it could work, because I did not trust myself. I did not trust my emotions. I did not want to lead with them for sure. But I had been stuck in the core of my story for so long that I was willing, even though reluctant and afraid, to lean into the learning. Usually my coach pushed me gently yet firmly in the direction of my own outcomes. Sometimes she pushed me hard. Once, I got angry. I was expecting her to validate my new awareness and the solutions I have devised for my problems. She challenged me instead. "Kathy," she said, "you have just put yourself in a box."

I did not understand her. I felt like I had been in a box, trapped. With this new thinking, I was finding my way out. She saw something I did not see—that I was desperately latching on to some idea that felt like a solution so I can get out of the "groan zone" I felt my life has become. She invited me to sit longer in my own confusion and chaos. I doubted my own capacity to do that, but she knew what was possible—things I could not see. I was a crying, frustrated mess. She said to me, "Kathy, the only reason I am doing this is because you have told me your current circumstances—how you live with yourself—are untenable." Harrumph! Fine. Be that way.

She demonstrated with me what she meant, what she wanted me to learn. In one session, she asked me, "What are you feeling right now? Where are you experiencing it in your body?"

I responded.

She asked me all over again in the next minute. I responded. And again. Finally I said, "I'm frustrated! Why are we doing this?"

She impressed upon me the value of knowing my own experience in any given moment.

Later I realized it is the difference between walking through my experience and living into my life. These are fundamentally different experiences. One is zombielike; the other is vibrant, free-flowing, and full of life.

Learning to work with my emotions brings me to this place. The previous few months have been such a rich and deep learning space, although they have not been without frustration. I realize that at some point, I want to be done. I have been doing personal development work and have been in a self-learning journey for twenty years. Some of it has been pretty intense. I want to graduate. I want someone to tell me that I have done a good job and I can be done now! *Here. Here is your graduation certificate.*

Lifelong learning. Ha! There is no jumping-off point. I mourn the lack of graduation. This is painful, hard work with no end in sight. I despair.

Like so many things, with the realization that I am holding this hope for graduation, this belief, something releases. I settle more deeply into my learning. I surrender, welcome, and embrace it. *Okay, let it come.* And come it does. Insights and revelations come so fast I can hardly keep up with them. This is beyond anything I ever expected was even possible. I become a sponge, and the journey becomes delightful and refreshing. *Oh, look what's popping up over here. Let me just take a look. What is that telling me? Let me inquire, observe, lean into.* This is powerful.

I know deep inside, not wanting to voice it, that I am preparing myself for what will likely be a separation. It is not a path I want, especially since this is my second marriage and we are business partners. I want to hang on to the hope and possibilities that permeated the early days of our relationship. I want us to find our way—together. But somewhere along the way, the spark in our marriage was lost. And our ability to find it or relight it becomes increasingly difficult, obscured by so many arguments, outright battles, and seemingly fundamental differences in our perspectives about our relationship, our parenting, and even how we work together.

It is the most challenging relationship I have been in. I am resentful of many aspects of it and of my husband. This lingering resentment at times has been so intense it has consumed me, made me feel like an ugly person, like someone I do not know and certainly not the person I want to be. The fear is that this is who I am at the core. Fear of this makes me want to run away. But how do you run away from something that lives inside you?

This is not the first time in my life that I have felt this ugly person in me, someone I do not know and do not want to be. I also felt this way as my first marriage ended. This time around, this feeling was at its height that day I had an epiphany in the laundry room. This was the moment when I first knew this marriage might not last, and that if I—we—could not fix the marriage, I had to work on me in order to understand why I had attracted this level of intensity into my life. My husband is a reflection to me of myself. My outer reality is a reflection of my inner reality. My challenge is to shift my inner patterns so the shape of my outer life also shifts. I want it to shift in a way that includes him. It is a desperate hope, and I hang onto it tenaciously.

Whereas I see upon reflection that I deliberately crashed and burned my first marriage and ran away as fast as I could, this time I am in no hurry. There is nowhere else I need or want to be. It is clear that this is the work I need to do. In case I might run away, our financial situation keeps me in my place even as I obsess over it and my perceived lack of options. I thought I had done my work after my first marriage, but really it was just the beginning—the beginning before the beginning; there is so much more to do. I am resenting the current situation, resenting my husband, resenting me, and regretting my decision to marry him with the joy of the early days of our connection obscured by the ongoing intensity of our relationship. Of all the choices I have made in my life, it seems this is the only one I regret. This, of course, gives it even more intensity.

The release point for me comes the day I have a new awareness: if I am really as powerful as people have been telling me I am, and given my propensity to want to stay out of the spotlight, hide in the shadows, and crash and burn my life to stay under the radar, if I am ever going to step into my power, strength, and path, I need this degree of intensity, disruption, and conflict to force me into the journey of embracing the stranger within. Otherwise, I might go my whole life with only glimpses of who she is, afraid of her, afraid to embrace her—the very essence of who I am and what is mine to do in the world.

The intensity of this second marriage and the incongruities in my life have been preparing me for this moment. By releasing regret, I am finally able to step into the conversation waiting to be had.

After arriving home from Ontario, I take a deep breath, invite a conversation—which he accepts—and dive in by sharing some of my learning and insight over the last little while. Then I say to him, "I believe the place a marriage needs to reside in is a place of emotional and physical intimacy that we do not have right now and that I do not think we can get back to." He agrees with me and goes further by saying he believes we have been brought together for a reason. Maybe we have not fully gotten to what it is we are to learn with each other.

I agree with the possibility that maybe there is still more to learn with each other. "I am willing to stay in this for a while, for more clarity, but not indefinitely," I say.

We leave the conversation in a surprisingly good place. We both seem to have been in a place of listening and hearing each other, something that has been a challenge for us, each of us rarely feeling heard, seen, or acknowledged by the other.

Following this conversation, I wake up in the middle of the night. I wonder if that conversation really took place or if I dreamed it. It seemed easy. I stop myself mid-thought. "Kathy," I say to myself, "You just said 'Yes to ease' in your life. It is showing up. Stop questioning it. Just say yes."

Days go by. Nothing really seems to change. We have a second conversation. New levels of clarity arise. More days go by, and he invites me into the third conversation. He says to me, "I think you might be right. We might be done."

I am not sure I am hearing correctly. "Okay," I say.

He goes on. "I realized that when I put the family calendar together this year, I forgot to put our anniversary date on it. And we've been married nine years, and nine is the number of completion."

He goes on to make suggestions about what a separation might look like. Much of what he suggests is congruent with my own thoughts. We think we will stay in the neighborhood to provide as little disruption to our son as possible. In the end, this is not possible.

Because of our financial situation, we decide to co-reside a while longer. We will use this time to sort out a few things, particularly around co-parenting. He moves into a different bedroom. We begin to think about how to separate our business. We agree he should keep the company name. It was his when we met. He offers the branding we worked out just the previous year because I felt so passionate about it at the time. Although appreciative of the offer, I feel it is time for me to move on to something completely different for me. I am willing, ready, and needing to let it all go.

We talk about when and how we will let people know, including the children and our parents. As the conversation winds down, I look at him and say, "You realize we have just agreed to separate?"

It is an incredulous moment. We both seem to feel the significance and completeness of it as well as new beginnings in the offing, although there is still much to work through before the new beginnings can really ignite.

We begin a truce that has greater and lesser degrees of ease and unease in it, finding our way in difficult circumstances, in our individual journeys, in a confined physical space. These are exactly the conditions we need to find our way to the next stage of collective and individual journey.

Chapter 11

Meeting the Ancestors at Gold Lake

I walk the road between the cottage I am staying in and the dining room of the retreat center. With each step I take, I feel the drumbeat rippling up through my body, hear it echoing in my mind. It is familiar to me from a vision from the past I had all but forgotten about. The image of the bonfire and the people singing, chanting, and dancing around the fire flashes into my mind, and I feel them here. I am completely present with the drumbeat, even as I am aware of my surroundings in Gold Lake, Colorado.

I do not realize it yet, but I have seen this land before. I traveled over it in my vision during my drumming experience, years before. It is a few days before this recognition fully grabs hold of me. When it does, it descends with waves and waves of shimmery shivers, indicating the truth of what I know, activating, as one of my friends tells me, blood memories.

The shaman at the drumming ceremony in 2000 said, "You never need to journey again. Your first journey tells you everything you need to know. But of course, we do journey again and again."

I had no idea of the power or significance of that drumming. It was an interesting experience at the time, it stayed in my awareness for a while and then faded away among the demands of everyday life—demands that showed up in creating a consulting practice, a difficult marriage, supporting my parents in their health challenges, finding out I was adopted, navigating my mother's dementia, and stewarding the life path of three children.

It was also lost in my own lack of knowledge as to what to do with this spiritual, energetic dimension of what was showing up in my life. Too many times my mind would go to the belief that it was not real and I was making it up.

Now here I am in Gold Lake. Undeniably, indisputably, it is a land I know without knowing it existed before now. I know it from my vision. I know it from my own memories of other times—memories activated by being in this space, on this land where the drumbeat reverberates in every step I take. The image of the bonfire and feeling of celebration is so palpable I do not even need to close my eyes to feel it in my being.

When I first see the invitation for the Art of Hosting on the subject of money in Gold Lake, I am immediately drawn to it. I lose track of how many times I open the invitation to reread it. Every time, I close it again because the incongruity of it does not make sense to me. Its main audience is financial planners—not a particularly compelling draw for me. Its hosting team is comprised of dear, dear friends who certainly do not need my help in hosting—although just to go to hang out with these good people would almost be enough.

Finally I draw tarot cards to give me guidance. I ask two questions: "What is the draw and what is the hesitation?"

The answer to the first question? Stop trying to figure it out logically. I laugh. Good answer.

The answer to the second question? Fear of rejection. I laugh harder. This is what was lurking in the background—fear that my good friends who love me will think I am interfering or inserting myself in a place I have no business being? This is a ludicrous thought. But there it is.

I call one of my friends on the hosting team, to share this with her and to let her know I have decided to come. I tell her she will laugh. She pauses for a brief moment and then she laughs—in a beautiful, welcoming, and delightful way. "Of course you should come," she says.

Days later she calls me back. "Kathy, I know why you are coming to Gold Lake. Because I am doing a one-day vision quest on the land, and you need to do it with me." The excitement in her voice carries across the continent, and I agree. "Okay, I have no idea what I am agreeing to, but I know you are right. Sign me up," I say.

Weeks go by. Now here I am, walking the land and hearing a long-forgotten drumbeat days before our adventure in this vision quest will begin.

Members of the hosting team are skilled at leading vision quests, the kind where there are days of preparation, then three days on the land and then days of debriefing and reintegration afterward. They are a bit concerned about us embarking on a one-day journey, and knowing us both, they fully trust the depth of our individual paths and how our journeys have connected to serve us well in what is before us now.

They are not able to stay on after the training to host us in our vision quest, but they want to make sure we are as prepared as possible. Early in the morning of the first day after my arrival in Gold Lake, we gather with them, the beautiful person who has offered to host us on the day of our vision quest, and others in our community who will be supporting us energetically from a distance during our questing time.

They mention the hole to the underworld. My shape-shifting lion unexpectedly and immediately appears, as if by magic. His appearance transports me back ten years to the drumming circle where he had served me so well. This is my first inkling that these two journeys are linked.

In Gold Lake, in the days leading up to the vision quest, the image of the bonfire and the people singing and dancing around it grows stronger. It vibrates in my being, bringing my attention to my physical surroundings and to the energetic quality of the place that is resonating in me.

One of my friends is in need of healing work. I know it the minute I lay on eyes on him. I ask him, "Tell me about your heartbreak."

He says, "Is it that obvious?"

"Yes, it's that obvious." It is seeping out of his very being.

We talk about when we might do the work, but there seems to be no obvious time because he is on the hosting team. We decide to be alert to opportunity, and of course, the moment to do the work becomes clear. It reaches the point where it must be done. We go for a walk off the trail and into the woods on the mountain, looking for a spot that feels right. We pause at several points along the way, sensing into the terrain.

Finally, we find a spot that feels right. We stop and prepare to do the work. There are sparse trees around the area, and there are stones embedded in the ground that we are walking across. There is a bit of a hill, on which are some rocks we can sit on. The sun is shining down on us. I worry just a bit about whether it will become too hot for us. Despite this, we decide this is the spot and this is the time.

We have been in conversation before about his guides. We already know many of them—what they look like and where they seem to be located in relation to him. We invite them into the space. My friend goes into conversation with each of them, to understand their purpose and what they have to offer him in this moment. By the time we are done a few hours later, his energy and his physical appearance have both shifted.

He calls the healing work shamanic. It is the first time I begin to think of the things I do and the way I can access spirit and guides and help others connect with their guides as shamanic.

Later I understand the significance of this to my journey in Gold Lake. He asks me, "Kathy, who are you?"

I hesitate before replying, with some thoughtfulness, "I am a healer." I know with certainty it is important for me to be involved with this healing work prior to my day on the land, as a reminder of the things I need to be present to, what I am being called to, and what wants to work through me.

At the end of the Art of Hosting training, everyone else prepares to go home. My friend and I and the third person, who has agreed to hold space for us at a base camp while we are out on the land, remain.

While they take care of other things that need tending to, I sit on a rocking chair on the porch of one of the cottages. As I rock, I tune in to the place and the drumbeat. As I hear the drumbeat, the vision of the people singing and dancing around the fire becomes even more vivid.

This is when I know this is the land and the people from my drumming circle vision ten years before. I also know that I heard that drumbeat even as a young child. It was sent to me as a reference point and a reminder. At that time, I did not know what it was. My memories of previous lifetimes and my connection to spirit had already been deeply suppressed; this was part of the walls of protection that had been building up around my heart since the time my birth mother left. The sound of the drumbeat scared me when I was little. I burst into tears as the shape of some of my life became visible in this moment, as I became aware of how the luminous stranger showed up even when I was too young to understand.

The afternoon wears on, and it is time to prepare. We need to purchase a few supplies, including water that we will take out to our questing sites and some food basics for that evening's supper and for when we return from the land. We also need to find and prepare a base camp and the individual sites for the next day.

We take a trip into the nearest little town. We buy water, nuts, dried fruit, granola bars, and a few other high-nutrient snacks to munch on. We also buy orange marking tape, whistles, some rain ponchos, and a few other things for safety during our alone time.

We have agreed between the three of us to honor our time together, from now until we depart, as sacred time, sacred space. After searching out our spots, we will enter silence to more fully enter our solitude.

Our task in this moment is to find our spots. Our host has already scouted out possible spots for the base camp—a place that we will depart from in the morning and return to at dusk and where our host will return to on and off throughout the day to see if we are in need of anything.

As we walk around the area, sensing into the energy, my friend and I both hone in on the same spot for the base camp. It is a spot that our host picked when scouting the area earlier. That message feels pretty clear.

We walk farther to find our solo retreat spots. My friend finds hers first. It is off the path and down into the woods a bit. I walk farther on and find my spot. We were told it would be good to be far enough away that we cannot see each other or hear each other so we will have complete privacy and can do whatever we feel called to do—even wail, if that is what rises up in us.

We mark the entrance points to both sites so we can easily find them the next day.

We return to the base camp site to prepare it. We collect rocks from around the area and create a big circle—big enough for four people to sit in comfortably. Our host finds an interestingly shaped piece of wood that we can use to symbolically mark the entrance to the underworld, an entry point for the journeys we will take.

We sit in the circle—each of us facing in one of the four directions. We try to light sage as an offering. It will not light. We tried earlier at the cottage as we began a check-in together; it wouldn't light there either. It seems this place does not need this kind of offering.

We are silent for a moment. My friend says, "I feel like there is another presence here. Maybe someone who wanted to be here but can't be?"

I tune in to the energetic presence in the same way I have learned to sense and "see" spirit guides. I sense the presence too. I sit with it for a moment. I have the feeling there is a shaman in the circle with us, occupying the empty spot. I check to see if this is my own shaman guide, but it feels different. I get the sense this is a shaman from this land, somehow related to my shaman guide but different. I speak this into our space.

I continue to tune in to the energy. The next thing I know, I am extending his greeting to all of us: "Welcome to this land, to this place. We have been waiting for you." And now, it is not just the shaman, but our circle is rimmed around with ancestors from the land. It dawns on me that these are the ancestors I have been "seeing" singing, dancing, and chanting around the fire. And I know in my heart that I am connected to them and to this land. They are my vision from ten years before. They still dance around the fire, shape-shifting, celebrating, preparing, holding a sacred ritual across time and space.

The shaman continues to speak. "This is a time of great turbulence in the world. It was not unexpected. It is no accident that you are finding each other now. This is a time of great awakening. Many are on this journey from all over. Many across the ages have agreed to congregate in this time to do this work, finding each other across vast geographical distances. It is a time of honoring contracts you have each entered into in a different time and space. You have been together before, more than once. Now is the time you have been preparing for. This is a time to walk with one foot in the physical world and one foot in the nonphysical world, traversing both with ease. It is time to renew yourselves, to wake more fully, to contribute to the renewal and nourishment the world and its people are craving now.

"We are here to assist you in this journey. You have important work to do in the world. You do not do it alone." I am really tapped into the energy of the place. These entities are clear to me on a visual plane beyond the physical. I "see" them, I sense them, and I feel like an extension of them.

I say to our host, "You do not need to be concerned when you are not at the base camp. If we need you, the shaman will let you know."

We eventually leave the base camp and head back to the cottage we are sharing to do whatever it is we need to do to settle into the night and prepare for dawn. We will be heading out before first light, around 4:00 a.m.

As we settle in for the night, thunder rumbles low and loudly over the cottage. Lightning flashes outside our windows, lighting up the room. While thunder and lightning storms are common in this place, they usually occur in the afternoon. One at night like this is unusual. But, of course, it is a raging storm. I take this as a sign—of welcome, of preparation for what is ahead of us this day. The shaman and the ancestors dance all night around the fire, preparing the space for us; they make a joyously raucous sound with the rhythmic pattern of the drumbeat. Even as I write this, years later, I am transported back to that time and place, and tears stream down my face.

As early morning approaches in that time just before the dawn, I find it easy to get up. I wear layers of clothing, prepared for the cool start of the day, heat later in the day, and the inevitable rain that comes midafternoon. I pack my journal and some tarot cards. I pick up my water and head out. I am ready. We had agreed we would each depart for the site separately. Our host left earlier to prepare himself and the site. Then my friend. Then me.

My shape-shifting lion joins me this morning, excited and spirited. We walk to the base camp together, looking for the markers leading into the site.

The path from the retreat center to our base camp is carved out of a hillside. On the right of the path is the lake—Gold Lake. To the left of the path is a sloped hill. The hill is barren for a spell—low-lying grass and the large rock surfaces that are so much a part of this landscape. Beyond that, higher up on the hill, are trees.

As I walk the path in the dim light of early day, something on the periphery of my vision on the left-hand side, up the hill, catches my attention. I pause to look. My breath stops. There is a deer running lightly down the hillside. She will cross my path. Except she does not. She catches sight of me and stops. For the longest moment, when I am sure I am not breathing, we stare into each other's eyes, both standing stock still. And then she turns around and runs back up the hill and disappears into the woods.

After a moment, I start breathing again and continue my walk to the base camp site.

Our host begins by asking again if we are ready for this day. He speaks to each of the directions and gives us some words of guidance. We are to leave something in the circle to represent our intention to come back from our journey. I leave a little rose-quartz angel. He tells us that as we leave, we are leaving ourselves behind and we will come back transformed.

As soon as he opens the circle, my lion jumps up excitedly and says to me, "What are you waiting for?" I laugh and immediately get to my feet. We head out down the path, my lion literally dancing all around me to the site I chose the night before for my solo time on the land.

I am here with deep intention. What is the portal I need to open in order to more fully step into my gifts—particularly my gifts as a healer?

We—my lion and I—arrive at my site. I sit for a moment, taking a breath. I walk around in a little exploration. Just down from the path is a level, secluded bit of land shaped like a platform. The ground is covered with brown needles from the trees, likely deposited over several years. This level platform is ringed with trees and feels like a protected space. It is a great place for me to set up camp. Before I do so, I wander around a bit more to get my bearings.

Beyond this little secluded sanctuary of space is open land. I feel as though I am literally at the top of a mountain looking down over a deep ravine, with grassy slopes all around leading down to a little valley-like area where a stream wanders through the land. In the distance, on either side of this little valley, are mountain ranges. The view is spectacular. As I stand on the mountainside, I feel stirrings within me, memories of other times in this place. The whispering of my spirit, the stranger within, calling me back to memories from other times.

On the other side of the path is more hill, covered with trees—the same trees the deer emerged from and retreated into just a short time beforehand. I can climb higher, though I will be surrounded by trees and unable to see the view of the valley.

After getting my bearings, I go back to the spot I have selected for my sanctuary space. I gather rocks to create a little circle, just for me. When the circle is complete, I lay out a blanket to sit and lie on as I feel moved. I am compelled to gather flowers to place in my circle as an offering. I find myself gathering little pinecones and building a symbolic bonfire at one side of my circle. None of this is planned. It emerges in the moment.

When my circle is complete, I sit in it and draw a breath. To my immense surprise, I feel the shaman sitting with me. This I did not expect. He is such a powerful entity; I am humbled.

I ask him, "Why are you here, with me?" I am under the impression he was to guide the overall questing experience, not specifically show up in my space.

He says to me, "I am partly responsible for calling you here. It is why the pull of the invitation to Gold Lake was irresistible. You are my people. We are your people. You have really important work to do today. I am here to help guide you through it."

What is it that I am supposed to work on? I wonder.

"You know that belief you have—that you are not really powerful, that this is not real, that you are not a healer? This is what you need to work on," he says to me.

"Oh," I say. "That one." Hmm, that little one. It rings so true for me; I know it is the work I am to do here.

At first it is hard to even sit. My body is unable to hold itself upright. I have to lie down. It is hard to hear the drumbeat and hard to feel the power and the energy of the land. I allow myself to rest on the land and enter a meditative state.

After a time, my work for the morning becomes clear. Past lives begin showing up in my awareness—some of which I have known about and some of which are just appearing in this moment. Integration is the work I am here to do; I am invited to integrate these past lives into who I am now, reclaiming the gifts that each of these characters brings, welcoming them home in their wholeness. Some, such as a barbarian,

I'm not quite sure what to do with at first, but I then realize this also provides aspects of me to welcome home. So I do. Some are entities from different dimensions, such as the fairy realm. I see connections between people I know and love in this lifetime and see also the connections from other lifetimes I shared with them—some in powerful circumstances.

For a while, I welcome clear and individual integration. Later I welcome all I have experienced but am not aware of in this moment with this silent invitation—*come home, bring your gifts and your wholeness.* I literally feel each successive integration in my body. I feel both the energetic impact within my body and a physical sensation related to each integration.

When it is complete, I sit for a while. I lie down again. This time I can feel the rhythmic drumbeat of the land, the power and energy of this place. After a spell, I gratefully thank the shaman for his guidance and support. I tell him I am ready to exit this circle for a bit. It is time to journal. He is gracious and releases me from the circle. I go higher on the mountain and sit in the warmth of sunshine to capture some of my impressions from this work.

Later, in another inquiry, despair, worry, guilt, and anguish arise in me. One of my guides helps me with this by putting them in separate labeled buckets. As these emotions are poured into their respective buckets, they are transformed into hope, joy, and inspiration. Then they are integrated back into my being in this transmuted form. It is surprisingly effortless as I allow my guides to do this healing work with me—gifts they are always ready and available to offer whenever I tune in.

The shaman tells me to go to the valley—that something will be revealed to me there. I head to the valley; marking my path as I go so I can later find my way back to my site. I find a tree to share space with. I hear the drumbeat of the land. As I look up at how far I have traveled, it appears to be a great distance, but the trip did not take an extraordinary amount of time.

I root with the tree and also move up its branches, where my lion finds me and travels with me again. I embrace the energy of this tree space—belief and trust—and wrap my arms around the tree, wanting to also integrate it into my being, my energetic field.

I am told during my time sitting with this tree that it is my job to go deep. The people I need to work with will find me. I will get to work on some extraordinary projects.

After a bit, I notice that dark clouds are moving in, and I must move back to my sacred space as a light rain begins to drizzle, before the lightning starts.

I move into my next inquiry, which is about the next level of consciousness that I am to work on. The shaman says to me, "It is time to go beyond the lone wolf, to really bring collaboration forth, and to request it in the work you do; to not be afraid of how much it costs. It is time to dive into your intuitive wisdom. As a natural healer, you can heal yourself too. You have a deep grasp of human nature. You have a deep knowledge of the world that comes from the heart."

As the day goes on, I am aware of my lack of consciousness of time. This day is like time out of time, like it is not part of chronos or chronological time at all. I am in kairos time, a time between, a moment of indeterminate time. I feel no hunger, no urgency, no restlessness. I am completely present to this day and what is unfolding.

In what I know is the afternoon, I find myself standing on the mountainside, looking out over the valley. Moment by moment passes. After awhile, I realize I have been standing in complete and utter stillness for a long time, maybe hours. My work in this spot is to be in conversation with each of the guides I know to be present for me in this work. They each have a story, and they each have gifts that I am to be made aware of.

I know as I stand in this place that I have stood here before. I have played in this valley. It is possible that in a time before time I was even a shape-shifter in this place, literally shifting form from human to animal spirit and back again, jumping off of cliffs and flying through the air with grace, agility, playfulness, and speed. I can see it my mind and feel the sensations of it in my body.

In an age after that, I am the medicine woman I have met before—the medicine woman who is related to my shaman guide, the one who has traveled with me for some years now. She is his granddaughter. She has been dormant in me—in my consciousness, in my lineage—for a long time. Even though I have known her, known of her, only now is she becoming activated in a big way. She also seems to be a granddaughter of the shaman I am meeting in this place.

She is with me, in me, and of me as I stand on the mountainside, entering into deeper relationship with the many guides who are ready to share the most amazing gifts with me. With each sharing, I grow a connection and understanding to the stranger in me.

The shaman says to me, "You are a very gifted medicine woman. You healed people. You could see into the future and knew this time was coming. It is part of your soul journey and part of your soul choices to be here now. You knew you would be born into difficult circumstances, and you accepted that as part of the journey, part of the awakening and illumination process.

"You are well protected by guides who love you very much, some of whom shared a lifetime experience with you where you shared a deep connection. You have great capacity for love, beauty, and grace. These are gifts. Your great capacity for love will be stretched by people, challenging circumstances, and other situations that will invite your heart to break open beyond anything you can imagine possible in this moment. It will carry you into and through situations you believe are next to impossible. You also have incredible courage and wisdom that comes from enduring depth."

I notice that I am afraid of these guides and their power. They are formidable. It is hard to acknowledge they are part of my retinue of support. Why me? How is that even possible? The guides say, "Our power is really your power. While it is formidable, you are quite capable of it. You are already growing into it. We will always be here to support, guide, and nourish you. You are allowed to trust."

New levels of integration and groundedness flow into my being. I can feel the energy of the mountain, of this place. It feels like home. I know I will bring it home with me, internalized in my being and my consciousness. I have stripped away aspects of who I am, who I thought myself to be, and will embrace an expanded view of who I am now, releasing the stranger within from the bonds I have ensnared her in.

As dusk falls, I feel the completeness of my experience on the land. I send waves and waves of gratitude to my guides for this journey, to the ancestors, and to the shaman, whom I have over the course of this day come to call the Shaman of Shamans or the Grandfather of Grandfathers. He was—is—a grandfather to me; of this I am certain.

I pack up my space, leaving the pinecone fire and the offering of flowers at my site. I walk back to base camp, greet our host, and sit with him for a few minutes before heading back to the cottage. Our agreement is that we will stay in silence until nine o'clock the next morning.

I am still in a sense of timelessness. I am not hungry, although the only thing I have taken in all day is water. And I have expanded my consciousness and awareness beyond anything I would have thought possible.

The next morning, the three of us convene at nine o'clock at our base camp for storytelling. The Shaman of Shamans and the ancestors join us. I sense that because of their awareness of what was coming in the ages ahead, they made a decision to shift out of this physical dimension and into another one to be watchful and provide spiritual guidance as invited. Many were part of that family and made the decision to continue the soul journey across lifetimes in this physical dimension. It is a story of my experience and of what I am sensing.

My friend and I each share stories of our experiences. Our host also has stories to tell that correspond to each of our experiences. One time, on a visit to the base camp, as he arrived back, there was a deer standing directly behind the spot in the circle where I had sat. I have no doubt it was the same deer I had met on the pathway as my solo day began.

Twice when our host came back to the site, the angel I had left behind had moved. The first time, he thought maybe he was imagining it, so he took special note. The next time he was certain. He asks me, "What is the significance of the angel?"

I say to him, "Before I came to Gold Lake, I left an identical one with my youngest son, to remind him I am close in his heart, even if geographically I am far away."

It is a beautiful round of storytelling that helps integrate the whole experience before we depart from Gold Lake. It is hard to leave the base camp. Our host asks if we want to visit our solo sites. Neither of us feels the need to. I cannot go back. My work there was complete. It is time to move forward now.

I have the good fortune of going to visit a friend in Boulder overnight before getting on a plane and heading home. It is an opportunity for more storytelling and witnessing, a greater depth of integration and preparedness to reenter the craziness of the world and the life awaiting me back home. I do not travel alone. The Shaman of Shamans and the ancestors come with me.

Their presence is immediately apparent the instant I turn my thoughts to them. Others can also sense them. After my Gold Lake experience, I go for a massage with a gifted friend to help ground this experience in my physical body. She focuses a lot of attention on my hands and feet. Afterward she says to me, "The ancestors wanted to bless your feet for the places you will walk, your hands for the people you will touch. They love you very much."

This I know. They love me. They help make my journey to openheartedness possible, inviting me to stretch in ways I never would have thought possible; to open in ways I would have thought damaging; to meet the stranger within in her truest form, as pure essence, soul quality; to strip away the fear, uncertainty, and shadow that are smoke and mirrors; to develop trust, strength, courage, and wisdom, and to embrace all that is showing up on my path with joy, love, delight, playfulness, and strength I did not know was in me. The depth of presence that begins to emerge for me is only possible because of the guidance and presence of these beautiful and amazing nonphysical guides.

CHAPTER 12

THE VEIL OF DEMENTIA

One day I am sitting with my mother in the long-term care facility that is now her home. She has lost most of her ability to string words together, let alone sentences or fully formed thoughts. I have met my sister but have not spoken to my mother about this journey. Early on, I did not know what impact it might have, and now I know there is nothing she can share with me, because her memories seem to be gone. Even if they are not gone, she no longer has a capacity to speak more than a few words before becoming confused about her own lack of communication ability.

This day we are sitting in a room that is used by families when residents die. When it is not in use by families, it is available for whoever chooses to go there. My mother likes this room and is in it a lot, usually by herself. She likes the quiet and the solitude. Today she is sitting in a wingback chair.

Out of the blue, my mother says to me, "How is your sister?"

I am stunned. I do not know how to respond. If there is an opportunity here to know something of my mother and her story in relation to me and my sister, I would love to have it emerge.

Warily, I ask her, "What sister, Mom?"

She looks confused. There is no moment. Carefully watching her, I decide on a different approach. "She's fine," I say.

My mother nods, looks away, is no longer confused. I am left with a question that is more like a certainty. My mother knows. Maybe the physical expression of her does not know, but the spiritual expression of her knows. Just as I was not supposed to know my birth mother, was my mother not supposed to be involved in my life after my sister reentered it? Who is to know? What I do know is that there is more going on here than the physical eye can see. There is a whole soul journey that supersedes the human tragedy story.

While my spiritual journey and physical walking of the path is deepening, life continues to unfold in its many twists and turns. It brings an abundance of opportunities for choice of story and of how to live into the experiences. Life calls me to consciousness and intentionality over and over again. I respond in the imperfectness of my humanity, sometimes well, sometimes less well, sometimes with more awareness, and sometimes with less awareness, but with a growing willingness to be on the edges of my own learning.

My mother's journey into long-term care is one that fully invites me into the exploration of perspective—story that arises from the human tragedy lens or soul-journey perspective?

I always thought I viewed her journey from soul journey, and that was true, to a certain degree. I discover I am barely scratching the surface and have so many deeper levels to traverse.

During the celebration of my parents' fiftieth wedding anniversary, Mom was pretty good during most of the gathering that my brother and I hosted in their home. She had a few inappropriate moments and made some strange comments to friends—bizarre little behavior quirks. We toasted their fifty years. I offered a few words of gratitude to my parents for their journey, their hospitality, their love, and their unconditional acceptance. Although the knowledge of my adoption was a new story to my brother and me, fresh in the days just previous to this celebration, this undercurrent is not obviously at play during our afternoon together.

My parents' friends were gracious. By the time people were getting ready to go, Mom decided she had also had enough. She headed out the front door with some of the guests. One of them came back in to let me know she was going out the front door. I had been watching her, so I was aware. I watched out the window as she walked down the driveway and disappeared for a few minutes. A bit later she came in the back door. When we asked her where she had been, she said, "In the car." In the car. As if it were perfectly normal for her to be there. It ass her pattern, one of them anyway. She was done, ready to go, so she went and sat in the car. Did she realize she was already home, or had enough time passed she figured she had arrived?

My parents' fiftieth anniversary was the same time we began the process for my mother to go into long-term care. Taking care of her was an increasing strain on my dad. He was unwilling to admit it, but he was exhausted. She was having problems holding her bladder—sometimes when she was out somewhere with Dad, and other times at night. She became more and more adamant about going home when she was ready. When Mom and Dad came to my house for special occasion dinners, when she ws ready to go, she put on her coat and went out to sit in the car. She needed to be distracted to keep her inside longer, but the pull in her to leave was strong.

One long weekend, Dad decided to take her to visit my brother in Prince Edward Island. The morning after they arrive, Robert called me. "Well. Just wanted to let you know they are headed home."

"What?" I am confused. "They only just got there."

Chuckling, Robert said, "Yeah, well . . . they took the ferry over, and Mom could not figure out why they had to drive and drive and then take the boat only to get off again after a few minutes. Then, after dinner, she put her coat on and got ready to leave. We convinced her to go to bed. It took a bit of doing, but when she got up this morning, she was still ready to go. So they are on their way home."

Is there a homing instinct that gets activated in us as we age? Or is that more likely to happen with people who are experiencing the veil of dementia? I do not know the answer, but it has me curious.

My mother developed all kinds of new idiosyncrasies in her behavior. One time when I was visiting we went upstairs to her room. I was taking stock of what she needed—bras, underwear, socks. We went through a lot of her stuff. She came across sweaters I had given her as gifts. She said to me, "Oh, here are your sweaters." I replied, "No, Mom. Those are your sweaters. I gave them to you as gifts."

She nodded. "Oh." And put them back in the drawer. She had enough awareness to know they came from me, but not so much as to connect it as a gift to her.

Every time I visited after this, Mom took me upstairs to go through her drawers. Every single time, she tried to give me back the sweaters I had given her. Every time. She also went into the living room and brought out a beautiful figurine of a woman dressed in a flowing blue dress. "Here," she said as she offered it to me. "This is yours."

"No," I said to her. Every time. "It is yours. I gave it to you as a gift."

She looked at it curiously, as if something does not make quite sense, turned around, and took it back into the living room. Every time I visited, this scene played itself out.

She also tucked little folded-up tissues and toilet paper everywhere. Under her pillow. In drawers. In her purse. Under things. And she filled the toilet with toilet paper. Dad had to go behind her to make sure she did not flush it all down, although flushing was another one of those simple everyday tasks she had forgotten how to do.

When we began the process for long-term care, we were told it would take six to nine months to have her placed in Harbourview Haven, which is in Lunenburg. I said to Dad, "You know, when they call, she will have to go. We will not be able to say no, or she will go back to the bottom of the list and we will have to start all over again."

You can know this intellectually, but it is a whole different story when you get the call. It came sooner than we expected, in just five months. Within a week of getting the call, we moved her out of her home of more than thirty years and into a little shared room in an institution that people move to when they are preparing to die. She never wanted to go there. No one ever does. There is only one way out.

It is one of the most heartbreaking decisions I have ever had to participate in, and easily the most difficult decision we have ever made as a family. The only saving grace is that it is in the town my mother lived in most of her life. Dear friends of our family work there. But that does not make it any easier as we all try to hold back the tears. Neither does the fact that she follows us out to the door, ready to go home with us.

When I leave Lunenburg the next day, I take the figurine of the beautiful woman in the flowing blue dress with me. Now it is mine. I put her on the shelf of my desk where other symbols of my journey also reside. I realize with a little flicker of recognition that this figurine looks like one of my spirit guides. Maybe my mother could see more than I knew or understood. I am awed.

At first, I am able take her out for little trips. I drive her to a neighboring town. We go for ice cream. She sits with her ice cream for a while before she figures out what to do with it. She watches me. She mimics my actions, whether it is eating ice cream or buckling her seat belt. She is sly about it, but I see what she does.

We even bring her to my home for Christmas dinner that first year. But it is not long before being out of Harbourview is just too difficult for her. She goes from walking to sitting in a wheelchair, which she uses to motor around the dementia ward, to moving less and less.

My mother, who never let me sleep in, now refuses to get out of bed most mornings—making up for lost time, maybe. She never complains—and almost never did—although now she is known to suggest that some people should be thrown out the window! Did dementia remove a filter, allowing her inside voice to become an outside voice, giving her freedom to say things she would have been horrified to say before dementia struck her?

I am only able to understand my mother's situation from the perspective of soul journey. Nothing else makes sense. The human story is pure tragedy. Why would an otherwise perfectly healthy individual lose her sense of life and of who she is, or who she was? It is senseless. This senselessness is what takes me more and more to soul-journey perspective. If, before she manifested into human form, she made decisions about what she wanted to experience in this lifetime, maybe decreasing cognitive awareness is part of that soul exploration. How do I know? How does anybody know?

I am aware that even though she does not talk much and her thoughts seem all jumbled and incoherent, she brightens up when she sees people she knows and loves. It takes longer as time goes by, but it still happens. When I walk into the dementia ward of the long-term care facility that is now her home, her eyes light up when she sees me. Does she know I'm her daughter? I do not know. But she sure knows that she knows me, and she knows that she loves me and that I love her back.

It is this language of love that is causing me to shift perspective on my mother and her dementia.

She still knows what she wants and is adamant about it. She goes on hunger strikes and refuses to eat. There is no forcing things. It would not work if they tried. The staff at Harbourview Haven know this. I have no doubt she wants to be acknowledged for her choices. She accepts the milkshakes they give her that are full of the nutrients she needs to minimally sustain her physical body. It is a choice she makes.

My mother's world shrinks dramatically. She does too. Physically she loses a lot of weight, shrinking to skin and bones. She loses her vibrancy and joy in life and her ability to comfort others.

She is still a human being. She is in her journey, in her way, in her soul's calling. I would only be fooling myself if I did not recognize that she is in a transition from the vitality of a full physical life to what is behind the veil. The rest of her will catch up when the timing is right, when she is ready.

I reconcile that this is no longer the woman who raised me. I need to be present to the woman who is here now. In the early days she still spoke, but her words were jumbled and incoherent, not making sense. If I respond to her incoherence as if it is a fully formed thought and create a repartee with her, her spirits are fine. If I get stressed or upset, she does too.

On one visit, I wonder if I can reach her in another way. What if I could shift my consciousness to a different plane, to a meditative state, touching the more universal consciousness? What might happen then?

I shift into meditation but keep my eyes on my mother, who is staring out the window. As I feel my consciousness shift, my mother turns to look directly at me, a look of surprise on her face. There is no doubt in my being that I have made contact with her. It is fleeting, but I know the pathway now. I know I can do it from anywhere; I do not have to be in the same room with her. Our consciousness travels beyond the geography of the physical world. I become more curious about consciousness and the nonphysical component of her journey—of anyone's journey. Long-term care is an intense learning laboratory for this inquiry.

To get to the dementia ward in what everyone in the town calls "the home," you enter the front door of the building, walk a short corridor past the administration offices, and enter through an electronically locked door into the main residential part of the building. You then have to walk down a long corridor to get to the dementia ward, which is behind yet another locked door.

As you enter the residential part of the building, your senses are assaulted. You come upon people—old people, and in some cases really old people—in wheelchairs or chairs, just sitting there for the most part, most of them nodding off. Those are the ones well enough to be sitting up. As you go down the corridor, rooms are on either side, and in most of them, someone is lying on a bed, oblivious to the rest of the world. Sleeping, snoring, unaware. And as good as this place is—and I do believe it is one of the best—it smells of old people waiting to die; sometimes less so, sometimes more so. It is a hard corridor to walk with regularity, knowing that the shape of these people's lives has shifted so dramatically.

I often wonder as I walk through the long-term care facility filled with very old, sleepy people, to the dementia ward in back, what the meaning of life is when you are so old and incapacitated, just waiting to die or living in your own little demented world with a whole bunch of other people also living in their own little demented worlds? Up to this moment, I have always thought of these people as waiting to die.

We all know the only way people come out of long-term care is in a coffin. This is where some of our population go to die when their loved ones can no longer take care of them.

During one visit with my mother, I sit on her bed with her, maintaining physical touch the whole time. When she looks at me, we hold eye contact. She smiles and even laughs. So do I, sometimes with my tears flowing. The rest of the time, I watch her lift her head to look very intently at things I cannot see all around her room. It is clear to me that spirit is gathering, although less clear to me is when she will finally decide to let go of her physical body. We, her family, are becoming more ready as we walk this path her.

For some reason, during this visit with my mom, I have a little revelation. I do not know why it never occurred to me before, but I am glad it has now. It expands my awareness of what else just might be going on in the corridors we walk to get to the dementia ward.

My spiritual journey over the last dozen years or so has shown me pathways to altered consciousness, to spirit journeying, and to spirit guides, angels, and other entities. I am aware that it is possible to "travel" in dream states—sleeping and waking—and that much good and healing work can happen in these states of altered awareness and consciousness.

As I sit with my mother and observe her looking at that which she can see and I cannot, I all of a sudden become aware that her physical body might be old and weak and her brain injured, as they say at the home, but her spirit or soul is strong. When I visit with my mother now, I am not visiting with the personality and the ego that inhabited her body for all those years before she developed dementia. I am visiting with her in the spirit of her soul's journey. If I can look past unbrushed teeth, unkempt hair, incoherence, and my own sorrow for the loss of this vibrant woman and mother in my life, I can be with her in spirit. It is her spirit that shines through her eyes with delight when she sees me. Her soul is connecting with my soul, and she is relating to me on the level of soul, not the level of this physical plane.

I begin to wonder just where, how far, and how often she may be journeying while her physical body sleeps or appears unconscious. That thought takes me to all the sleeping bodies throughout the whole facility. A curiosity dawns within me. Where might some of those souls be journeying to while their physical bodies sleep? I am sure some of them may well be wrestling with their own demons, so to speak, but who is to say that most of them are not off doing much-needed soul work in ordinary and extraordinary reality.

This is a soul's journey obscured by the human tragedy story; it is so obvious when entering this building. The human tragedy story is so apparent that it obliterates the soul-journey perspective for many. It is hard to see beyond the sights, sounds, and smells assaulting your senses as you walk the halls. For many, this is so blinding that it is impossible to see anything more. It is impossible to see the fullness and vibrancy that exists just beyond the veil.

It is such a small leap for me that I do not know why it has not occurred to me before. Now I am aware of a bubble of light surrounding this home. The notion that these beautiful souls might be making contributions to the world that most of us cannot see or understand makes my own spirit more joyful. Now I hold my mother's journey with an added degree of lightness and joy that I have no doubt she feels. She is journeying well and will continue to do so; I have no doubt about that. She is a great teacher for me. I love her, and she knows it.

CHAPTER 13

EMBRACING THE STRANGER IN ME

In the year and a bit since I found out I was adopted, my journey has been intense. The adoption story is only part of it, of course. I never know when the intensity of the journey will hit me or what the focus will be.

In a phone session with the coach, the one who helped me connect or reconnect to my spirit guides, amplifying my spiritual journey, I find myself in healing work around my mothers—my birth mother and my mother who raised me.

We are in a visualization process to access the deep sorrow I am experiencing now. I see three females standing on an arc—my birth mother on one end, my mother in the middle, and a young girl at the other end. The young girl is some form of me, of the stranger in me. In my years of lost joy, too much responsibility, and too much tension, she has been hiding, stashed away in a closet somewhere.

It has not been safe for her to come out and play. She has not felt invited or welcome anyway.

I did not expect to see her. She is here to observe. What will happen now?

I am with them, standing on the straight line that stretches from one end of the arc to the other.

I turn first to my mother. As I step into her energy, it is as if a veil of emotion lightly sprinkles over me, starting at the top of my head and moving down to my toes—sadness and fear. She is holding a baby, and she is connected to my father by an elastic rope. She moves toward and away from him. If she moves too far, the rope snaps her back. She is remorseful that she has been given this gift (me) and that she carries so much fear around the gift. She also fears that she has not done as good a job with her gift as she hoped or has not lived up to some standard she felt she was entrusted with. We work with what she needs now. I see a shimmer of joy and peace come back into her. She stands straighter. When it is time to release the cord that attaches her to my father, she has to do it on her own time. She takes several deep breaths, turns toward him, plants her feet firmly, and removes the cord timidly. She is both afraid of him and for him and is concerned about what might happen as she releases the cord. One of my guides—the one represented by the figurine my mother insisted I have—works with her, embracing her, offering her the relief of forgiveness.

Then my attention goes to my birth mother. The emotional experience with her is one of conflict, confusion, and deep shame. I have an image of these emotions within her, beginning with her head, going down through her body and out her feet, and emanating right into her lineage—as though she carries shame that is hers and is also well beyond her as part of her lineage. This image of energy flow comes several times.

An image of two sets of bookends arises—one is from around the period of time starting when my birth mother left when Deb was three years old and then after she and Deb reconnected thirty years later. The other set is around both ends of my life, with no overlapping experience with my birth mother.

Her message to me is that I was born very gifted and she was not to tarnish my gifts. She carried deep shame around her two girls throughout her life.

When we work with what she needs, I see layers and layers peel off and drop away until this shimmering, very beautiful woman stands there. I see a cord between her and Deb—who is angry that she was twice rejected by her mother and never publicly acknowledged as her daughter. I invite her to release this cord. She does so with loving tenderness, blowing kisses in Deb's direction.

I can feel the release and surrender in my own body as well as see it in hers.

As she releases, the little girl who has been standing on the other side of the arc, observing, jumps right into me! I feel it immediately. She stretches into my body to see what it feels like. I move with her, my body and my facial expressions reflecting her experience. She says "I'm *free!*" Truly, truly amazing.

I have shifted once more and moved more deeply into who I am and what I am being called to do.

The last message to me during this visualization is about confirmation. As my birth mother is leaving, she opens a portal showing me how much more support is available to me and the potential for my gifts. She invites me to continue to step fully into those gifts and to bring them to the world in all their beauty and glory.

It remains to be seen if I am courageous enough to do this.

Almost three months after my Gold Lake experience, I attend the first Shamanic Convergence in Nova Scotia. I had seen a flyer for this event a few months before. Once I went Gold Lake, I knew I had to attend this gathering.

I am stressed about attending. It is September, the beginning of a year. My soon-to-be ex-husband and I are still co-residing, and business is scarce for both of us. We are in the deepest debt load and our lowest capacity to be responsive to arising needs that we have been in during our whole marriage and business partnership. I cannot see my way on this path. I do not see how we will ever find the financial resources to begin to live each in our own home.

I am not living the gift of knowing I received years before between my first and second marriages as I began to walk the path of starting a business, as I was trying to understand my way into that next movement in my life: knowing that stress comes from living in my head, and projecting what I am living now into my future because I cannot see what has yet to unfold on that path. It is hard to move beyond feeling trapped by circumstances at times. Yet knowing myself and my journey beyond the confines of this projection is essential, as is letting go of fear and calling my attention to living in this present moment.

In this present moment I am fine. It is a lesson I need to call myself back to over and over again. In this moment, I am fine. I do not serve myself by creating a future story about my life that traps me. Stress keeps me stuck. It feeds off itself. Letting go of the projection of this stressed current reality is not irresponsible—although my mind would have me believe so. Facing the facts in my current reality does not help me imagine into a new story. Imagining into the future that is calling me is the story that inspires the present moment.

I arrive at the Convergence stressed. Dollarwise and timewise, I should not be attending another conference, although both time and money were committed months before. Guilt tells me time should be spent in developing business materials or writing or some other "doing" thing. But the doing inspired by fear and stress is frantic, desperate activity, not intentional journey or path, not acknowledging knowing that comes from being grounded and centered.

Worry and fear impact lines of communication with spirit and with my ability to receive. I feel more stuck. More trapped. I do not know how to move, how to release the fear or surrender into the uncertainty. As I arrive at the Shamanic Convergence and settle in, I relax into where I am. I decompress. I open up and become ready for new experiences.

I have brought my drum. After returning home from Gold Lake, a friend suggested I make a drum and told me who could help me with this. I felt called to make this an activity with my youngest son. We spent a day with a friend who is also at the Shamanic Convergence. I bring my drum; this is the first opportunity I have to use it in a group, in ceremony, with ritual.

I experience what it is like to become a hollowed wood to receive spirit flowing through me. I witness another participant resisting the call of spirit and see how challenged, almost tortured, he is in his being because of his resistance. I do not feel a call of my own to be a messenger on behalf of our group. I feel a bit disappointed, but witnessing the struggle in this other person makes it clear to me that I have not been called in this moment. If I had been, I would know.

A sweat lodge is being offered. I know I am to take part, although I have no idea what to expect. I am a bit trepidatious. I do not fare well in heat. I have no idea if I will be able to withstand the intense heat of the sweat lodge.

I surprise myself. We are led in the offering of prayers. There are three or four rounds of sweat with the opportunity to step outside between rounds. I step out after the first round for a breath of air. I return.

In the second round, deep in the prayer, we are invited to speak or sing out loud, trusting no one is specifically listening to any other individual but we are all there for our own journey, our own healing.

Somewhere in this round, I discover a new voice in me. But it is not new. It is ancient. The sound emanating out of my throat is not a sound I could consciously make or replicate. I am in a primal place with a primal voice. It is new to me now, but it is not new to me at all. It is the voice of my timeless self—the voice of the medicine woman who has been emerging since my Gold Lake experience. This call, which I have uttered forth from my throat in ceremony and ritual, is not forgotten in my blood memories, in my cellular memories. I have come back to a new level of integration, a new level of healing. And she is just beginning to emerge, this medicine woman. She will become more prominent over the next few months as I journey to Bowen Island and Brazil and other places in between. She will show up unexpectedly and beautifully until I capture her essence to stand in her power and strength in the way she is calling me. She is one manifestation of the glorious stranger in me.

I leave the Shamanic Convergence with an unexpected gift: the articulation of a personal purpose statement. It is full of meaning. "From this place of deep rootedness in my spiritual lineages, I boldly bring my healing gifts to the shifting shape of the world and the regeneration of its people." As this statement emerges for me, it carries energetic surges. Each part of the statement carries deep meaning. It resonates in my being, singing to my soul, inviting me to my path, compelling me.

It leaves a residue easily activated now. It stays with me in the challenges that continue to show up.

My soon-to-be ex-husband and I continue to co-reside for a few more months, trying to get a handle on our situation and our finances. I still feel stuck. A friend tells me I need to let go of the house we are living in. I am reluctant to do so. We have both agreed that I will stay in it and he will find another house in our neighborhood. We are both challenged in manifesting the financial resources to make this happen. It seems we may be in this living arrangement indefinitely, if logic and finances are our guiding influences. However, a lesson in manifestation is looming.

The day of decision leading to movement dawns clearly. There is a wicked blowup between us that shakes loose the stuckness. Without knowing how, it becomes abundantly clear to me that it is time to let go. In tears that refuse to stop, I tally the finances, call a lawyer, and find a handyman. He calls a real estate agent. We draft a separation agreement, the basis of which is to sell the house and pay off all the debt, knowing that once the debt is paid off, there will be little remaining; this is part of the "reality" that has kept us stuck—the story we have individually and together been giving life to. Now we begin to look at options for moving to a neighborhood we can afford to move into separately.

The handyman is amazing. He works with us to figure out exactly what needs to be fixed or modified. He finds ways to work small miracles that I am sure save us thousands of dollars—like salvaging a shower stall in our basement I was sure would need to be completely replaced because it had been used extensively by a motley collection of teenagers over the years and was dirty looking no matter how hard I scrubbed.

While little repairs are being done to the house, I energetically say my good-byes and prepare it for new owners. Each time I go for a run in our neighborhood, when I come back, I circle around back to the stream, sit on my little meditation rock in the middle of the stream, and do energetic releasing work. Then I circle round the other side of the house, saying good-bye and inviting the house and property to be welcoming for whoever comes next.

Our real-estate agent has the most amazing pictures of our house taken for the listing. The house is listed on a Saturday afternoon. Sunday we have two showings, and Sunday night we have an offer. The person making the offer wants to move quickly. We accept the offer. Our house sells in just twenty-four hours, even though others on our street have been for sale for months, even a year. I knew it would sell quickly; I just did not imagine it could be this quickly.

While the showings are being held, I find my new home. I saw it on the Internet, just recently listed. My youngest son and I drive by it Sunday morning and notice that there is an open house in the afternoon. We come back for the open house. I love the house—the look, feel, decorating, backyard, size. It feels as though it were made for me and my children. It is waiting for me. There is an offer on the house already, but it is conditional.

When we accept the offer on our old house, I make an appointment with the agent to come back and look at my house again and to also look at two others. The other houses have no real appeal to me. I know my new home.

I put an offer in, asking the owner to move within three weeks. This means he will have to put his stuff in storage for a month until he can move into his new place. He accepts the offer. The house is mine!

I am dazed and amazed. For a long time I have been muddling around in my journey, feeling stuck, feeling the unchanging nature of my core story. In a matter of moments, it seems, things have moved at lightning speed. The stuck things, the impossible things, have all moved so swiftly that it almost does not seem real. What has put life in motion with such speed? I am deeply curious. This is a lesson I want to embody. There was absolute clarity; the conditions were in place to take the leap into the void, because there was no staying in the current circumstance any longer and there was no going back. The path had to emerge.

I am amazed at what has happened; I never could have imagined it once I let go of the "how" and the next movement or breath in my life became crystal-clear. How much, really, am I prepared to allow and accept? I see how mountains move seemingly effortlessly. Is it really possible to allow that into my life on a regular basis? I am paying attention to what has transpired here. What is here for me to learn and grow from?

It is an intense few weeks. I am cohosting a one-week training in this period of time. My newfound sister, Deb, comes to help with the move. I am grateful. Other friends show up to help pack, move, and unpack. My ex-husband has found a house too but will leave his stuff in storage for a month, as he is traveling a lot. This allows our son to be fully in one place and then the other as we all get used to new living arrangements.

I am grateful. It is a deep, joyful gratitude. My house is a visible symbol of this convergence point in my journey—a five-year transition period that has been full of tension, conflict, healing, resolution, and growth has come to an end. It now feels like a softer, gentler unfolding process. My soul is singing, delighting in the inner transformation and emergence that has occurred.

A newfound sense of freedom manifests in me. I wake up every morning feeling joyful. I turn around, and something about my house catches my eye. A shiver of delight runs through me. The thought *I love this house!* flows into my mind. And I do. And it feels as if I am loving it without being attached to it.

About six weeks after moving in, I wake up one morning, still feeling this sense of joy. But this morning I wonder, *When will this sense of joy and delight pass and "normal" set in?* I am not sure what "normal" means. I give my head a shake and say to myself, "Kathy! Who is to say that joy and delight are not the normal state and that every now and then you blip out of it temporarily but then come back to joy and delight? Why can't that be normal?"

Since that time, I have come to study the law of attraction in a deeper way. No matter what source you look to, this is exactly the message. Joy is our natural state of being. Emotions are our guidance system. This is exactly what my coach told me and helped me live into more fully a few years before. Good-feeling emotions tell us we are aligned with our inner essence or soul quality. Bad-feeling emotions tell us we are not aligned. It is as simple as that. The law of attraction brings to us things that resonate with our own vibration—good or bad. When we understand and know our emotional state, we have the conscious choice to shift it intentionally to a better-feeling state. It is always a choice. No good comes from staying stuck in bad feelings. It does not make anyone else feel better, no matter what guilt trip they lay on you, or you on them. It does not serve your own abundant success. Reach for better-feeling thoughts. As this awareness rises up in me, my heart opens more fully—not to any person in particular, but to life.

I take a deep breath. A quotation by Rumi comes to mind: *Your task is not to seek for love, but merely to seek and find all the barriers within yourself that you have built against it.* Love is what fills my senses and I find myself falling in love, everywhere I go, with so many I meet. Falling in love with life itself.

A few months after moving into my house, I find myself on back on Bowen Island, five years since being introduced to my first Art of Hosting Training. This time I am here for a Warrior of the Heart training. Warrior of the Heart has flowed out of Art of Hosting and Aikido. It has been calling me for a while, but I have not been ready to do much more than try to find my center. I certainly have not been ready to wield a sword. But now that I am stepping into the journey to openheartedness, I am readier to step into this. I have heard that a warrior of the heart is someone who courageously steps up to be of skillful service to what is needed now, while actively perfecting powerful and wise actions in community, in the world, and in life. It is a pathway for me to continue to connect to my spiritual lineages and step into boldly bringing my healing gifts to the shifting shape of the world and the regeneration of its people.

I step into this circle to play and to wield the sword of my courage with strength and compassion, to see the metaphor of my soul's journey in this extension beyond me. The timing is right. I step into this circle surrounded by friends who are also stepping in. One friend is the friend from my Gold Lake vision quest. We are weaving more threads of journey and connection together.

We are in a retreat center built around a 1,100-year-old tree. It is the oldest tree on the island. Its spirit and energy are alive in the place. It invites reverence. Much of our practice happens in the field in front of this tree. There is also a meditation hut and a labyrinth. The tree, the hut, and the labyrinth are in service of the local community and in service of us.

The training is powerful, and there is more to come. My guides are strong in my awareness, preparing for the next phase of this trip—a gathering of many from around the world who have been stewarding the movement of the Art of Hosting, its patterns and practices, both through work in the world and through training and practice grounds. For me, the journey is about to intensify.

Some of us who have been in the Warrior of the Heart training are staying on for the stewards gathering. More are arriving, including more friends and colleagues I have worked with. One in particular has been carrying unspoken, unresolved issues from a time we worked together months before.

He invites me for lunch. Not knowing he has something specific in his mind, I come to lunch to say hello, to reconnect. He begins to give me feedback, suggesting that my contribution to our previous work together put him at risk with clients of his in attendance. I was too spiritual—or something. Dumbfounded, I do not know how to respond. Tears stream down my face. I have been ricocheted out of my sense of grounding, peace, and contentment that has been building in the days before during the Warrior of the Heart training. I am most grieved that this has been in the field between us for months without my knowledge, but it explains the strange quality of our occasional contact since then.

Questions arise in my mind. Even as they do, I realize it does not matter. I do not need to know these answers. Somewhere, somehow, I know this is not about this conversation. This is about more—much more. This is fundamentally important to me in embracing the stranger within and the journey to openheartedness.

I need to find a quiet spot to quell the inner turmoil that has risen up in me, to find my way to my heart's wisdom.

We are surrounded by people I love and who love me. Any one of them could be a good confidant or support in this, but as I consider whether I want to send for someone, I know the answer is no. There is something for me in sitting with it myself to see what emerges, to not make the story any larger than it is already looming in and around me, to understand it from the human tragedy perspective or to lean into the soul journey's invitation that has just showed up, with boldness. I have choices to make.

I find my way to the meditation hut, tears still streaming down my face. I light a candle and lie down on the floor with a bare awareness of time, hoping no one will come at this time, wanting to be alone in my solitude. The tears continue to flow. My mind is mostly quiet. I am not playing and replaying scenes or conversations over in my mind. I am simply trying to stay with my emotional experience, to see what it is telling me and what I am being invited into. Breathing. I wish for more time, and I know I am already late for the beginning of the afternoon Open Space session.

I make my way back to our meeting space, my tears barely stopped and my eyes still brimming, ready to spill over. I cannot look at anybody, because I know that if I do—because they all love me and they are all compassionate—the tears will flow again. Something is stirring deep within me. I do not yet understand what it is.

Emotionally exposed, I am willing to stay with it, to know I am in my vulnerability without needing to share the story of why. This is significant learning for me.

I understand that despite an inexhaustible supply of tears, I am okay. Throughout the day, insight and understanding percolate. I have been invited into a choice. One choice is to only live into the story that has been brought to me by my friend of our experience in that training, to doubt myself, to put my stranger back in hiding. Another choice is to see other stories that were also alive in that training—the story that takes me to Brazil, the story that shows the beginning of new friendships and new opportunities.

It becomes clear. I am being shown two very different possibilities and being invited to choose. The choice? Stay on the path I have been traveling, step more fully into who I am and what is mine to do and not be sidetracked by what some may or may not like or be comfortable with. Their journey is not my journey. It is not my responsibility to appease anyone else. It is my responsibility to respond to the call of my path. Do I have the courage within me to do that—to take the path that someone else seems to disapprove of or find threatening?

I know, from a deep place of knowing, I will find my way with friends and colleagues whose journeys will align or coincide with mine. People I am meant to work with will show up along the way. I was told that in Gold Lake. I cannot go back into hiding. I would shrivel up and die, bit by bit. I can only emerge more fully. I would not have seen the depth of this without this story being brought to me in the way it was. It is a gift. I am invited to embrace my stranger, set her loose, and continue the journey to openheartedness.

As I am sitting in this next level of my own tension and journey, there is also tension in the stewards gathering. It arises from debate about the various methodologies to get work done or to be in circle council with each other the whole time we are together since such opportunities are rare. The question has been raised a few times. The decision has always been to continue with the path we started on, but the tension sits in us and with us.

On our last day together, the field takes on a life of its own. We all bow to what wants to happen rather than any notion of what we think we might like to have happen. Design and plan for the day are set aside as we gather in the ambience, energy, and ancestry of the 1,100-year-old tree. Scars from where a woodsman tried to cut it down but the ax broke instead are visible on the trunk. Scorch marks are evidence of a fire that came through a hundred years before but did not bring this tree down. And, if we look high enough, we can see that the very top of the tree broke off at some point in its history. And still the tree stands. Its very life force vibrates for a good distance around it. It is truly a reverent space.

We find ourselves deep in council on the morning of our last day. When it begins to rain, we shift into the meditation hut—not a place we would normally find ourselves for a meeting, because it is open to the public. However, the reverent conversation we are in seems appropriate to the space, and the rain will possibly keep others away, so we enter.

My whole body is vibrating during this morning. The essence of spiritual energy and of one of my guides in particular is streaming into my back. The intensity is palpable. I am visibly shaking with a shift in consciousness. I feel it within me. I am fueled by the exchange I had with my friend and the deep learning that has transpired, as well as by the place, space, and time we are in. The shift is in me. It is in our field. A new time is being birthed; consciousness is shifting from a few who have held the field, even when they did not want to, to the field itself. We feel it in each of us individually and all of us collectively.

Threads of my spiritual path have taken me from the drumming circle in 2000, to my spirit guide journey in 2007, to Gold Lake in 2009, to the Shamanic Convergence also in 2009, and now to this sacred space on Bowen Island in 2010.

The next step on my path is Brazil. I have never been. It has never been on my radar as a place to visit. It began to show up in my life a couple of years before when I met a couple of Brazilian friends for the first time at an Art of Hosting gathering in Nova Scotia. A strong connection emerged that year that included a few conversations and almost a trip.

A couple of years later, more Brazilian friends came into my life, attending the training I was part of cohosting before I moved into my house. An invitation was crafted at that time for me to go to Brazil to cohost a training focused on the inner journey first and then how that inner journey shows up in the outer world. That is to say, it was about hosting oneself before diving into practices and methodologies. I was captivated by the idea. A hosting team of six of us emerged—four Brazilians and two international hosts, one of whom would bring Warrior of the Heart into our work together.

Soon after my time on Bowen Island, I take my first trip to Brazil. The retreat center where we hold the training is a couple of hours outside of Sao Paulo and is stunningly beautiful. We decide not to use an official translation service, but a new member is added to the team who has offered to provide translation for us. We agree that the training will be in Portuguese and that when my American friend and I speak, what we say will be translated for the full group. He and I will have whispered translation for the whole gathering.

I am completely comfortable and at ease during my arrival in Sao Paulo and in all our conversations up to when I become aware of the arrival of participants at the retreat center. Then I begin to notice my own nervousness. Concern about language surfaces in me. I am uncomfortable in not knowing other languages and coming to another country presuming that the locals will accommodate me. I worry I am imposing my own ignorance on a group of people and am concerned that I will be perceived as arrogant, or even that I truly am arrogant in assumptions I have not even been aware I was making.

My Brazilian friend who first invited me to come cohost this training invites me to host the opening world café with her. I appreciate this invitation to dive into the work, and I am anxious about it at the same time. We agree on what parts of the café we will each do. She will do translation for me.

I say to her, "I am really wrestling with this. I feel it in me. I am adding an extra layer that is not even necessary. You are going to translate a process that you could easily introduce on your own without me." A desire to retreat, to hide, and to not put myself out there in my own uncertainty and uncomfortableness is rising up in me.

My friend is amazing, as I knew she would be. She encourages me and supports me in beautiful ways. We move into the café process together. I am introducing café etiquette. I find myself speaking the first principle of etiquette. My friend translates. As I am speaking the second principle, something registers in me. I say to myself, "Kathy, you would never just say the café etiquette without using story. Slow down. Pause. Use story in the same way you would if you were doing this for any other audience you might work with." I back up. I begin to tell a story and feel myself surrendering into the work, the place, the people, and the rhythm of the translation.

I surrender into the physical place, letting go of my insecurities as they arise. My heart breaks open wider. This is crazily possible in this place because my Brazilian friends live into the relational field in a way I have not experienced in North America. There is a beautiful depth to the field.

The stranger in me is emerging with more boldness and more love. I am learning that embracing her releases her, releases any limiting beliefs I have about her, and makes her fully a part of who I am. Embracing her shatters the illusion of fragmentation within me, allowing me to feel more and more of the integrated whole of who I am. The journey to openheartedness is a natural expression from this place. Love, joy, and delight flow as they are embodied and as layers of illusion fall away. This reveals the power of openhearted vulnerability to protect in ways walls never could, to embrace others in ways walls would never allow. As I embrace this stranger in me and open my heart more, I create relationship with people across a room, with a deep gaze and a welcoming energy. I notice. I enjoy. I appreciate. I fall in love. I sense rhythms and patterns in relationship. My heart energy spills into the space, beyond time, beyond words. I am not exposed; I am present.

A part of our training, hosted by participants, is a visualization process and then a fire-and-water ceremony under the stars at a fire pit. During the visualization, my medicine woman from Gold Lake arises up out of me, luminously large, hovering over me. She completely has my attention. She follows me to the fire pit, and when it is my turn, she invites me to dance around the fire, just as I did in my vision with my shape-shifting lion more than a decade before, just as I did for eons in past lives with ancestors I have been coming to know over these last few years. I am compelled to dance as her strength and her heritage emerge more completely onto my essence. This is one more step in embracing the stranger in me becoming one with all that is already present in me; one more way my first drumming experience shows its lasting resonance in my journey and in my being. It is one more step in my journey to openheartedness.

The medicine woman calls to me. "Draw me."

"I don't draw," I say to her.

"Draw me," she whispers louder.

The compulsion is strong. In the way that paths unfold, the next morning space is created to draw or create some image from our experience the night before.

267

"Here I am," she says. I see her, looming large in my awareness. I pick up markers and paper. I draw her—far better than I could possibly have imagined. I know she has drawn herself in order to make herself symbolically visible to me through art. She is in me, one of the manifestations of the beautiful stranger within, inviting my embrace. I am in her, leaning into her embrace. She is ready to be more vibrant, alive, and accessed. I am ready to be more vibrant and alive, more visible.

I leave Brazil enamored with the people and the depth of relationship that has emerged, even with people who speak only Portuguese. I am certain there is more work for me to do in this beautiful country and know I will return.

There is also more work for me to do at home and in other places that call. There is more for me to do within myself to continue to take down barriers, continue to step out of the shadows, and more fully come into the essence of who I am and what it is that is mine to do in the world.

My heart is more open than it has ever been. I am told I have a depth of presence that is beautifully strong in helping others to center and ground. There is no turning back as I move into the second half of my life. The stranger is illuminated in love and light. I am extraordinarily blessed to be witness and journeyer at the same time.

EPILOGUE

RETURN TO SOUL JOURNEY

When my older boys were young children, their grandfather on their father's side died. Their dad and I had already separated. They went to the funeral, and afterward I asked them how it was. We began to talk about death. They said to me, "We think it's kind of like this. You know when you dream and when you are in the middle of a dream it seems real? But then you wake up and you know it was just a dream. We think life is like that. It's really just a dream, but it seems real. Then you die, but really it's like waking up and realizing it was just a dream." Such wisdom from out of the mouths of babes. They are closer to source.

My nine-year-old also understands death and dying enough to ask to visit his grandmother with me when I tell him I am going to see her in what are likely to be her final days, maybe even her final hours. He has not been there much lately. I remind him what his grandmother looks like and that she is on her deathbed. He still wants to come, even when the call comes to say this might be her last day. And my oldest son and his girlfriend come too. My middle son is away at university; otherwise, he would come too. We all sit vigil the day before my mother dies, for hours. All of us watch my mother with sidelong looks every time her breathing stops—for the eternity that shows up in a moment. We laugh together with relief when I point it out, naming the obvious.

February 8, 2012. My mother dies. Never having been present at a death before, I do not know what to expect and it is not what I expected. My brother, father, and I hold vigil, practically holding our collective breath as my mother, Mary Patricia Ann Ritcey Jourdain, draws her last, peaceful breaths. She falls quiet at 12:30 pm.

Then there is silence. Her silence. No more rattling breaths drawn with some effort through her lungs into her body, which has been ravaged by dementia for many years and the refusal to eat for many months.

We hold our silence in reverence for my mother, her journey, and the honor of witnessing the final stages of her transition from physical form into spirit. I already believed much of her consciousness was active in the subtle realms even as her physical presence diminished. With her last breaths, I imagine her spirit gently tugging until the last wisps of it are finally released into a delightful little dance of joy and freedom.

My mother's journey with dementia was a long one. My journey through hers was an inspired one. Her greatest teachings for me may have come in the last few years, when she could no longer string coherent sentences together, during the contrast of those times when she seemed to have no awareness of my presence to when I knew she was aware I was there.

I have one of those moments of her awareness the night before she dies. We had moved her to a special room where I could stay with her overnight. My father asked me to stay with her, and I was more than willing to do so. I did not expect this gift. Months ago we were told she could die any day, maybe in her sleep at night. I have been traveling extensively. I might have missed her death. I had only just returned from my most recent trip days before this.

When we transferred her to a different room, we missed one of her medication times. I was aware of this, but she did not seem to be in distress. So I sat on the arm of the couch, at eye level with my mother, who was lying in her bed. I looked into her blue eyes. She held my gaze.

When I say she held my gaze, I mean she held my gaze. For a woman who had been increasingly less present over the years, she was just as present as I was. I was mesmerized. I could not take my gaze away.

I talked to her. I told her about things and people in my life. I told her how beautiful she is—not was, but is. I told her how gifted and how loved she is. I thanked her for being in my life, for being my mom. Mostly, I held her gaze with love until she began to exhibit signs of distress. Then I went for the nurse. Then she was gone again until the moment of her final breath.

While I sat with her, I meditated. I allowed my consciousness to tune in to what more was happening in that moment. I sensed some of her guides. They were celebrating as they got ready to receive her. There was a beautiful young woman, a little black dog, and one other. There were points of light—candles or stars. They shimmered, sparkled, and lit the way. There was such joy. Such readiness. It was calm and beautiful—just like my mother in the final hours of staying with her physical body. She was preparing to let go. It is a gift to sit vigil with her.

My brother, Robert, arrived from Prince Edward Island. I called him earlier in the day. Someone from Harbourview Haven had asked me when he was arriving. He was waiting for the call, but in an instant it occurred to me she might be waiting for him instead of the other way around. I told him to come now. And he did. He came directly to see Mom when he arrived late at night. We visited for a while. I shared my experience with our mother and her guides. He eventually left to stay the night with Dad, planning to come back early the next morning.

The staff at Harbourview Haven teach me about human dignity and respect through how they relate to my mother. Even up to the last moment, they treat my mother as if she is fully present and aware. They call her by her name. In the middle of the night, they come into our room. "Mary," they say, "we're going to turn you over now." "Mary, we are going to give you your meds now. It might sting a little."

On the morning of her death, a care worker comes in to wash her face and freshen her up, providing a depth of love, care, dignity, and respect to a woman in her last moments on this physical plane. They understand about death and dying. They know that it is a process and a transition as much a part of life as birth and life itself. I am now aware that dying and death require the same kind of loving care and attention as birth does. It is birth—birth back to spirit. It happens when the soul is ready, not necessarily when those who are waiting think they are ready. The same is true when we await the birth of a newborn; the child arrives in its timing, not ours.

With my mother's last breath, four of us—me, my brother, my father, and my mother—are still in the room. But now the shape of our lives has fundamentally shifted. As long as we stay sitting in the room, it is like she is still there in her emaciated form. But, of course, she is now free of form. Eventually we have to move and leave her next steps in the capable hands of the Harbourview Haven staff, who transfer her into the equally capable hands of the funeral home.

That night, as I drive from Lunenburg to Bedford, the full moon is shining brightly. I do not feel sorrow. I feel euphoric joy—just as when my youngest son was born. I am driving home by the light of the moon and my mother's joyous spirit, free from form and fully reunited with her stranger within. This is something she could not embrace on her physical life path this time around.

Her journey illuminated for me one of the threads in the weave of embracing the stranger in me, in each of us: journeying to openheartedness. Embarking on this journey allows us to find soul-journey perspective amid the human tragedy story; to choose the lenses, filters, and stories we need to live into in order to make sense of the journey; choose the better-feeling stories; write the endings that celebrate the journey, life, and many other things; and invite the inquiry and curiosity of what more becomes possible when embracing the stranger within and journeying even more deeply, lightly, and joyfully into the openhearted embrace of journey.

CPSIA information can be obtained at www.ICGtesting.com
Printed in the USA
LVOW05s1314230713

344088LV00002B/28/P